Security in the Pacific is complex and highly contested sociologically, geopoliti-
cally and scholastically and the book compre‍‌   ‍‌ ‍‌these complex
and often competing discourses in a brilliant
those seeking to be enlightened with original
multi-dimensional and intersectional nature of
mational, culturally resilient and sometimes p

— **Prof Steven Ratuva**,
for Pacific Studies
Sociology, University of Canterbury, —
Political Science Association Research Committee on
Security, Conflict and Democratization.

This important and timely book provides a comprehensive theoretical and empirical examination of security and insecurity in Pacific Island countries. The book's
editors and contributors elucidate the complex, interrelated and multidimensional
dynamics and forms of security in these countries at different levels of analysis
from the global to the local. *Mapping Security in the Pacific* challenges us to
rethink issues of security and insecurity in the Global South, including how security is defined and approached; the role of local and international organisations;
and the gendered nature of security, making this volume a must-read for both
students and established scholars.

— **Nathan W. Pino**, *Professor of Sociology, Texas State University, USA*

*Mapping Security in the Pacific: A Focus on Context, Gender and Organisational
Culture* provides an important contribution to understanding a wide range of security concerns and contexts from the perspective of the Pacific Islands. The mul-
tidisciplinary/multidimensional focus on different dimensions of security allows
the reader to gain an understanding of the context, gender and organisational culture of Pacific Island security through a diverse range of contributions on issues
ranging from policing, climate change, military reform and economic (in)security.

— **Fiona Hukula**, *Senior Research Fellow, Building Safer Communities
Research Program National Research Institute-Papua New Guinea*

The Pacific region is a large geographical area but very little remains known of
the social structures and social relations of its many small nations. Even less is
known of the way in which security is maintained, challenged, transformed and
reformulated in this region. This book remedies these deficiencies by providing
important essays that shed clear light on these concerns.

— **John Pratt**, *Professor of Criminology, Victoria
University of Wellington, New Zealand*

Mapping Security in the Pacific

This book examines questions about the changing nature of security and insecurity in Pacific Island Countries (PICs). Previous discussions of security in the Pacific region have been largely determined by the geopolitical interests of the Global North. This volume instead attempts to centre PICs' security interests by focussing on the role of organisational culture, power dynamics and gender in (in)security processes and outcomes.

Mapping Security in the Pacific underscores the multidimensional nature of security, its relationship to local, international, organisational and cultural dynamics, the resistances engendered through various forms of insecurities, and innovative efforts to negotiate gender, context and organisational culture in reducing insecurity and enhancing justice. Covering the Pacific region widely, the volume brings forth context-specific analyses at micro-, meso- and macro-levels, allowing us to examine the interconnections between security, crime and justice, and point to the issues raised for crime and justice studies by environmental insecurity. In doing so, it opens up opportunities to rethink scholarly and policy frames related to security/insecurity about the Pacific.

Written in a clear and direct style, this book will appeal to students and scholars in criminology, sociology, cultural studies, social theory and those interested in learning about the Pacific region and different aspects of security.

Sara N. Amin is Senior Lecturer and Coordinator of Sociology at the University of the South Pacific. Her research focusses on migration; identity politics, violence and security; gender relations; and education. She has two ongoing projects: *Religion and Policing in the Pacific* and *Changing Gender Relations in Families in South Asia*.

Danielle Watson is Lecturer and Coordinator of the Pacific Policing Programme at the University of the South Pacific. She conducts research on police/civilian relations on the margins with particular interests in hotspot policing, police recruitment and training as well as many other areas specific to policing in developing country contexts.

Christian Girard, PhD, is an independent researcher and development practitioner based in Fiji and a former assistant professor in development studies at the Asian University for Women in Bangladesh. His professional experience and research interests include vulnerability, poverty, informality, housing, governance and public policy in Asia-Pacific, Africa and Latin America.

Routledge Studies in Crime and Justice in Asia and the Global South

Edited by Wing Hong Chui
City University of Hong Kong

Russell Hogg
Queensland University of Technology

John Scott
Queensland University of Technology

Crime and justice studies, as with much social science, has concentrated mainly on problems in the metropolitan centres of the Global North, while Asia and the Global South have remained largely invisible in criminological thinking. This research series aims to redress this imbalance by showcasing exciting new ways of thinking and doing crime and justice research from the global periphery.

Bringing together scholarly work from a range of disciplines, from criminology, law and sociology to psychology, cultural geography and comparative social sciences, this series offers grounded empirical research and fresh theoretical approaches and covers a range of pressing topics, including international corruption, drug use, environmental issues, sex work, organized crime, innovative models of justice and punishment and penology.

Punishment in Contemporary China
Its Evolution, Development and Change
Enshen Li

Criminal Legalities in the Global South
Cultural Dynamics, Political Tensions and Institutional Practices
Edited by Pablo Ciocchini and George Baylon Radics

Organized Crime and Corruption Across Borders
Exploring the Belt and Road Initiative
Edited by T. Wing Lo, Dina Siegel and Sharon I. Kwok

Mapping Security in the Pacific
A Focus on Context, Gender and Organisational Culture
Sara N. Amin, Danielle Watson and Christian Girard

For more information about this series, please visit: www.routledge.com/criminology/series/RSCJAGS

Mapping Security in the Pacific

A Focus on Context, Gender and Organisational Culture

Edited by Sara N. Amin, Danielle Watson and Christian Girard

Routledge
Taylor & Francis Group

LONDON AND NEW YORK

First published 2020 by Routledge

2 Park Square, Milton Park, Abingdon, Oxon OX14 4RN
605 Third Avenue, New York, NY 10017

Routledge is an imprint of the Taylor & Francis Group, an informa business

First issued in paperback 2022

Publisher's Note

The publisher has gone to great lengths to ensure the quality of this reprint but points out that some imperfections in the original copies may be apparent.

British Library Cataloguing-in-Publication Data
A catalogue record for this book is available from the British Library

Library of Congress Cataloging-in-Publication Data
A catalog record for this book has been requested

ISBN: 978-0-367-14392-3 (hbk)
ISBN: 978-1-03-233693-0 (pbk)
DOI: 10.4324/9780429031816

Typeset in Time New Roman
by Apex CoVantage, LLC

Contents

Figures

Tables

Contributors

Sara N. Amin is Senior Lecturer and Coordinator of Sociology at the University of the South Pacific. Her research focusses on migration; identity politics, violence and security; gender relations and education. She has two ongoing projects: *Religion and Policing in the Pacific* and *Changing Gender Relations in Families in South Asia*.

Paul J. Carnegie is Associate Professor of Politics & IR, Universiti Brunei Darussalam-Institute of Asian Studies and the former Director of Postgraduate Governance Studies at USP. His research specialises in comparative democratisation and human security. He has published widely including the co-edited volume *Human Insecurities in Southeast Asia*.

Richard A. Davis, is Senior Lecturer in Theology and Ethics at The Pacific Theological College. He earned a PhD in political theology from the University of Edinburgh in 2013. He has research interests in political theology and Christian social ethics and teaches across the range of theology and ethics.

Sinclair Dinnen is Professor in the Department of Pacific Affairs at the Australian National University. His research and publications have focussed on regulatory pluralism, justice and policing reform, conflict and peacebuilding and post-colonial state formation in the SW Pacific.

Greg Dvorak is Professor of Pacific/Asian History and Cultural Studies at Waseda University. His research focusses on militarism, memory, gender and art in post-colonial Oceania. He is the author of *Concrete and Coral*: *Remembering Kwajalein Atoll between Japan, America and the Marshall Islands* (University of Hawai'i Press, 2018).

Michael Fink is a cultural geographer and recently worked as a lecturer at USP (Fiji) and Göttingen (Germany). His research interests include socio-ecological transitions and adaptation to climate change and natural hazards in the Pacific Islands region.

Miranda Forsyth is Associate Professor at the School of Regulation and Global Governance (RegNet) in the College of Asia and the Pacific at the Australian National University. Miranda's research investigates the possibilities and challenges of the inter-operation of state and non-state justice and regulatory systems.

Nicole George is Associate Professor in Peace and Conflict Studies in the School of Political Science and International Studies at The University of Queensland. Her research examines the gendered impacts of conflict in Pacific Island contexts and the roles played by women in peacebuilding, conflict transition and post-conflict governance.

Christian Girard, PhD is an independent researcher and development practitioner based in Fiji and a former assistant professor in development studies at the Asian University for Women in Bangladesh. His professional experience and research interests include vulnerability, poverty, informality, housing, governance and public policy in Asia-Pacific, Africa and Latin America.

James Johnson is a social psychologist who has published extensively in the area of interpersonal stereotyping processes in America and the Pacific region. He has also secured over four million in external grant funding. Finally, he has served as a consultant for various American and Pacific region government agencies.

Natasha Khan is the coordinator for the Leadership, Governance and Human Rights Programme at The University of the South Pacific. Her research focusses on SIDS conflicts, transitional justice, amnesty, coups d'état, security sector reform, human rights and development, human rights defenders and faith, corruption, culture and human rights.

Victor T. King is Chair Professor of Borneo Studies, Universiti Brunei Darussalam-Institute of Asian Studies. During the last six years, he has edited/co-edited seven books on topics ranging across tourism in Asia, UNESCO World Heritage sites in Southeast Asia, ethno-development, Southeast Asian studies, Borneo studies and human insecurities in Southeast Asia.

Andreas Kopf is an environmental sociologist and Lecturer at The University of the South Pacific. His research interests include research on the social and human dimensions of contemporary global climate change, particularly in relation to sustainable development and human security in the Global South.

Penelope Schoeffel is Associate Professor in the Centre for Samoan Studies at the National University of Samoa, where she teaches in the development studies programme. The focus of her research for many years has been on gender, culture and social change.

Tanya Trussler is Associate Professor in the Department of Economics, Justice and Policy Studies at Mount Royal University, Canada. Her PhD dissertation examined geotemporal factors affecting homicide and homicide clearance in Canada. Her research involves interpersonal violence, recidivism, policing violence, quantitative criminology, spatial risk, distribution of crime and crime-reduction methods.

Danielle Watson is Lecturer and Coordinator of the Pacific Policing Programme at the University of the South Pacific. She conducts research on police/civilian relations on the margins with particular interests in hotspot policing, police recruitment and training as well as many other areas specific to policing in developing country contexts.

Eberhard Weber is Associate Professor in Human Geography at the School of Geography, Earth Science and Environment at The University of the South Pacific. His research interests include research on vulnerability and resilience to climate and natural hazards and disasters as well as on environment-induced migration in the Pacific Island region.

Introduction

1 (In)security in the Pacific

Danielle Watson, Christian Girard
and Sara N. Amin

Background

Traditionally tackled and understood more through the frame of politics and inter-national relations at the state level (Jacob, 2017; Bogarti, Spring, & Brauch, 2016; Martin & Owen, 2013; Brauch & Scheffran, 2012; Dupont, 1997) the concept, study and understanding of security have expanded over time to broader areas, risks and challenges, including the very central issue of climate change and its impact and implications for different types of security. This includes human secu-rity (Behnassi, Gupta, & Pollmann, 2019; Elliott, 2015, 2018; McLellan, 2018a, 2018b; Tazreiter, Weber, Pickering, Segrave, & McKernan, 2016; Martin & Owen, 2013; Brauch & Scheffran, 2012; Scheffran, Brzoska, Brauch, Link, & Schilling, 2012), food security (Sarkar, Sensharma, & vanLoon, 2019; Yadav, Redden, Hatfield, Ebert, & Hunter, 2019; Dhanarajan, 2017; Campbell, 2015, Kaldor & Rangelov, 2014; ADB, 2011; UN, 2009), water security (Brisman, McClanahan, South, & Walters, 2018; Bogardi, Spring, & Brauch, 2016; Manton, 2014; Ayson & Ball, 2006), energy security (McCauley, 2018; Heath et al., 2014; Kaldor & Rangelov, 2014; Anceschi & Symons, 2012), health security (Savage, McIver, & Schubert, 2019; O'Manique & Fourie, 2018; Rushton & Youde, 2014), environmental security (Behnassi et al., 2019; Dalby, 2017; Elliott, 2015, 2018; Watson & Pandey, 2015; Trombetta, 2008) and the recognition of transnational threats (Masys & Lin, 2018; Jacob, 2017). Although these have been the object of substantial literature and research in the last few decades, it is more recently that these challenges and concerns have been linked to policy discussions on security (Behnassi et al., 2019; Dalby, 2017).

This book contributes to this growing literature by focussing on the Pacific Island Countries (PICs), a region for which the literature is less abundant, even for the literature on Asia-Pacific that frequently focusses on Asia without discussing the PICs. While contributors to this volume will specify how security is defined in the context of their respective chapters, the following questions and distinctions can frame the discussion and reflection on security.

The first question is about whether the focus of security ought to be on the state or the individual, what Dupont (1997, p. 31) refers to as the "'who' of secu-rity". Bogardi et al. (2016) associate the broader understanding of security and the rise of human security to a postmodern perspective versus the longstanding modern perspective that is centred around the state and national security. This book embraces both perspectives, taking a broad approach to security, especially as many non-traditional security risks and threats also have an impact on national security (for example, climate change is often seen as a threat to national security by governments [Dalby, 2015; Brauch & Scheffran, 2012]). In addition, this book widens the scope of the "who" of security to include (indigenous) communities.

The second question is related to the "nature and hierarchy of threats", what Dupont (1997, p. 31) defines as the "'what' of security". In the introduction of The Handbook of Security, Gill (2014, p. 1) insists that the first priority is the "need to thoroughly catalogue the range of threats that security must address". As such, the multiple perspectives taken in this book contribute to mapping a wide range of security concerns in the PICs, from gender-based issues to policing, nuclear contamination, climate change and more.

A third question can be framed around the idea of security as "what actors make of it" (Wendt, 1992, 1999 in Brauch & Scheffran, 2012, p. 3). For example, this is the approach Chmutina, Lizarralde, Dainty and Bosher (2016) took to analyse the resilience policy discourse in the UK through stakeholders' interviews, meetings and documents, as well as the one taken by Boas and Rothe (2016) on resilience thinking and its understanding and use by practitioners, specifically in the UK. In addition to authors in this book highlighting how on-the-ground activists and policing institutions adapt to changing security contexts, the book's focus on praxis is achieved through unique interview chapters with practitioners.

A fourth question relates to the multifaceted nature and the interconnectedness of security issues, as many affect each other or even share some causes and implications. The work of Savage et al. (2019) is an example of this interconnectedness in the context of the PICs, where they look at the links between climate change, food and nutrition security and non-communicable diseases (NCDs). One specific way this book highlights the interconnectedness of security issues is to examine the (re)productive outcomes of tensions between "tradition"/change, local/global and individual/community/state concerns.

As Gill (2014, p. 1) points out, "every academic discipline has a contribution to better understand some aspect or manifestation of security and in providing theories and frameworks which can help enhance our comprehension of security and insecurity". In security studies, political sciences and international relations, a key tension in thinking about security has been related to debating the relevance and value of expanding the concept of security to human security, where individual welfare, freedom from want and fear are centred (Brauch & Scheffran, 2012; Pettman, 2005; Miller, 2001), a shift that has however become widespread in development studies (Bogardi et al., 2016). Evaluations of whether new actors in the field of security provision are a source of insecurity or not continue to also be a site of debate (Abrahamsen & Williams, 2006, 2007), as do questions related to the place of women and gender in (violent) political conflict, conflict resolution and peacebuilding (Cohn, Kinsella, & Gibbings, 2004; Kirby & Shepherd, 2016; Shepherd, 2016). In other disciplines such as sociology and anthropology, security–insecurity are linked to concepts of risk, precarity, safety, uncertainty, surveillance and competing cultural/legal/moral authorities as experienced by communities and individuals, and their consequences for nation-states, governments, governance and civic order (Bauman, 1992; Forsyth, 2009; Giddens, 1990). Criminology brings into focus the crime–justice–security nexus and both critical criminology and Southern criminology emphasises the need to think beyond legal and formal policing institutions in considering crime prevention, delivery of justice and security provision (Carrington, Hogg, & Sozzo, 2016).

While dialogue on security varies in understanding, approaches and focus, what is consistent throughout the literature is an acknowledgement of existing threats to security that have far reaching impacts, which extend beyond the remit of any single discipline. As such, a multidisciplinary approach is important to look beyond familiar knowledge spaces for solutions to unconventional and complex problems to formulate appropriate responses. In relation to this book, this suggests a need to map security to determine the issues, identify how they overlap across focal areas and develop strategies that pay attention to the specific physical, economic and human resources in the Pacific Island Countries (PICs), a relatively unique context in the Global South.

Keeping these questions and issues in mind, *Mapping Security in the Pacific* aims to provide a collection of multidisciplinary perspectives on security in the Pacific region. The volume presents a diverse range of theoretical and empirical studies, along with specialist views on security-related issues. The book examines how security and insecurity are produced and resisted and their implications for theorisation of and policymaking on security. The volume underscores the multidimensional nature of security, its relationship to local, international, organisational and cultural dynamics, the resistances engendered through various forms of insecurities, and innovative efforts to negotiate gender, context and organisational culture in reducing insecurity and enhancing justice. It presents context-specific perspectives from a wide range of scholars with shared interests in issues pertinent to varied dimensions of security in PICs, often characterised as countries with complex and enduring historical legacies, remote populations facing environmental challenges, high rates of gender-based violence, globalisation and political structures embedded in tensions between (neo-/post-) colonial, "modern", "religious" and "indigenous" authority structures.

It is important to underscore that both insecurity and security in the PICs have been framed in part through ideas of small and remote, leading often to policies and approaches that are paternalistic, demand "protection" from "big" geopolitical powers and reproduce dependency (Fry, 1997). Moreover, scholarly discourses reproduce the PICs as failed states and communities incapable of providing social protection. Ratuva (2014) has argued that such a characterisation is a product of Western ideologies of "formal and institution-based social protection policies", which fail to recognise the "culture-based indigenous social protection systems used by subaltern Pacific communities as a means of building resilience and developing adaptation strategies. The major plank of the argument here is that far from being 'failed', Pacific communities have over the years developed culture-based mechanisms, not captured in Western-based classificatory schemas, which provide them with resilience and adaptability in the face of neoliberalism and globalisation" (p. 42). More broadly, Teaiwa (2014, p. 73) illustrates that colonialist framings of the PICs have been repeatedly challenged by peoples in the Pacific to emphasise "Pacific autonomy, resistance and creativity (Teaiwa, 2014, p. 73)", in which "smallness" and "remoteness" are reframed through "sea of islands" to centre vastness, global significance and influence, connections and strengths located in indigenous knowledge, relations and practices (Hau'ofa, 2008).

These reframings are gaining traction in larger policy spheres as evidence by SIDS' rebranding themselves as "Large Ocean States" (Chan, 2018), the centring of the ocean in climate change and sustainable development policies globally and the strengthening of Pacific regionalism among PICs. *Mapping Security in the Pacific: A focus on context, gender and organisational culture* brings forth voices and perspectives in the PICs about what are (in)security issues in their own context, how these are seen, understood and defined, what kind of challenges are faced and what solutions are proposed for action and policy.

Structure of the book

The chapters explore security as a multidisciplinary and multidimensional construct; the gendered sources of security and insecurity; the role of various contexts (religious, political, economic, etc.) and organisational culture of security providers and partners in impacting on security–justice outcomes; and the tensions and negotiations between modern, traditional, national, international, legal, religio-cultural security and justice institutions. Chapters are presented under three sub-themes specific to the conceptualisation of security in the contexts of PICs. While we acknowledge that these three areas do not cover the full scope of security-related issues specific to the Pacific, we recognise the importance of presenting chapters rich in topical and disciplinary diversity as a basis for future dialogue across real, imagined, theoretical or philosophical borders. Following is a summary of the chapters' contributions under each of the three selected themes: 1) Reframing Security in the Pacific; 2) Sources of Gender Insecurity in the PICs; and 3) Organisational Culture, Security Providers, Partner Institutions and Security Outcomes.

Part 1: Reframing security in the Pacific – For the Pacific region as a whole, security-related discussions are primarily centred on insecurities related to geopolitical and geostrategic interests, porous borders, climate change and gender. In addition, within the region, countries tend to place emphasis on other security issues related specifically to their contexts, as priorities vary based on different economic, political, social and geographical factors. The chapters in this section emphasise the importance of reframing security in the Pacific in ways that underscore the importance of interconnections between the different dimensions of security, as well as the ways Pacific actors are reframing security to assert their own agency.

Paul J. Carnegie and Victor T. King argue that the field of human security needs to engage more fully with a range of disciplinary concepts to maintain its relevance and gain greater analytical purchase on the multiple forms of lived and day-to-day insecurities of the twenty-first century in Oceania. They highlight issues of vulnerability and precariousness which underscore discussions of "safety" and "risk" and their complex relationship to "trust" and "uncertainty".

Matthew Dornan examines how the concept of human security interacts with economic development in its various forms, drawing on economic and social indicators from different Pacific island economies. By exploring vulnerability and low incomes of households, he brings into focus the centrality of shocks, informality and informal social protection.

Greg Dvorak reflects on the historical roots of insecurities within PICs by revisiting Marshall Islands' history of colonialism, militarism and environmental challenges. He draws attention to how stakeholders navigated and negotiated insecurities over time, identifying the important role women and their mobilisation of indigenous culture have had in asserting autonomy and seeking justice related to displacements, health and food insecurities brought about by nuclear testing. The chapter also shares Pacific specific adaptations to insecurities over time with currency in the twenty-first century and beyond.

Anand Chand and Tauisi Taupo confront issues of environmental insecurities faced by the two PICs often described as the most significantly impacted by climate change, Tuvalu and Kiribati. They explore the links between natural disasters, climate change and security and elaborate on the consequences of such issues to economic, food and water insecurity, while highlighting how environmental (in)security ultimately has implications for nationhood security and sovereignty.

Part 2: Sources of gender insecurity in the Pacific – Gender insecurity continues to be a priority of the international agenda. Underrepresentation of women, culturally-enforced discrimination and inadequate working conditions continue to be among problems faced by women in PICs. For many of these countries, traditional and cultural ideas about gender and gender roles underscore much of what accounts for insecurities faced by women. The value of empowering women has been accepted as a prioritised area for many countries from a standpoint of promoting gender equality as a catalyst for human development and national capacity building. However, this presents challenges in many contexts as equality is championed without considerations of its implications for organisational frameworks, human resources' capacity and contexts beyond professional spaces that continue to be influenced primarily by religion, culture and accepted ideas about gender roles. Dialogue about the need for equality tends to only scratch the surface of the multifaceted nature of the problems faced by many PICs when actioning the gender balance mandate within historically male-dominated professional and personal spaces. What is also not explicit is the problems posed by lacking supporting legislature, vague polices that work in the disservice of marginalised genders and sexual minorities, the absence of gender sensitive workspaces and marginalised individuals championing a poorly conceptualised cause.

The chapters in this section traverse security issues related to women's place in state and nation building, religion and spirituality, intimacy and sexual prejudices and climate change vulnerability. Contributors offer scholarly positions rich in cultural specificity and awareness as follows:

Penelope Schoeffel examines how donor and international agendas influence the "formula" for aid delivery in the Pacific. She highlights a reality of aid provision for women empowerment uninformed by contextual variables, which works in the disservice of the desired empowerment outcomes. Detailing examples from Samoa that also critique the "the good man" gender and development discourse, she puts forward recommendations to improve women empowerment agendas, and highlight key considerations necessary for the formulation of appropriate and applicable responses.

Sara N. Amin, Tanya Trussler and James Johnson present a country-specific study exploring the prevalence and variations in attitudes towards sexual(ized) violence in Fiji. They document the gendered nature of (in)security, bringing into focus both the normalisation of violence against women and the rationalisation of exclusion of sexual minorities in Fiji, the relationship between the two and their association with key socio-economic factors.

Nicole George examines the importance of gender considerations in security sector reform. She highlights how gender has been incorporated into peacebuilding initiatives in Bougainville and the Solomon Islands in an attempt to create improved opportunities for women. She also draws attention to how informal gendered logics work in the (dis)service of reform objectives.

Andreas Kopf, Michael Fink and Eberhard Weber present arguments which explore women's disproportionate vulnerability to climate change impacts, focussing on the case of Tropical Cyclone Winston (2016) in rural Fiji. They identify specific social, economic and cultural factors that contribute to vulnerability and highlight the need for these factors to be addressed to effect more permanent and broad social change that will go beyond policy priorities and action and prevent them from being exacerbated by natural disasters and climate change.

Richard A. Davis explores the possible role of Christian theology in reducing rates of violence against women and increasing their security. He presents the contributions of non-governmental stakeholders towards the elimination of violence against women and points to the complementary contribution of theology, specifically in PICs' contexts characterised by very high rates of Christian adherence and church attendance.

Sara N. Amin and Christian Girard put forward the position of transgendered individuals in Tonga through the perspective of the founder of the Tonga Leitis Association (TLA). They highlight insecurities developed as a result of multiple forms of discrimination and present *talanoa* (dialogue) as an important aspect of advancing the transgender agenda of freedom from discrimination, in addition to the key role of businesses and the private sector to support and create opportunities for leitis in Tonga.

Part 3: Organisational culture, security providers, partner institutions and security outcomes – State and non-state actors have long placed emphasis on addressing security-related concerns impacting law, order, peace and security within and beyond jurisdictions. Both scholarly and policy dialogue has stressed the importance of state responses, non-state stakeholder responses and the partnering of state and non-state actors for necessary security outcomes. It is also important to look at how service security provision evolves over time in different contexts and to acknowledge that state providers of security cannot exist in isolation. The chapters in this section explore responses to security involving state actors as well as non-state actors with influence on state responses. Contributors offer perspectives on policing which transcend ideas about policing as an act performed by the most visible arm of state governance to include other dimensions of policing involving the military, communities and other social actors. Scholarly positions are offered as follows:

Danielle Watson and Sinclair Dinnen explore security outcomes by highlighting the impact of external interventions on security and security service provision in Melanesia. They focus on the realities specific to small island territories and discuss the dangers of transposing first-world policy philosophies and practices to these contexts.

Miranda Forsyth explores the interface between security service provision and community beliefs about (in)security in relation to sorcery accusation related violence in Papua New Guinea. She explores the importance of relational networks as opposed to or alongside state resources in ensuring security outcomes. The chapter highlights the challenge of navigating different organisational and cultural norms and supports arguments about the importance of contextual considerations in devising strategies to improve security outcomes.

Sinclair Dinnen expounds on security service providers and partner institutions as critical to dialogue about security in Papua New Guinea (PNG). He highlights the role of non-state actors alongside the state and its law enforcement agencies in security service provision. He references the political economy of private security in PNG, its implications for "public security", and the likely beneficiaries and likely losers from such developments.

Natasha Khan traverses the terrain between organisational culture and security providers by examining the role of the military in state (in)security in Fiji. She presents arguments to support consideration of multiple factors in security sector reform, particularly its timing, and shows how poorly or overlooked/omitted variables are likely to present undesired outcomes.

Danielle Watson and James Johnson put forward the position of a key stakeholder in Guam on partnering for optimal security outcomes. They present effective security service provision as dependent on the relationship between policing organisations and the community. Here, organisational culture is also presented as a key factor for successful security providers.

The chapters in *Mapping Security in the Pacific* go beyond the issues of jurisprudence, international relations and political security by drawing on the security–insecurity framework and examining the role of organisational culture, power dynamics and gender. They bring forth analyses at micro-, meso- and macro-levels, allowing us to interrogate security beyond a political framework and examine the interconnections between security, crime and justice as well. It has a wide geographical focus and covers the Pacific region more widely, as well as points to the issues raised for crime and justice studies by environmental insecurity. The volume presents literature on a range of security issues specific to the Pacific from multidisciplinary standpoints, making it relevant as an undergraduate and graduate academic reference text for faculty and students across the University of the South Pacific's 12 member countries and other education institutions interested in these issues beyond the Pacific region. Although context-specific, many conclusions, recommendations and conceptualizations are relevant to the broader theorisation and understanding of security and insecurity, their multiple forms and the ways to tackle them. They can also speak to other contexts with different yet similar structures where these issues are at stake.

We hope *Mapping Security in the Pacific* contributes to the overarching aim of the book series, Routledge Studies in Crime and Justice in Asia and the Global South, by opening up opportunities to rethink scholarly and policy frames related to security/insecurity about the Pacific, in which context, complexity, connections, indigeneity, "smallness", traditions and faith, are not conceptualised as problems to be solved, but that they are understood as key means to better understand local realities and challenges of security and achieve adaptation and resilience.

References

Abrahamsen, R., & Williams, M. C. (2006). Security sector reform: Bringing the private in: Analysis. *Conflict, Security & Development, 6*(1), 1–23.

Abrahamsen, R., & Williams, M. C. (2007). Securing the city: Private security companies and non-state authority in global governance. *International Relations, 21*(2), 237–253.

ADB. (2011). *Food for all: Investing in food security in Asia and the Pacific – Issues, innovations, and practices*. Mandaluyong City, Philippines: Asian Development Bank.

Anceschi, L., & Symons, J. (2012). *Energy security in the era of climate change*. London: Springer.

Ayson, R., & Ball, D. (2006). *Strategy and security in the Asia-Pacific*. Crow's Nest: Allen & Unwin Book Publishers.

Bauman, Z. (1992). Interview with Zygmunt Bauman. In *Intimations of postmodernity* (pp. 205–228). New York: Routledge.

Behnassi, M., Gupta, H., & Pollmann, O. (2019). *Human and environmental security in the era of global risks: Perspectives from Africa, Asia and the Pacific Islands*. London: Springer.

Boas, I., & Rothe, D. (2016). From conflict to resilience? Explaining recent changes in climate security discourse and practice. *Environmental Politics, 25*(4), 613–632.

Bogardi, J., Spring, Ú. O., & Brauch, H. G. (2016). Water security: Past, present and future of a controversial concept. In C. Pahl-Wostl, A. Bhaduri, & J. Gupta (Eds.), *Handbook on water security* (pp. 38–58). Cheltenham: Edward Elgar Publishing.

Brauch, H. G., & Scheffran, J. (2012). Introduction: Climate change, human security, and violent conflict in the anthropocene. In J. Scheffran, M. Brzoska, H. G. Brauch, P. M. Link, & J. Schilling (Eds.), *Climate change, human security and violent conflict: Challenges for societal stability* (Vol. 8, pp. 3–40). London: Springer Science & Business Media.

Brisman, A., McClanahan, B., South, N., & Walters, R. (2018). *Water, crime and security in the twenty-first century: Too dirty, too little, too much.* London: Springer.

Campbell, J. R. (2015). Development, global change and traditional food security in Pacific Island countries. *Regional Environmental Change, 15*(7), 1313–1324.

Carrington, K., Hogg, R., & Sozzo, M. (2016). Southern criminology. *The British Journal of Criminology, 56*(1), 1–20.

Chan, N. (2018). "Large Ocean States": Sovereignty, small islands, and marine protected areas in global oceans governance. *Global Governance: A Review of Multilateralism and International Organizations, 24*(4), 537–555.

Chmutina, K., Lizarralde, G., Dainty, A., & Bosher, L. (2016). Unpacking resilience policy discourse. *Cities, 58*, 70–79.

Cohn, C., Kinsella, H., & Gibbings, S. (2004). Women, peace and security resolution 1325. *International Feminist Journal of Politics, 6*(1), 130–140.

Dalby, S. (2015). Climate change and the insecurity frame. In S. O'Lear & S. Dalby (Eds.), *Reframing climate change: Constructing ecological geopolitics* (pp. 83–99). London: Routledge.

Dalby, S. (2017). Environmental (In)security. In Richardson, D., Castree, N., Goodchild, M. F., Kobayashi, A., Liu, W., & Marston, R. A. (Eds.), *International encyclopedia of geography* (pp. 1–10). London: John & Wiley & Sons.

Dhanarajan, A. (2017). *Sustainable agriculture towards food security.* Singapore: Springer.

Dupont, A. (1997). New dimensions of security. In D. Roy (Ed.), *The new security agenda in the Asia-Pacific region* (pp. 31–50). London: Macmillan press Ltd.

Elliott, L. (2015). Human security/environmental security. *Contemporary Politics, 21*(1), 11–24.

Elliott, L. (2018). Harm and emancipation: Making environmental security "critical" in the Asia-Pacific. In A. Burke & M. McDonald (Eds.), *Critical security in the Asia-Pacific.* Manchester, England: Manchester University Press.

Forsyth, M. (2009). *A bird that flies with two wings: Kastom and state justice systems in Vanuatu.* Canberra: ANU E Press.

Fry, G. (1997). Framing the islands: Knowledge and power in changing Australian images of "the South Pacific". *The Contemporary Pacific*, 305–344.

Giddens, A. (1990). *The consequences of modernity.* Cambridge: Polity Press.

Gill, M. (2014). Introducing the handbook of security. In M. Gill (Ed.), *The handbook of security* (pp. 1–17). Palgrave-MacMillan.

Hau'ofa, E. (2008). *We are the ocean.* Honolulu: University of Hawai'i Press.

Heath, L., Salinger, M. J., Falkland, T., Hansen, J., Jiang, K., Kameyama, Y. . . . White, I. (2014). Climate and security in Asia and the Pacific (food, water and energy). In M. J. Manton & L. A. Stevenson (Eds.), *Climate in Asia and the Pacific: Security, society and sustainability* (pp. 129–198). New York City: Springer.

Jacob, E. D. (2017). *Rethinking security in the twenty-first century: A reader.* New York City: Springer.

Kaldor, M., & Rangelov, I. (2014). *The handbook of global security policy.* Chichester: John Wiley & Sons.

Kirby, P., & Shepherd, L. J. (2016). Reintroducing women, peace and security. *International Affairs, 92*(2), 249–254.

Manton, M. J. (2014). Introduction. In M. J. Manton & L. A. Stevenson (Eds.), *Climate in Asia and the Pacific: Security, society and sustainability* (pp. 1–16). London: Springer.

Martin, M., & Owen, T. (2013). *Routledge handbook of human security.* Routledge.

Masys, A. J., & Lin, S. (2018). *Asia-Pacific security challenges: Managing black swans and persistent threats.* London: Springer.

McCauley, D. (2018). *Energy justice: Re-balancing the trilemma of security, poverty and climate change*. London: Palgrave MacMillan.

McLellan, B. (2018a). *Sustainable future for human security: Environment and resources*. Singapore: Springer.

McLellan, B. (2018b). *Sustainable future for human security: Society, cities and governance*: Singapore: Springer.

Miller, B. (2001). The concept of security: Should it be redefined? *The Journal of Strategic Studies, 24*(2), 13–42.

O'Manique, C., & Fourie, P. (2018). *Global health and security: Critical feminist perspectives*. London: Routledge.

Pettman, R. (2005). Human security as global security: Reconceptualising strategic studies. *Cambridge Review of International Affairs, 18*(1), 137–150.

Ratuva, S. (2014). "Failed" or resilient subaltern communities?: Pacific indigenous social protection systems in a neoliberal world. *Pacific Journalism Review, 20*(2), 40.

Rushton, S., & Youde, J. (2014). *Routledge handbook of global health security*. London: Routledge.

Sarkar, A., Sensharma, S. R., & vanLoon, G. W. (2019). *Sustainable solutions for food security: Combating climate change by adaptation*. London: Springer International Publishing.

Savage, A., McIver, L., & Schubert, L. (2019). Review: The nexus of climate change, food and nutrition security and diet-related non-communicable diseases in Pacific Island countries and territories. *Climate and Development*, 1–14.

Scheffran, J., Brzoska, M., Brauch, H. G., Link, P. M., & Schilling, J. (2012). *Climate change, human security and violent conflict: Challenges for societal stability* (Vol. 8). London: Springer Science & Business Media.

Shepherd, L. J. (2016). Making war safe for women? National action plans and the militarisation of the women, peace and security agenda. *International Political Science Review, 37*(3), 324–335.

Tazreiter, C., Weber, L., Pickering, S., Segrave, M., & McKernan, H. (2016). *Fluid security in the Asia Pacific: Transnational lives, human rights and state control*. London: Springer.

Teaiwa, K. (2014). Reframing Oceania: Lessons from Pacific studies. In *Framing the Global: Entry points for research*. Bloomington, IN: Indiana University Press.

Trombetta, M. J. (2008). Environmental security and climate change: Analysing the discourse. *Cambridge Review of International Affairs, 21*(4), 585–602.

UN. (2009). *Sustainable agriculture and food security in Asia and the Pacific*. Bangkok: United Nations Economic and Social Commission for Asia and the Pacific (ESCAP).

Watson, I., & Pandey, C. (2015). *Environmental security in the Asia-Pacific*. London: Palgrave Macmillan.

Yadav, S. S., Redden, R. J., Hatfield, J. L., Ebert, A. W., & Hunter, D. (2019). *Food security and climate change*. London: Wiley-Blackwell.

Part 1

Reframing security in the Pacific

2 Mapping circumstances in Oceania

Reconsidering human security in an age of globalisation[1]

Paul J. Carnegie and Victor T. King

Introduction

In 1994, the United Nations Development Programme (UNDP) launched an ambitious attempt to expand the concept of "security" to include the day-to-day lived insecurities experienced by numerous different peoples and communities globally. "Human Security" entered the lexicon of world affairs by way of the now much cited *Human Development Report 1994* (UNDP Report). A key observation of the UNDP Report was that many nation-states continued to privilege military expenditure and traditional security concerns over and above the human development and welfare priorities of their populations (Roberts, 2007). The primacy of the state-centric security paradigm was identified as increasingly at odds with contemporary sources of conflict and insecurity (Kaldor, 1999).

The UNDP Report's attempt to shift the reference point of agenda setting from that of traditional security to individual freedom and development underscored a growing awareness that international security and development are interdependent. As the Commission for Human Security (2003) concluded, the interrelated nature of economic, food, health, environmental, personal (in relation to crime and violence) and community (particularly in relation to inter-ethnic issues, minority group rights and gender) security along with political surety (with reference to basic human rights) are mutually supportive of human well-being.

There is recognition within the international community in normative terms, if not always in practice, that human security is an essential part of sustainable development and poverty reduction in the twenty-first century. As growing evidence further indicates, the disruptive inequalities of globalisation's underbelly and the forces it unleashes have also perpetuated instances of poverty, emboldened criminality and deepened shadow economies in tandem with the upside's many benefits (Heine & Thakur, 2011; Stiglitz, 2002). Large numbers of humanity do not have ready access to alternative livelihoods and forms of support, nor do they have receptive channels of communication to voice their concerns (Standing, 2011). The high levels of risk and insecurity that the global "precariat" find themselves living through are the real outcomes of a range of largely unacknowledged sociocultural-economic transformations (Harvey, 2006; Standing, 2016). It is a precariousness largely beyond their control. One that often permeates by gradual and debilitating increments in the oceans, rivers, forests and fields of our planet and plays out in anonymous corners and alleyways (Carnegie, King, & Ibrahim, 2016). Their plight is the localised consequences of interlinked national, regional and global forces and interests.

Nonetheless, expanding security beyond the level of international relations between nation-states and their traditional security concerns is not without its critics and sceptics (Buzan, 2004, pp. 369–370; Chandler, 2008, pp. 427–439; Krause, 2004, pp. 367–368; Paris, 2001, pp. 87–102). One of the primary charges is that as a concept, human security is too open-ended and imprecise for practical application. Its protean character is seen as having limited analytical utility for prioritising and apportioning valuable resources. As Yuen Foong Khong (2001, pp. 231–236) neatly surmises, trying to prioritise everything means nothing is prioritised. Others have gone even further by arguing that the adoption of a discourse of human security by certain states can operate to mask an ongoing entrenchment of elite interests (Chandler & Hynek, 2011). Moreover, rather than give voice to the voiceless, privatised reform packages to developing countries often resemble more of a case of protecting "us over here" from "those over there" (Duffield & Waddell, 2006, pp. 1–23).

Evidently, real tension exists between the ways in which local, community and individual level insecurities are understood and the transferability of the human security agenda to particular settings. Each country or region confronts a different context of human security and faces a set of specific challenges. However, action in developing countries is formulated largely with the backing of international donors and tends to be generic, imitative and overly ambitious (Cammack, McLeod, Menocal, & Christiansen, 2006). If the threats and impediments to human security are part of the daily-lived experience of large numbers of people and their vulnerability and precariousness are neither readily understood nor measurable, how are we to proceed? What is becoming clearer is that it is not possible to encapsulate the range of issues confronting regions, countries, communities and individuals within a neat conceptual framework of human security. Histories, cultures and ethnicities differ, configurations of politico-business elites and patterns of civil-military relations also vary, as do the respective positions within the international system of power and privilege. Yet, what we can do is identify specific concepts to deploy in developing our understanding of the range of uncertainties, insecurities and risks currently exercising us.

In this chapter, we contend that the field of human security (which tends to be dominated by the disciplinary concerns of international relations, development and security studies) needs to engage more fully with a range of sociological and anthropological concepts to maintain its relevance and gain greater analytical purchase on the multiple insecurities facing Pacific Island Countries (PICs) of Oceania in the twenty-first century. We do so by considering the utility of theoretical and empirical contributions generated by such scholars as Zygmunt Bauman, Anthony Giddens, Mary Douglas, Olivia Harris, James C. Scott and Edward P. Thompson. This allows us to situate vulnerable and precarious circumstances (human insecurities) within conceptual discussions of "safety" and "risk" and their complex relationship to "trust" and "uncertainty". While we readily accept that our selection of works displays a certain idiosyncrasy and remain open to charges of Anglo-centric bias, the choices are informed. They are based on the import of their insights to the task at hand and their ability to encapsulate much about contemporary marginality and the range of human insecurities confronting us. They should in no way be read as definitive templates but rather indicative of a path ahead.

Recalling useful concepts for uncommon times

Before going further, a few remarks need to be made about the ways in which concepts in the social sciences particularly sociology and anthropology can relate to our considerations. "Insecurity" triggers conceptions of higher levels of uncertainty, vulnerability and a lack of protection; more particularly, higher risks attached to the exercise of one's everyday routine and a lack of trust in social, political, economic and other kinds of relationships. This is especially so if those who are experiencing higher levels of risk are having to deal with those who exercise power, influence or control over their life chances and opportunities. For those who experience insecurity, or perceive themselves to be insecure, there is a sense of an absence of the ability to make decisions about their own life. They do not have a say in the way in which their community and, at a higher level, the nation-state is run. This reinforces a sense that their lives lack meaning. They detect an absence of generally accepted norms and values that were previously considered to govern every day relationships. They may even develop an inability to identify with and acknowledge the legitimacy of the dominant norms of society. Overall, those who experience insecurity in these ways feel a sense of isolation and marginalisation.

For those schooled in critical traditions, the concept of "alienation" comes to mind. The loss of connection between what workers produce and why they are producing it (Marx, [1844] 1968). A loss of control over their working lives, their destinies and identities and their relationship with other workers finds a parallel in the vulnerability and uncertainty of many contemporary and increasingly temporary employment conditions. When lives are fragmented and mediated through money relationships or global capital forces, a sense of separation and loss ensues.

This also resonates with the related concept of "anomie" and in turn ideas of "normlessness" or "estrangement" (Durkheim, [1893] 1977). A sense of disconnection from the social world can develop by way of modernisation, urbanisation and individualisation. The breakdown of social bonds between an individual and their society or a mismatch between individual expectations, desires and behaviour and the wider society is a symptom of this process. If you lack identification with the dominant values and ideals of the developmental state in which you live, then marginalisation and a precarious existence become a real possibility. *In extremis*, of course, this could lead to the taking of one's own life (Durkheim, [1897] 1951).

Significantly, these frequently ignored concepts retain relevance with our current and, in many ways, silent predicaments of vulnerability and precariousness (human insecurities). The World Health Organisation (WHO) provides figures of over 800,000 deaths globally every year due to suicide. It is the second leading cause of death among young people from the age of 15 to 29 (WHO, 2017). The WHO identifies vulnerable groups in low and middle-income countries as especially prone to suicide: those experiencing conflict, disaster, violence, abuse, loss, discrimination and a sense of isolation. This is the case in PICs that have some of the highest suicide rates globally with an incidence of 30 per 100,000 in places such as Micronesia, Guam and Samoa (Pacific Report, 2014). That is nearly double the global average and the rates of youth suicide are even more acute (Chand, 2015). Sociologically, we can point to several key stressors including unemployment, changing socio-cultural expectations, familial breakdown, bullying and various forms of violence and abuse, especially sexual and gender-based. These stressors are amplified through intergenerational conflict as modern individualistic lifestyles jar with the traditional conformity demanded from Pacific communal social hierarchies and associated behavioural obligations and conventions (Lowe, 2019, pp. 105–138).

At least some of these problems must be laid at the door of the governments that preside over their citizens because either they have generated some of these very problems themselves or they have simply failed to address them. They usually assign them a low priority or quite simply they do not have the capacity, the political will, support or interest to help solve them.

A central problem in examining such multiple insecurities is the question of at what level do we address them? There is tension between the levels and spaces of insecurities in both discourse and practice. The actions taken to ensure the security and integrity of the nation-state or increasingly international peace, stability and cooperation, may work against the rights, freedoms and security of individuals and communities. In short, such actions may create insecurities at the local level. Ideally, the security of individuals and communities and the political and physical integrity and security of the nation-state within which they live should be mutually reinforcing, but this is certainly not always the case.

Decisions of political leaders, taken, as they argue, in the interests of the nation-state often cut across and compromise an individual or community sense of what is needed to ensure local-level collective "security". People intuitively know what that latter "security" means but it is hardly surprising that national-level policymaking in a complex society will invariably have an adverse effect on the interests and the perceptions of security of some segment of society. The compromise can take many forms. For instance, the need to cut the public deficit can lead to a reduction in the resources provided for the police force. As a result, this can increase fear and anxiety about crime levels and heighten the threat felt by individuals to their security and well-being. The pressure from global financial institutions to prioritise interest payments on national debts can lead to reductions in public funding of health services or education and concomitant increases in charges and fees. This in turn makes it difficult for families to ensure that their children will have access to the health services and education necessary to ensure their future occupational and economic security. As a result, they may begin to disassociate themselves from the dominant values and ideals of the developmental state in which they live and jeopardise themselves further.

In places like Solomon Islands and PNG, pre-existing social, economic and political grievances are magnified by rural-urban drift and youth bulges. School-leavers have about a one in eight chance of joining the formal labour force in Port Moresby. The pressure to seek out alternative income can push youth into the embrace of armed groups or "raskol gangs" and street crime (Hayward-Jones, 2016). Honiara continues to be a magnet for disaffected youth where an estimated 20 % are officially unemployed (SPC, 2017). Mis-matched expectations and hamstrung governance realities continue to pitch livelihood contraction against the risk of violent conflict (IDMC, 2014)

Embarking on the promulgation of an international norm and operationalising a safety and security regime to embody the right to feel and be safe and secure does raise expectations of delivery. It also leads us into paradoxical terrain. The more secure we make the world appear, the less its image can tolerate risk. Over-protectionism on all levels tends to breed a debilitating inability to cope with difficulty and complexity. Arguably, this is the opposite of what our contemporary condition demands.

On the face of it, this might seem a somewhat trite conundrum when the perceptions of security–safety and insecurity–risk vary so widely and brutally, especially in the developing world or areas beset by warfare and conflict. There is no easy response to such a comparative dilemma. Some developing nation-states, more than others, live with risk and insecurity and create a populace that sees itself as largely independent of the state. To survive they are forced to make their own way and develop their own creative solutions to address insecurities. The state does not support them and indeed may exploit them in a range of contexts through corrupt practices.

Nonetheless, we can begin on a conceptual level at least to think our way through the impasse between norm promulgation and practical application. How much more pressing is the safety-risk dilemma for those countries in which one's very life is at risk because of inter-ethnic conflict, civil war, uncontrolled violence and crime, poverty and unemployment, disease, environmental destruction and loss of rights in land? Situating vulnerable and precarious circumstances (human insecurities) within conceptual discussions of "safety" and "risk" and their complex relationship to "trust" and "uncertainty" can assist in this endeavour.

The following sections draw on theorists in sociology, anthropology and socio-political history, who not only conceptualise and address issues of risk, insecurity and marginality, but each in their own way were marginal or saw themselves as marginal from mainstream society.

From Bauman to Giddens and the late modern condition

Many writers and scholars have documented issues of trust, risk and uncertainty in the age of late modernity (Beck, 1992; Bhide & Stevenson, 1992; Endres &

Six-Hohenbalken, 2014; Watson & Moran, 2005; Zinn, 2008). But none more elo-quently and extensively as the Polish Jewish exile, Zygmunt Bauman, for whom uncertainty was an immediate and everyday experience in communist Poland in the 1950s and 1960s. Antoni Gramsci influenced him among other social thinkers but Bauman brought together a range of ideas from social and political philosophy (Forgacs, 1988). If we are to gain purchase on the largely unacknowledged range of contemporary insecurities, he deserves our attention.

For Bauman, the major task of modernity (which he refers to as "solid" in that it emphasises matters of control and order rather than alienation and anomie) has been to remove unknowns and uncertainties; to make order. This means allocat-ing people a place in the division of labour, to rationalise, bureaucratise, catego-rise and address personal insecurities. The implication was that following rules and regulations is a morally good thing to do in the modern condition. However, Bauman was fully aware that the process of order-making is never complete; the devastating logical corollary is that some people are never administered in this way; they remain "strangers", "outsiders", "other" and in certain cases become identified as people to be feared and coerced.

From this Bauman begins to identify that rules and regulations that ordered "solid" modernity experience slippage in the increasingly "liquid" world of "post-modernity". Having said this, it is worth noting that both Anthony Giddens and Bauman view post-modernity or "late modernity" as an extension of the same forces which shaped modernisation (Giddens, 1990, 1991; Hutton & Giddens, 2000). But significantly, late modernity is a "reflexive modernisation" in which people are less concerned with the precedents that were set by the generations that went before them; this requires some qualification of course.

Late modernity may provide individuals with freedoms to choose (an era of liberation if you will) but simultaneously it generates uncertainties, risk and emotional stress that have become ever more diffuse and unpredictable. Bauman attempted to capture these increasingly uncertain circumstances in several inter-related works (Bauman, 2000, 2003, 2005, 2006, 2011). A recurring motif for Bauman throughout was the problem of outsiders. This is relevant in situating the relational qualities of contemporary human insecurities.

To elaborate, in a world of consumers (or those who can afford to consume), those who live in sink estates, squatter settlements, banlieues, slums or favelas are increasingly closed off and marginalised. They are unemployed, spatially and socially segregated, involved in crime, are feared; they live in a world of insecu-rity and uncertainty themselves and they inflict it on others. Consequently, those who can afford to consume, increasingly live in walled and gated communities, employ private security with surveillance technology, alarms and guard dogs. In PNG for instance, security services are its fastest growing sector worth about one billion Kina (US$ 360 million) (Pacific Report, 2015). And if you walk around the Fijian capital of Suva you will get an immediate sense of its burgeoning pri-vate security guard sector. The salient point here are the connections between both the experience and the perception of uncertainty among various social and cultural groups (King, 2016, pp. 25–42). The frailty of human bonds in late or liq-uid modernity is a precursor to the situations we seek to manage but rarely avoid.

Douglas to Harris on risk, ways of life and ties that re-bind

Another concept that overlaps with some of Bauman's work is that of "risk". Just as our experience of uncertainty is coincidental to our construction of it, so to with risk. If we accept that perceptions of risk are socially constructed, then they represent different evaluations. In other words, there are different estimates of life chances within different institutional and historical contexts, and with reference to sets of cultural values and ways of life. How do we decide upon what is potentially dangerous or harmful and what is not? The approach of Mary Douglas and her co-author Aaron Wildavsky to risk is interesting here. Their construction of "ways of life" in terms of "group" and "grid" comprise different permutations of social organisation that endow people with perceptions that serve to strengthen the very institutional context within which they are embedded (Douglas, 1992; Douglas & Wildavsky, 1982). Douglas' work, situated in the anthropological tradition, speaks to the condition of "solid" modernity, and the aversion to subversive or marginal behaviour. Like Bauman, she draws attention to the tendency to focus resentment and blame on those who are perceived to be different, who defy authority and institutions and who live on the edge of what is defined as "society". Although not without explanatory limitations, as a frame this helps explain people's outlook on risk and uncertainty, and the apportioning of blame if things go wrong (Boholm, 1996, pp. 64–84). It depends then on cultural ways of life and what levels of uncertainty people are prepared to tolerate and how they organise themselves to cope with them.

This takes on resonance in Melanesia where sorcery/witchcraft practices and beliefs remain prevalent. Adherence to and suspicion of these beliefs and practices intersect with a wide array of social deprivation issues and uneven economic development combined with a dearth of public health awareness and limited national cohesion amongst diverse kinship groups. It is a situation that generates fertile environments for fear, distrust and violence (Forsyth & Eves, 2015).

Olivia Harris further connects to the above concerns from an anthropological perspective as she also emphasises the point that in response to uncertainty, social groups "defend continuity, and their rights to claim and express particular links with the past" (Harris, 1996, pp. 1–16).

We know that renewed claims to ethnicity and indigeneity are keenly felt in many PICs especially over customary land ownership and entitlement. These feelings can become amplified by rural–urban drift in peri-urban areas and growing resentment towards exclusionary national government policies. Divisive mining and logging operations or "new" migrant Chinese business activities can also prove potent catalysts for such claims (Firth, 2018, pp. 1–26). Though sometimes frail, bonds of cultural identity, connection with the past, celebration of tradition and the mutual support which underpins these claims for continuity, are sometimes all that can be mustered to counter feelings of insecurity.

What bears on the theme of insecurities, are the ways in which identities and ethnicities are constructed or crystallise. Often, they do so in the face of perceived threats and insecurities, and the domination of some by others (Carnegie,

2016, pp. 1–25). Certain group identities can forge and crystallise in opposition to the emergence of the modern nation-state and its coercive-exclusionary practices. In turn, the cultural expressions of these inter-ethnic identity formations, as we know, have frequently resulted in forms of violence (Carnegie, 2017, pp. 733–747). The five-year civil conflict in Solomon Islands (1998–2003) or the 1990s conflict in Bougainville were largely underpinned by competitive struggles over land and identity.

From a human security perspective, addressing complex and deeply rooted types of insecurity takes more than coercive state action. The latter is potentially counter-productive in the long term. On its own, it fails to address effectively the conditioning factors and social imaginary underlying insecurity and violence. If over-utilised, it runs too high a risk of antagonising and further polarising oppositional segments of the population by perpetuating a "ghettoised" sense of enmity and alienation towards the state and wider society (Carnegie et al., 2016, pp. 53–68).

Scott through Thompson on trust, respect and coming in from the margins

James C. Scott's work (1977, 1985, 1990) provides another reference point for our considerations. His central idea, though probably not expressed in quite this way is "trust" and one might add "respect", from which flow safety and livelihood security. For Scott, "peasant" values and the ways in which they evaluate the behaviour of others are oriented to the need to secure an adequate level of subsistence (the "subsistence ethic"); the concern therefore is with the security of supplies of basic foodstuffs and other essential needs (shelter, support and mutual reciprocity). Local elites provide charitable donations and other gifts or provisions to their dependents. Scott's thesis was persuasive and bold in its comparative perspective, but it was certainly not without conceptual and empirical problems (King, 1978, pp. 123–149; Popkin, 1979; King, 1981, pp. 249–251). Scott and his co-researcher Benedict J. Kerkvliet focus on the character and quality of patron–client relations, and the consequences of the breakdown or breach of these relations for "peasant" security (Kerkvliet, 1977). Once the traditional paternalistic "moral order" begins to break down with the intervention of market relations, capital and profit (in other words, modernity), then the likelihood is resistance and possibly protest and violence. For Scott, "peasant" society and culture placed an emphasis on respect for the subsistence needs of the rural poor, on mutual support and a reciprocal sense of give-and-take fairness in the face of the potential and actual insecurity of one's livelihood. In short, it draws attention to the contextual bonds of trust, safety and security.

Scott's thesis drew significantly on the influential work of Edward P. Thompson ([1963] 2013, 1971, pp. 76–136). Thompson sought not simply to re-write history from the perspective of the downtrodden ("history from below") but to capture the values, perspectives and culture of those living at the margins, those who had been left out of history. As Thompson ([1963] 2013, pp. 12–13) declared, "I am seeking to rescue the poor stockinger, the Luddite cropper, the 'obsolete' hand-loom weaver, the 'Utopian' artisan, and even the deluded follower of Joanna Southcott, from the enormous condescension of posterity. Their crafts and traditions may have been dying. Their hostility to the new industrialism may have been backward-looking. Their communitarian ideals may have been fantasies. Their insurrectionary conspiracies may have been foolhardy. But they lived through these times of acute social disturbance, and we did not". Recently, Norbert Götz (2015, pp. 147–162) has sought to extend the concept of "moral economy" from the narrow historical and economic contexts of Thompson's, and indeed Scott's and Kerkvliet's work, to explore the moral dimension of such fields as "welfare", "humanitarianism" and "civil society". Having said this, it should be noted that for Thompson, class was not a predetermined structure but a relationship. He saw it arising in different times and places, but never in quite the same manner. In significant ways, the contemporary expression of this is the growing distance between the "haves" and the "have-nots". It begs the question, who speaks for the latter in the apportioning of ever-scarcer resources when the walls go up? For PICs, the very real spectre of climate-induced forced migrations and threats to water and food security on future livelihoods will bring into sharp relief the starkness of these inequalities (Birk & Rasmussen, 2014, pp. 1–13; Reuveny, 2007, pp. 656–673).

What does all of this have to do with human security in Oceania?

In an era of globalisation, there is a telling relationship between uncertainty, insecurity and violence. What we confront is an unsettling human moiré patterned by a range of often unseen and overlapping local, national, regional and global interests and forces. In many countries, political elites wish to promote agricultural modernisation and large-scale commercial plantations. Given that a high percentage of populations in PICs are engaged in subsistence agriculture (in Vanuatu about 80 % of the population relies in some way on household food gardens and fish-of-the-day catches), the apportioning of land to intensive, industrial scale agrobusiness is a sensitive and divisive matter. The tension between the security and interests of the nation-state and the need to address individual, community and local insecurities is evident across Oceania (UNDP, 2014). It is a deeply contradictory matter and invariably exacts a high price on human development aspirations.

The substantial agroforestry concerns in PNG, Fiji, Solomon Islands and New Caledonia are not without controversy. In PNG, the Special Agricultural and Business Lease (SABL) system introduced in 1979 was supposed to benefit traditional landowners through a leasehold system of rents for productive use of customary land. However, insidious levels of corruption have led to large-scale "land grabs" on the part of avaricious business interests. It is estimated that over 5.2 million hectares of customary land has been alienated (Filer, 2017, pp. 169–203). The likes of Fiji and Hawai'i also have significant tracts of land turned over to sugar cane and copra production.

The case of atoll microstates such as Kiribati, Tuvalu or Nauru is rather different. They have little land mass for large-scale agricultural operations but huge territorial waters. With few other national resources for generating income, the selling of fishing licences for exclusive economic zones to overseas commercial fishing fleets raises much-needed revenue but little in the way of long-term food security (Barnett, 2011, pp. 229–237).

Political elites also seek to maintain and enhance national integrity and incorporate minority populations into the majority or dominant culture. In a region defined by its ocean and the mobility of its inhabitants, this is a thorny issue in some of the larger archipelagic states of Oceania. For example, in Fiji, ethno-culturally distinct Rotuma and the historically displaced Banabans on Rabi island face pressure to assimilate within the unitary state. Moreover, central governments define who qualifies as a citizen and who does not; policing and monitoring territorial borders and exerting punitive action and sanctions for those who do not conform.

If we are to take our evaluations of risk and insecurities seriously in PICs it is not enough to reach into the generic solution cupboard. Whether it be marginalised communities, subsistence fishermen and farmers or insecure migrants who traverse borders, they depend on those who govern to recognise their rights as human beings to protection and support and their need to conduct their daily lives in safety and security, and if migrants to provide a safe and welcoming haven. Their realities occupy a range of local struggles to survive in environments where ruling political elites are often preoccupied with securing economic growth, shoring up configurations of politico-business dominance and preserving territorial state-sovereignty against threats (real and perceived).

Addressing these situations means doing more than solely relying on strictly scientific or measurable calculations of uncertainty and risk. It involves considering the knowledge of the probable consequences and possibilities of an event or process. We must then link that to the perceptual dimension of those calculations, based on values and beliefs, and importantly the political dimension of framing risk (in which the risk under scrutiny is subject to negotiation and contestation among political actors who have specific interests, goals and agendas). Which brings us to what is related intimately to uncertainty and risk in the context of human security. The tentative response is safety and trust, which are also social constructs. If we are to get a handle on uncertainty and risk, we must strive for trust in our relationships and the establishment of an environment of safety.

But there is the rub. In our globalising age, transnational corporations, international organisations and economists are constantly concerned and berating others about the reliability or trustworthiness of transactions, especially in relation to developing countries, and expound on the virtue of this reliability as a pillar of good economic governance. Yet, we have lamentably witnessed the extent to which uncertainty, debt and risk (including risk-seeking behaviour) inhabit our international financial system. Driven by global electronic technology, the triumvirate of uncertainty, debt and risk are now deeply embedded in a range of interrelated but largely invisible transactions from the global to the local.

Our trust in political, financial and even cultural institutions have increasingly diminished. And trust is something which we usually rely on when we negotiate the edge between having confidence in what we think we know and sampling the contingencies of new possibilities. Without the stability that trust induces, uncertainty creeps into everyday lives and we develop a growing dependency on the need for protection. But if we are dependents of others more powerful and influential than us, can we trust those we are dependent upon? Can we trust them not to undermine community or collective security and livelihoods?

These are serious questions given that the total population of PICs is forecast to grow from 11 million to an estimated 17.7 million by 2050 (predominantly in four countries: Papua New Guinea, Solomon Islands, Vanuatu and Kiribati) (UNFPA, 2014). And the recent Boe Declaration (the official 2018 communiqué from the Pacific Islands Forum in Nauru) stated that "climate change remains the single greatest threat to the livelihoods, security and well-being of the peoples of the Pacific". If the Pacific Ocean warms at a rate even below current conservative estimates this will impact coral reefs and mangroves and bring about major shifts in precipitation patterns and the frequency and intensity of cyclones. The overall prognosis is deeply troubling with the prospect of rising sea levels, forced migrations, degradation of aquatic ecosystems and declining fish stocks from ocean temperature rises and plastic pollution, contamination of freshwater through saltwater inundation, land degradation and loss (impacting food security, livelihoods and cultural life) and an increasing incidence of water-borne and vector-borne diseases such as dengue, chikungunya, malaria and typhoid (Campbell & Bedford, 2014, pp. 177–204).

It has become clear to many PICs that dealing with the macro-threat of climate change and its attendant host of associated and intersecting human insecurities requires a more honest form of brokering and mutual support than previously afforded them. New forms of diplomacy, coalition building and action are emerging (Melanesian Spearhead Group; Polynesian Leaders Group; UN Group of Friends on Climate and Security; Alliance of Small Island States) but whether it is sufficient to counter and mitigate the former hegemonic influence and interests of the likes of Australia, France, UK, NZ and US over security and economic matters in the region remains to be seen.

Conclusion

Reconciling ambition with messy realities is never straightforward. As mentioned at the beginning of our discussion, the ways in which vulnerability and precariousness (human insecurities) play out across Oceania are not readily understood or easily measurable. It is not possible to encapsulate the range of issues within a neat conceptual framework of human security.

When thinking about human insecurities in PICs and the ways in which to address them, it is important to remember that the Pacific Ocean is no monolithic, empty expanse. Its islands are not inconsequential specs in a vast briny abyss but oceanic states of imagination in the minds and hearts of their inhabitants. The life-sustaining inevitability of the ocean in reality and the imaginaries of its people is ever present. Coming to terms with the human insecurities of "large ocean states" and their developmental, political and ethnocultural diversity is a different proposition than generating homogenised responses for supposedly similar "small island developing states".

Trying to visualise this in your mind's eye is like contemplating an Alexander Calder "Mobile". The reality defies and confuses expectation in equal measure. What confronts you are disparate fragments of uneven form and colour that float and fluctuate. Weighted and light. A kinetic assemblage that seems improbable but somehow isn't. Oddly balanced maybe, yet vital and buoyant.

If we are to expand effectively the scope of "security" towards addressing the day-to-day inequities and lived insecurities experienced by many people across Oceania (now and into the future), then gaining a better understanding of the complex and largely hidden nexus of interrelated conditioning forces and interests underlying them constitutes a significant step forward.

Our brief sojourn through the work of some influential and pioneering scholars shows there are specific concepts we can deploy in developing our understanding of the range of uncertainties, insecurities and risks currently exercising us. We have drawn on a set of interrelated readings not previously brought together in this form and for this purpose. And we attempted to re-situate human security not necessarily within a coherent theory but a "collage" of concepts relevant to the central preoccupations of the social sciences. Conceptually locating threats and impediments to human security within relationships of risk, uncertainty, safety and trust, opens a way to understand more fully the context of human insecurities in PICs, their communities and for the individuals who populate them.

We hope to have demonstrated that identifying multiple insecurities resonates directly with some of the crucial concepts in the social sciences. In our terms and as we have sought to use and interpret them here: "uncertainty, risk, safety and trust". Without trust, which in turn entails respect in relationships, then uncertainties and threats abound and the everyday lives of the populace are constantly engaged in coping with risk. These are the central concepts which underpin human security and provide a direction for future research and practice in Oceania.

Note

1 This chapter is published with the kind permission of the Japanese Association of Human Security Studies. An earlier version of it appeared in the *Journal of Human Security Studies*, 7(1), pp. 1–17.

References

Barnett, J. (2011). Dangerous climate change in the Pacific Islands: Food production and food security. *Regional Environmental Change*, *11*(1), 229–237.
Bauman, Z. (2000). *Liquid modernity*. Cambridge: Polity Press.

Bauman, Z. (2003). *Liquid love: On the frailty of human bonds.* Cambridge: Polity Press.

Bauman, Z. (2005). *Liquid life.* Cambridge: Polity Press.

Bauman, Z. (2006). *Liquid fear.* Cambridge: Polity Press.

Bauman, Z. (2006). *Liquid times: Living in an age of uncertainty.* Cambridge: Polity Press.

Bauman, Z. (2011). *Culture in a liquid modern world.* Cambridge: Polity Press.

Beck, U. (1992). *Risk society: Towards a new modernity.* London: Sage Publications.

Bhide, A., & Stevenson, H. (1992). Trust, uncertainty and profit. *The Journal of Socio-Economics, 21*(3), 191–208.

Birk, T., & Rasmussen, K. (2014). Migration from atolls as climate change adaptation: Current practices, barriers and options in Solomon Islands. *Natural Resources Forum, 38*(1), 1–13.

Boholm, A. (1996). Risk perception and social anthropology: Critique of cultural theory. *Ethnos, Journal of Anthropology, 61*(1–2), 64–84.

Buzan, B. (2004). A reductionist, idealistic notion that adds little analytical value. *Security Dialogue, 35*(3), 369–370.

Cammack, D., McLeod, D., Menocal, A. R., & Christiansen, K. (2006). *Donors and the 'fragile states' agenda: A survey of current thinking and practice.* Report submitted to the Japan International Cooperation Agency. London: Poverty and Public Policy Group Overseas Development Institute.

Campbell, J., & Bedford, R. (2014). Migration and climate change in Oceania. In E. Piguet & F. Laczko (Eds.), *People on the move in a changing climate: The regional impact of environmental change on migration* (pp. 177–204). Singapore: Springer.

Carnegie, P. J. (2016). *Of social imaginary and violence: Responding to Islamist militancy in Indonesia.* IAS Working Paper 22, pp. 1–25.

Carnegie, P. J. (2017). State, security and militancy in Indonesia. In S. N. Romaniuk et al. (Eds.), *Palgrave handbook of global counterterrorism policy* (pp. 733–747). New York: Palgrave Macmillan.

Carnegie, P. J., King, V. T., & Ibrahim, Z. (Eds.). (2016). *Human insecurities in Southeast Asia.* Asia in Transition 5. Singapore: UBD-Institute of Asian Studies and Springer.

Chand, R. K. (2015). Access to information: Questions on equality, gender and geographical gap in relation to suicide prevention. *Journal of Pacific Studies, 35*(1), 1–19.

Chandler, D. (2008). Human security: The dog that didn't bark. *Security Dialogue, 39*(4), 427–439.

Chandler, D., & Hynek, N. (Eds.). (2011). *Critical perspectives on human security.* PRIO New Security Studies. London: Routledge.

Commission on Human Security. (2003). *Human security now.* Washington, DC: Communications Development Incorporated.

Douglas, M. (1992). *Risk and blame: Essays in cultural theory.* London and New York: Routledge.

Douglas, M., & Wildavsky, A. B. (1982). *Risk and culture: An essay on the selection of technical and environmental dangers.* Berkeley, CA: University of California Press.

Duffield, M., & Waddell, N. (2006). Securing humans in a dangerous world. *International Politics, 43*(1), 1–23.

Durkheim, E. [1893] (1977). *the division of labor in society* (W. D. Halls, trans.). New York: Free Press.

Durkheim, E. [1897] (1951). *Suicide: A study in sociology* (J. A. Spaulding & G. Simpson, trans.). Glencoe, IL: The Free Press.

Endres, K. W., & Six-Hohenbalken, M. (2014). Introduction to risks, rupture and uncertainties: Dealing with crisis in Asia's emerging economies. *Cambridge Anthropology, 32*(2), 42–48.

Filer, C. (2017). The formation of a land grab policy network in Papua New Guinea. In S. McDonnell, M. G. Allen, & C. Filer (Eds.), *Kastom, property and ideology: Land transformations in Melanesia* (pp. 169–203). Canberra: ANU Press.

Firth, S. (2018). *Instability in the Pacific islands: A status report* (pp. 1–26). Sydney: Lowy Institute.

Forgacs, D. (Ed.). (1988). *The Antonio Gramsci reader: Selected writings 1916–1935.* New York: Schocken Books Inc.

Forsyth, M., & Eves, R. (Eds.). (2015). *Talking it through: Responses to sorcery and witchcraft beliefs and practices in Melanesia.* Pacific Series. Canberra: ANU Press.

Giddens, A. (1990). *The consequences of modernity.* Cambridge: Polity Press.

Giddens, A. (1991). *Modernity and self-identity: Society in the late modern age.* Cambridge: Polity Press.

Götz, N. (2015). "Moral economy": Its conceptual and analytical prospects. *Journal of Global Ethics*, *11*(1), 147–162.

Harris, O. (1996). The temporalities of tradition: Reflections on a changing anthropology. In V. Hubinger (Ed.), *Grasping the changing world: Anthropological concepts in a postmodern era* (pp. 1–16). London and New York: Routledge.

Harvey, D. (2006). Neo-liberalism as creative destruction. *Geografiska Annaler. Series B, Human Geography*, *88*(2), 145–158.

Hayward-Jones, J. (2016, March 17). *The future of Papua New Guinea: Old challenges for new leaders* (pp. 1–28). Lowy Institute for International Policy.

Heine, J., & Thakur, R. (Eds.). (2011). *The dark side of globalization.* New York: United Nations University Press.

Hutton, W., & Giddens, A. (Eds.). (2000). *On the edge: Living with global capitalism.* London: Jonathan Cape.

IDMC. (2014, December 11). *Papua New Guinea: Invisible and neglected protracted displacement* (pp. 1–13). Internal Displacement Monitoring Centre, Norwegian Refugee Council.

Kaldor, M. (1999). *New and old wars: Organized violence in a global era.* Cambridge: Polity Press.

Kerkvliet, B. J. (1977). *The Huk Rebellion: A study of peasant revolt in the Philippines.* Berkeley and Los Angeles, CA: University of California Press.

Khong, Y. F. (2001). Human security: A shotgun approach to alleviating human misery? *Global Governance*, *7*(3), 231–236.

King, V. T. (1978). Moral economy and peasant uprisings in South-East Asia. *Cultures et développement*, *10*(1), 123–149.

King, V. T. (1981). Review of "The rational peasant: The political economy of rural society in Vietnam", by Samuel L Popkin. *Journal of Development Studies*, *17*(2), 249–251.

King, V. T. (2016). Review article: Conceptualising culture, identity and region: Recent reflections on Southeast Asia. *Pertanika: Journal of Social Sciences and Humanities*, *2*(1), 25–42.

Krause, K. (2004). The key to a powerful agenda, if properly defined. *Security Dialogue*, *35*(3), 367–368.

Lowe, E. (2019). Epidemic suicide in the context of modernizing social change in Oceania: A critical review and assessment. *The Contemporary Pacific*, *31*(1), 105–138.

Marx, K. [1844] (1968). *Economic and philosophic manuscripts of 1844* (M. Mulligan, trans.). Moscow: Progress Publishers.

Pacific Islands Report. (2014). *Suicide rate in Pacific Islands among highest in the world.* Pacific Islands Development Program, East-West Center, Honolulu.

Pacific Islands Report. (2015). *Security services fastest growing industry in Papua New Guinea*. Pacific Islands Development Program, East-West Center, Honolulu.

Paris, R. (2001). Human security: Paradigm shift or hot air? *International Security, 26*(2), 87–102.

Popkin, S. L. (1979). *The rational peasant: The political economy of rural society in Vietnam*. Berkeley and Los Angeles, CA: California University Press.

Reuveny, R. (2007). Climate change-induced migration and violent conflict. *Political Geography, 26*(6), 656–673.

Roberts, D. (2007). *Human insecurity: Global structures of violence*. London: Zed Books.

Scott, J. C. (1977). *The moral economy of the peasant: Rebellion and subsistence in Southeast Asia*. New Haven, CT: Yale University Press.

Scott, J. C. (1985). *Weapons of the Weak: Everyday forms of peasant resistance*. New Haven: Yale University Press.

Scott, J. C. (1990). *Domination and the arts of resistance: Hidden transcripts*. New Haven: Yale University Press.

SPC. (2017). *Solomon Islands country report: Summary of results* (pp. 1–12). Noumea: Pacific Community.

Standing, G. (2011). *The precariat: The new dangerous class*. London: Bloomsbury Academic.

Standing, G. (2016). *The corruption of capitalism: Why rentiers thrive and work does not pay*. London: Biteback Publishing.

Stiglitz, J. (2002). *Globalization and its discontents*. New York: Norton.

Thompson, E. P. (1971). The moral economy of the English crowd in the eighteenth century. *Past and Present, 50*(1), 76–136.

Thompson, E. P. [1963] (2013). *The making of the English working class*. London: Penguin Books, Modern Classics.

UNDP. (1994). *Human development report 1994*. United Nations Development Programme. New York and Oxford: Oxford University Press.

UNDP. (2014). *The state of human development in the Pacific: A report on vulnerability and exclusion in a time of rapid change*. Suva: United Nations Development Programme Pacific Centre.

UNFPA. (2014). *Population and development profiles: Pacific Island countries*. United Nations Population Fund. Suva: Pacific Sub-Regional Office.

Watson, S., & Moran, A. (Eds.). (2005). *Trust, risk and uncertainty*. Basingstoke: Palgrave Macmillan.

World Health Organization. (2017). *Suicide fact sheet*. Geneva: WHO Media Centre. Retrieved March 15, 2017 from www.who.int/mediacentre/factsheets/fs398/en/

Zinn, J. O. (Ed.). (2008). *Social theories of risk and uncertainty: An introduction*. Oxford: Blackwell Publishing.

3 Economic (in)security in the Pacific

Matthew Dornan

Introduction

No discussion of human security is complete without examining economic security, or the stability and sustainability of people's livelihoods and material well-being. Low incomes are often associated with an absence of economic security. Throughout much of the Pacific Islands region, hardship and poverty accentuate the vulnerability of households to external shocks, both natural and man-made, thus generating economic insecurity. At the same time, limited economic opportunities constrain the ability of households to respond to these external shocks. It is for this reason that economic development forms an important objective in the efforts of governments to improve human security across the region, though it is worth noting that higher incomes are not necessarily synonymous with improved security as the cash economy can carry its own risks.

Economic security is also closely linked to the provision of key public goods, such as health and education services, and to social protection systems. The failure in many Pacific island countries to provide such public goods limits the ability of households and individuals to productively participate in the national economy, constraining economic opportunity and contributing to economic insecurity. The lack of such services also contributes to a more immediate lack of economic security: inadequate healthcare and the absence of formal social protection means there is no safety net beyond that provided by traditional social structures, and these are increasingly ill-equipped to deal with external shocks.

Pacific island economies are inherently vulnerable to external shocks. Small size means that their economies are undiversified and susceptible to shocks in any one sector. The export base of most Pacific island economies is particularly limited, with reliance on just one or two main exports. Pacific island governments source most of their revenue from resource rents (in fishing, logging and mining) or from international development assistance, both of which are known for their volatility (Iulai, 2014). This situation exposes Pacific island governments to fluctuations in their revenue base, affecting government spending. At the same time, Pacific island countries are also highly exposed to the effects of climate change, with sea level rises and increasing intensity of cyclones already impacting island states.

This chapter examines these causes of economic (in)security in the Pacific. In so doing, it explores how limited economic opportunities and climate change impact economic security. The chapter also discusses informality and its complex relationship with economic security. The chapter first discusses the inherent vulnerability of Pacific island economies to external shocks and links this to poor development outcomes. The effects of climate change and natural disasters on economic (in)security are then examined. The chapter also examines how these vulnerabilities affect individuals and households, and how informality and the prevalence of subsistence agriculture interact with economic security. The chapter concludes by arguing that social structures that protect against such threats, including traditional social safety nets, are not an adequate substitute for formal social protection measures which to date have limited reach in the Pacific.

Pacific island economies are inherently vulnerable to external shocks

Pacific island economies are inherently vulnerable to external shocks, due to their small size and consequent lack of diversification. The logic of this is simple enough. In a large economy, the performance of one firm or industry has a limited impact on overall economic activity, as that firm or industry will typically account for only a small portion of total economic activity. In a small economy, that is not the case. The performance of just one firm or industry can have an enormous impact where that firm/industry is responsible for the bulk of economic activity in that economy.

The terms of trade of Pacific island states are thus by definition subject to volatility. Industries that have been a mainstay of Pacific island economies are often highly vulnerable to changes in the global economy and trading environment. Tourism, for instance, an important sector for many Pacific island states, is well known for volatility (see Figure 3.1). Tourism is especially vulnerable to natural disasters and political instability. In Fiji, for example, visitor arrivals fell 26% and tourism earnings declined by 21% after the 1987 coup. After the 2000 coup, visitor arrivals fell 28% and tourism earnings 29% (Harrison & Pratt, 2010). Declines of a similar magnitude were averted after the most recent coup, but only due to a combination of heavy discounting and a 30 % devaluation of the Fiji Dollar, which increased prices of imported goods and services for ordinary Fijians.

The resource sector, another industry subject to price volatility, is also very important for Pacific island countries. Papua New Guinea (PNG), with its considerable mining and gas resources, is the second most resource-dependent nation on earth (after Mauritania), with mineral rents equal to more than 30% of its gross domestic product (GDP) (Osborne, 2014). Papua New Guineans have recently experienced considerable hardship owing to the collapse of commodity prices and with that, lower government revenues, which have led to severe cuts in key government services. But it is not just Melanesian countries which are

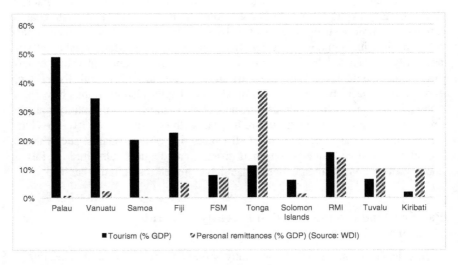

Figure 3.1 Tourism and Remittances as % of GDP

heavily reliant on natural resources subject to price instability. Countries like Kiribati, Tuvalu, the Republic of the Marshall Islands (RMI) and the Federated States of Micronesia (FSM) are also increasingly reliant for their revenue on licencing fees from tuna fishing, which historically has also experienced considerable price volatility. In these countries, changes in global commodity prices are also of economic significance due to their impact on supply costs, with reliance on imported fuel and food exposing consumers to changes in price (Tumbarello, Cabezon, & Wu, 2013).

Remittances form another important source of income in the Pacific, particularly in Polynesia. Nowhere in the world are remittances more important to the economy than in Tonga, where they routinely measure between 35 and 45 % of GDP (Curtain, Dornan, Doyle, & Howes, 2017). However, remittances are also a source of income that is subject to volatility, with a tendency to be pro-cyclical, with their quantity following the global business cycle (a feature that is also shared by foreign aid and commodity prices). Remittances to Tonga fell considerably as a result of the global financial crisis of 2008, owing to its employment and wage effects on Tongans living in metropolitan countries.

Historically, industries built on preferential trade access have also been important for Pacific island countries. Fiji's garment industry, for example, was relatively successful due to favourable access to markets through the Lomé convention and SPARTECA (with Australia and New Zealand), employing a workforce of 19,000 at the end of the 1990s (Storey, 2006). Over the same period, Fiji's sugar industry was successful for similar reasons – with the European Union paying above-world prices for sugar exports. Samoa's auto-parts manufacturer, Yazaki EDS Samoa, once the largest private sector employer in Samoa, was also successful due to preferential access to the Australian market (Connell, 2013).

Such arrangements, though beneficial for those involved, are also vulnerable to changes in the external environment. The gradual erosion of these special access arrangements as destination markets liberalised their economies and reduced import tariffs for larger developing countries has seen many such industries decline. The Yakazi EDS Samoa factory closed in 2017. Fiji's sugar industry appears to be in terminal decline. Its garment industry persists and is possibly an example of relative success in niche markets (supplying niche Australian markets with just in time orders), but it is much smaller than it once was, employing less than half the workers it did at its peak.

The most important economic sector in most Pacific island countries is the public sector. Government is normally the largest employer in Pacific island countries, with wages paid by government higher than those in other sectors. Public sector employment also comprises the largest share of formal sector employment of any sector in most Pacific island states, ranging from 30 % in Solomon Islands to 80 % in Kiribati. This makes Pacific island economies vulnerable to changes in government spending and employment, and associated with this, to revenue challenges that might be caused by declines in foreign aid or taxation revenue from the resources sector or industries that are vulnerable to external shocks. There are multiple examples in the Pacific where reductions in the size of government – generally precipitated by fiscal crises – have caused economic downturns, including in Vanuatu, Cook Islands, RMI and Samoa.

External vulnerability contributes to poor development outcomes

The vulnerability to external shocks outlined above has contributed to poor development outcomes in the Pacific. Real GDP growth is more volatile in Pacific island countries than in non-small states and other (non-Pacific) small states. The difference in volatility of weighted terms of trade is even larger, with Pacific island economies again disadvantaged relative to larger economies. The IMF has shown that volatility in GDP growth is associated with lower rates of GDP growth over time. This relationship is especially evident in Pacific island countries, where countries subject to extreme levels of volatility in GDP growth have also averaged low growth (Tumbarello et al., 2013).

It is unsurprising, therefore, that Pacific island economies have performed poorly since independence, with income growth lower than that in other regions and neighbouring countries (see Figure 3.2). The IMF notes that "real average income per capita in PICs has increased by less than 10 percent since 1990, compared with 40 percent in the Eastern Caribbean, 25 percent in the group of all small states and about 150 percent in Asia's emerging market economies" (Kronenberg & Khor, 2014). At the same time, productivity growth has been slow, meaning limited wage growth and improvement in living standards.

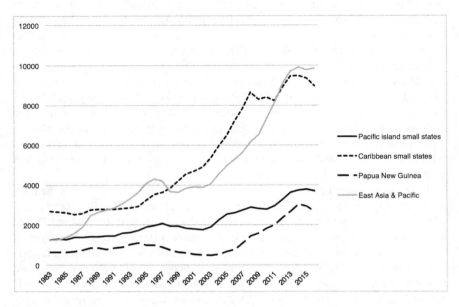

Figure 3.2 Gross National Income Per Capita (current USD)

This lack of growth is not something easily addressed through policy. While there is certainly scope to improve the policy and business environment, Pacific island countries also face geographical constraints to growth owing to their remoteness and small size (World Bank, 2014a). This combination of smallness and remoteness is unique to the Pacific. There is no other region or set of countries in the world that are both so distant to major markets and so small as to lack economies of scale (World Bank, 2014a). This small size contributes to the vulnerability of Pacific island economies. Winters and Martin (2004) also show that small size disadvantages Pacific island producers on world markets, as they are unable to benefit from economies of scale. Winters and Martin (2004) argue as a result that many Pacific islands are unable to compete in international markets, noting that in the extreme:

> there may be some very small economies that face such great absolute disadvantages that exporting at world prices is either impossible or generates factor incomes that are too low to subsist. In the limit free trade could mean no trade for these economies.
>
> (Winters & Martin, 2004, p. 348)

For such countries, foreign exchange must instead be earned through other means, including foreign aid, sovereignty rents (for example, sale of passports) and remittance income. Bertram and Watters (1985) argued decades ago that such entrepreneurship had served many Pacific island countries well, with per capita incomes higher than what might be otherwise expected. At the same time, such activities are inherently exposed to developments and actions overseas – a point which emphasises the vulnerability of Pacific island economies to external shocks.

A final point worth noting is that small size also has implications for the cost of delivering public goods and basic government services (World Bank, 2014a). Key government functions such as support for legislation, regulatory structures and the legal system require a minimum number of people for their delivery. In small countries, this means more public servants relative to the population served than in larger countries, which in turn means higher per capita service delivery costs (World Bank, 2016). Once again, such employment, and the important services such employment delivers, is vulnerable to shortfalls in government revenue resulting from external shocks.

Climate change and environmental stressors are increasingly significant

Pacific island countries have always been highly exposed to natural disasters, particularly cyclones in the South Pacific and droughts and flooding caused by El Niño weather patterns. The intensity of the strongest cyclones has increased in recent years in the South Pacific, consistent with predictions of the Intergovernmental Panel on Climate Change (2014). Tropical Cyclone Pam, which hit Vanuatu and parts of Tuvalu and Kiribati in 2015 causing extensive damage, was the second strongest cyclone ever recorded in the South Pacific (when measured on the basis of sustained wind speeds) and led to economic costs equal to 64 % of GDP in Vanuatu (Dornan & Cain, 2015). The following year, Tropical Cyclone Winston made landfall in Fiji: the most intense tropical cyclone in the Southern Hemisphere on record.

The increasing intensity of natural disasters, coupled with flooding caused by sea level rises, are already affecting Pacific island economies. These effects are expected to worsen as the level of greenhouse gases in the atmosphere increase. The ADB estimates that by 2100, if the world stays on its current fossil-fuel intensive growth path, climate change will cost the Pacific 12.7% of GDP each year – an amount that far surpasses annual rates of economic growth and which therefore has the potential to reverse development gains made in the region. Approximately half of that reduction is associated with agriculture, meaning that households in rural areas, including those that depend largely on subsistence livelihoods, will be particularly exposed (ADB, 2013).

A recent modelling exercise undertaken by the Fiji government with support from the World Bank examined the implications of climate change-related disasters for households with different income levels (Government of Fiji, 2017). Unsurprisingly, the study found that the poor, or households that have the lowest levels of economic security, are most severely affected by natural disasters. The study found that in response to natural disasters, low-income households disproportionately reduce their consumption. The aggregate effect is that for each

$1 of damage incurred as a result of a natural disaster, consumption spending declines by $1.80, meaning that the F$500 million in average annual asset losses from tropical cyclones and floods in Fiji equates to a reduction in consumption of F$900 million.

An associated challenge in the Pacific is the limited coverage and availability of insurance. In countries like Fiji, where home insurance is available, most households (approx. 90 %) cannot afford insurance premiums, meaning they are exposed to the full financial impacts of natural disasters and must rely on savings and informal social safety nets, which take the form of support from kin and the local community, in order to rebuild their homes. In many smaller Pacific island countries, there is no insurance available to be bought; households are forced to bear the full cost of damage associated with climate-related natural disasters. Even in Fiji, where the financial system is more developed, there is no insurance available for agriculture (Government of Fiji, 2017). Farmers, who were among the groups worst affected by TC Winston, bore all of the losses associated with damage to crops and farming equipment. Sugar farmers in the Rakiraki area, which was directly impacted by the cyclone, were further affected by the Fiji Sugar Corporation's decision not to re-open the Rakiraki mill, meaning sugar from the area must now be transported a significant distance to the Ba mill.

Household impacts and informality

Discussions of national-level impacts on the economy are often not well linked to the household level. However, vulnerability of the types described above impacts individuals, households and communities first and foremost, with these impacts aggregated in the economy-wide measures referred to above. Natural disasters affect households, destroying assets and livelihoods. External economic shocks similarly impact the employment and income of households. Low rates of economic growth manifest themselves in low-income growth for households and individuals, whose choices and opportunities are subsequently constrained. And poor service delivery, worsened by revenue constraints and external shocks, directly affects people on the ground, with long-term implications for the economic opportunities and incomes of individuals and households so affected.

Not discussed so far in this chapter is the extensive informal sector and reliance by Pacific island households on subsistence agriculture. This informal sector is commonly considered to be a strength in the Pacific and a source of resilience to external shocks. This is true in some ways. Subsistence agriculture is a source of food security for households affected by economic downturn. Certain root crops are also resilient to natural disasters and a source of food when other crops are destroyed. The diversity of traditional crops protects households from diseases that affect homogenous cash crops. Lastly, traditional social structures provide a source of informal social protection for households and individuals in times of crisis – as discussed below.

Notwithstanding these benefits, the relationship between informality and resilience is complex and there are limits to the benefits that informality provides households. While subsistence agriculture is considered less risky than cash cropping, it is also associated with low incomes, which constrain the opportunities and choices of households. It is well known that the poorest households in the Pacific are those that are least integrated into the broader economy and which rely on subsistence agriculture (Gibson & Rozelle, 2002). These households are also disproportionately affected by natural disasters, given their reliance on agriculture. In PNG, for example the 2016 drought is likely to have caused or contributed to the deaths of thousands of people, with most being reliant on subsistence agriculture for their livelihoods and having no source of cash income to fall back to when crops failed (Broughton, 2017).

Informality also has other downsides. Jobs in the informal sector by definition lack the protections associated with formal sector employment, such as sick leave, maternity leave, pension payments, disability insurance and protection from unfair dismissal (World Bank, 2019). The economic security of workers in the informal sector is typically lower than that of workers in the formal sector, with no rules and laws in place to constrain the actions of employers. Workers in these situations are potentially one accident away from unemployment and the poverty that entails.

Informal safety nets, provided by traditional social networks that are based on blood relation, village, language and other factors are without doubt of great importance in the Pacific (Nanau, 2011; Sviridova, 2013). Reciprocity and gift exchange relationships are commonplace across the Pacific, with meeting requests for goods and services from one's network considered an "important obligation of extended kinship networks" (World Bank, 2014b, p. 52). Gift exchange takes many forms, including *communal collection* for ceremonies and community projects, *specialised collection* where goods of equal value are exchanged, thus helping households diversify their asset base and *generalised reciprocity*, where households and individuals are provided with goods and services in times of need. The latter means of exchange is especially important for social protection, with such reciprocity generally disproportionate and redistributive, meaning well-off households and individuals are expected to give more to those that are less well-off (World Bank, 2014b). Gift exchange relations thus provide a form of informal insurance, whereby those that experience hardship or economic shocks are supported (World Bank, 2017).

Informal social protection is especially important given the near absence of formal safety nets or a welfare state in most Pacific island countries, with Fiji being an exception. Formal non-contributory safety nets in the region (excluding Fiji) are limited to payments for people with disabilities in Tonga and old-age pensions, which are provided in Kiribati, Samoa and Tonga. New Ireland province in PNG has also established such schemes. As noted, Fiji is an exception, with a large-scale poverty targeted cash transfer programme and child benefit in place, in addition to disability support schemes and an old-age pension (World Bank, 2017). The absence of significant formal safety nets in most of the Pacific means that when the livelihoods of households are affected by a shock, such as an illness or accident which affects a "breadwinner", informal social protection systems are typically called on to provide relief. The resultant value placed on informal social protection partly explains a reluctance in the region to use the term poverty (though hardship, effectively a synonym, is accepted).

The limits to informal or traditional social protection need also be recognised, however. Informal social protection is often accessed on unequal terms, with some people excluded from appropriate support. Local elites often have considerable influence over how informal social protection is distributed (Calder & Tanhchareun, 2014). Furthermore, informal safety nets do not function well when an adverse shock affects all members of the community, such as in the case of natural disasters, the impacts of which are expected to increase as climate change worsens (Calder & Tanhchareun, 2014; IPCC, 2014). In such cases, assistance from unaffected actors is particularly beneficial (as in the case of formal social protection or assistance from government).

The key difference between formal and informal social protection can be found in the relationships which characterise them. Formal social protection involves citizen–state relationships. Informal social protection involves relationships between individuals and groups which exclude the state. Of ongoing debate is the interaction between the two types of social protection, and in particular, the impacts on informal social protection of introducing formal social protection systems. While impacts are sometimes said to be negative, there is little evidence to support this argument, though some studies have been critical of poverty targeting methods (Calder & Tanhchareun, 2014). Indeed, there is reason for thinking that formal social protection can help to support informal social protection, by addressing gaps and enabling especially poor individuals and households to better participate in traditional social networks (Calder & Tanhchareun, 2014).

What is clear is that limits to informal social protection are increasingly being recognised in the Pacific. The establishment of old age pensions in a number of Pacific island countries over the last decade acknowledges the inadequacy of informal networks in supporting older members of the community. Similarly, growing awareness of climate change and adverse experience with major disasters is likely to lead people to question whether traditional safety nets are an adequate response to such shocks. As economies develop over time and people migrate to urban areas, reliance on traditional safety nets is likely to decline further – as has occurred in other parts of the world (Calder & Tanhchareun, 2014). Such change suggests a growing need to expand formal social protection in the Pacific.

Conclusion

This chapter has explored economic (in)security in the Pacific Islands region and the link between economic development and human security. Pacific island economies are inherently vulnerable to external shocks as a result of their small size and reliance on certain economic sectors and sources of income. Regionally, widespread hardship and poverty accentuate the vulnerability of households to external shocks, both natural and man-made, with limited economic opportunities constraining the ability of households to respond to external shocks. Climate change and climate-related disasters are further reducing economic security in the region through their impacts on livelihoods.

The informal sector, including traditional social protection systems and subsistence agriculture, is widely viewed in the Pacific as providing households with a measure of protection from external shocks. However, the relationship between the informal sector and resilience to external shocks is complex, with informality also associated with low income and lack of job (and livelihood) protection. Informal or traditional safety nets are important in the Pacific given the near absence of formal social protection systems. However, they should not be viewed as an adequate substitute. As populations move to pursue economic opportunity, the need to establish formal social protection for disadvantaged households and individuals will only increase.

References

ADB. (2013). *The economics of climate change in the Pacific.* Mandaluyong City, Philippines: Asian Development Bank.

Bertram, G., & Watters, R. (1985). The MIRAB economy in South Pacific microstates. *Pacific Viewpoint, 26*(3), 497–512.

Broughton, B. (2017). *Evaluation of Australia's response to El Niño drought and frosts in PNG 2015–17.* Prepared for Australian Department of Foreign Affairs and Trade.

Calder, R., & Tanhchareun, T. (2014). *Informal social protection: Social relations and cash transfers.* Department of Foreign Affairs and Trade. Canberra: Commonwealth of Australia.

Connell, J. (2013). *Islands at risk: Environments, economics and contemporary change.* Cheltenham, UK: Edward Elgar.

Curtain, R., Dornan, M., Doyle, J., & Howes, S. (2017). *Pacific possible. Labour mobility: The ten billion dollar prize.* Canberra: ANU and World Bank.

Dornan, M., & Newton Cain, T. (2015). Vanuatu and Cyclone Pam: An update on fiscal, economic, and development impacts. *Pacific Economic Monitor,* 23–27.

Gibson, J., & Rozelle, S. (2002). *Poverty and access to infrastructure in Papua New Guinea.* Davis, CA: University of California.

Government of Fiji. (2017). *Climate vulnerability assessment: Making Fiji climate resilient.* Suva: Government of Fiji.

Harrison, D., & Pratt, S. (2010). Political change and tourism: Coups in Fiji. In R. Butler & W. Suntikul (Eds.), *Tourism and political change* (pp. 160–174). Oxford: Goodfellow Publishers Limited.

Intergovernmental Panel on Climate Change. (2014). *Climate change 2014: Impacts, adaptation, and vulnerability. Part B: Regional aspects* (pp. 1757–1776). Contribution of Working Group II to the Fifth Assessment Report of the Intergovernmental Panel on Climate Change. Cambridge: Cambridge University Press.

Iulai, L. (2014). Aid volatility: Is it a problem in Tuvalu? *Asia and the Pacific Policy Studies, 1*(2), 379–394.

Kronenberg, R. P., & Khor, H. E. (2014). Economic growth in the Pacific Island countries: Challenges, constraints, and policy responses. In H. E. Khor, R. P. Kronenberg, & P. Tumbarello (Eds.), *Resilience and growth in the small states of the Pacific.* Washington, DC: International Monetary Fund.

Nanau, G. L. (2011). The Wantok system as a socioeconomic and political network in Melanesia. *OMNES*, *2*(1), 31–55.

Osborne, D. (2014). *An analysis of the PNG Sovereign Wealth Fund's process of formulation and progress towards establishment*. NRI Issues Paper #9, 2014. Port Moresby: National Research Institute.

Storey, D. (2006). End of the line?: Globalisation and Fiji's garment industry. In S. Firth (Ed.), *Globalisation and governance in the Pacific Islands: State, society and governance in Melanesia*. Canberra: ANU Press.

Sviridova, T. (2013). *Review of traditional safety nets in Pacific Island countries*. Background Paper for Pacific Hardship and Vulnerability Report. Washington, DC: World Bank.

Tumbarello, P., Cabezon, E., & Wu, Y. (2013). *Are the Asia and Pacific small states different from other small states?* IMF Working Paper, 2013/123.

Winters, A., & Martin, P. (2004). When comparative advantage is not enough: Business costs in small remote economies. *World Trade Review*, *3*(3), 347–383.

World Bank. (2014a). *Well-being from work in the Pacific islands*. Haque, Tobias and Packard, Truman. Washington, DC: The World Bank.

World Bank. (2014b). *Pacific hardship and vulnerability report*. Washington, DC: The World Bank.

World Bank. (2016). *Pacific possible background paper: Financing for development*. Washington, DC: The World Bank.

World Bank. (2017). *Asia and Pacific social protection report: Pacific background paper* (unpublished). Washington, DC: The World Bank.

World Bank. (2019). *Pathways to better jobs in IDA countries*. Washington, DC: The World Bank.

4 Resisting the tides

Responding to nuclear and environmental "insecurity" in the Marshall Islands

Greg Dvorak

Prelude: insecurity

When we think of "security" in an Oceanic context, what do we really mean and for whose sake? Security is often defined by outside actors when discussing the Pacific Islands regional situation. As former New Caledonia president Philippe Gomès once said, "Security is external security, and the major powers with which you and we are linked unfailingly are the warranty that we most need" (Hegarty & Tryon, 2013, p. xviii). Often security becomes a narrative about how small, vulnerable Pacific states in the centre of the ocean have no choice but to "link unfailingly" and ally as a "warranty" against the big bullies who dominate their waters from the "rim". This kind of narrative about security tends to distract us from the deeper, more personal, local realities of life in and between Pacific Islanders and their islands. Especially when Pacific Islanders are portrayed as mere victims or pawns in a "fatal impact"-style[1] global game of chess, international relations observers often pay too much attention to the big global actors while shrugging their shoulders and writing off the struggles of local Pacific communities as unfortunate but inevitable.

In recent years, China has increasingly been portrayed as the bully on the playground of Oceania. Hegarty comments on how the concerns of renewed Chinese power in the region is ultimately "unsettling the established order", a worry that precipitated former US President Barack Obama's strategic/security "pivot to Asia" (Hegarty, 2013, p. 4). Like many other analysts of security in the "Asia-*hyphen*-Pacific" region, Hegarty goes on to describe the destabilisation of Pacific Island nations' circumstances caused by the influx of inexpensive goods and aid money from China. China's increasing military presence on the high seas and a number of territorial disputes have also precipitated policy shifts by Australia and Japan toward a larger "Indo-Pacific" strategy that attempts to surround and contain this expanding Chinese influence.

This "pivot" to China in response to a military and economic threat to "security" takes much-needed attention off the long extant instability within and between Pacific Island Countries – insecurities which were paradoxically the direct result of the "security" constructed largely by and for the western hegemony we know as "the established order" in the first place. China may present new elements of unpredictability and instability in contemporary times, but from an Islander perspective, long before it had any influence in this part of the world, hundreds of years of European colonialism had already wreaked havoc in these islands. Upon these legacies of European colonisation were also layered several decades of Japanese imperial and military expansion that led to a horrific war with the United States (US) and its allies, a trauma that still haunts and pains Pacific Islanders today, especially in the parts of Micronesia and Melanesia where these scars are the deepest. And no sooner had that war finished, the US and a number of other countries embarked on nuclear wars upon the Pacific Islands during the Cold War. The industrialisation, nuclearisation and globalisation of the world have also led to "environmental colonialism", the devastation of local Pacific island ecosystems for the sake of enriching large nations, as a direct or indirect result of urbanisation, manufacturing, overfishing and pollution.

Postwar American discourses of security are perhaps the most apparent in Northern Oceania, although the US has saturated the majority of Oceania with its military infrastructure since the 20th century, swallowing all of the Pacific Island nations, Australia, New Zealand, Indonesia, Philippines, Japan, Korea, China and much of Asia into a vast sphere of military power called "PACOM", the Pacific Command. In northern Oceania, the US maintains extensive military bases from Hawai'i across Micronesia to Guåhan (Guam) and into Japan, Okinawa and Korea. Arguably, what looks like security from an American perspective is in fact experienced as little more than *insecurity* from the perspective of the Pacific people who live in these islands. Not only are lands and livelihoods appropriated for American military purposes, but these places have become a target of aggression for American enemies, the strategic bullseye. Even in the very recent past, Hawai'i, Guam, and Micronesia in general were all threatened with nuclear annihilation by North Korea.

At the epicentre of this "arc of insecurity" lies the Republic of the Marshall Islands. At its centre is Kwajalein Atoll, the largest inhabited atoll on earth and site of a major American intercontinental ballistic missile test range since 1964– previously a support base for the atomic weapons tests that were conducted by the US Department of Energy at Bikini Atoll and Enewetak Atoll in the 1940s-50s. This chapter revisits and articulates nuclear narratives from all of the Marshallese places most directly affected by American weapons testing from the immediate aftermath of World War II to the present. It also aims to honour and remember the resilience and courage of Marshall Islanders themselves amidst this instability, and how Marshallese activists, thinkers and artists – especially women – have been the true guardians of their peace and security despite the persistent onslaughts of violence and injustice wrought by larger and more powerful nations. It is important to remember the deep commitment Marshallese have for environmental security of their lands and seas – not only safety and recovery from nuclear trespasses but also security from rising and warming seas. Especially when the Bulletin of Atomic Scientists' Doomsday Clock has been reset to the closest it has been to midnight since the Cold War, and when environmental scientists all around the world warn of impending catastrophe, these Marshallese pasts and presents demand our attention.

Swimsuits and sea monsters

In naming his skimpy, sensational swimsuit "the bikini", a Frenchman shamelessly reduced the entire ancestral heritage and pride of a people into a fetish garment meant to objectify women and titillate heteronormative men's sexual appetites. His publicity stunt capitalised on the unspeakable trauma and pain of a nation of resilient people whose sacred and beloved home lands and waters had been permanently poisoned. Would global consumers have as easily accepted a bathing suit named "the auschwitz" or "the hiroshima"?

The Republic of the Marshall Islands is a vast and stunningly beautiful oceanic nation of 33 atolls consisting of thousands of islands that span 2 million square kilometres of the Central Pacific Ocean, and Bikini is but one of those atolls, settled over 3,000 years of sophisticated Pacific Islander navigation and voyaging. Together with many of the atolls of the *Kapin Meto* northwestern Marshall Islands, Bikini figures prominently in Marshallese creation cosmologies as a sacred place of origins and a full pantheon of gods, a cradle of civilisation. The name Bikini actually means "the lands of many coconuts" in Marshallese, referring to its symbolism as a place of great abundance. But only less than a year after the airplanes *Enola Gay* and *Bockscar* dropped their atomic payloads onto the civilians of Hiroshima and Nagasaki, the US Navy designated Bikini as a site for testing and refining atomic weaponry further, initiating the environmental devastation of that atoll and launching an era of unimaginable hardship for the Marshallese people. And literally days after the first test at Bikini in July 1946, Parisian industrial engineer and fashion designer Louis Réard decided upon a new name for his "explosive" swimsuit after reading the newspaper headlines (Lal & Fortune, 2000, p. 259).

If the Internet is any indication of contemporary public awareness, it is worth noting that searching the web for the keyword "bikini" yields nearly 30 million hits in English, roughly 99% each of which reference only bathing suits, not Bikini Atoll and the Marshall Islands. Eclipsed by a hegemonic gaze that trivialises and objectifies both women's bodies and tropical islands as little more than sites of pleasure, the real Bikini Atoll is largely unknown or forgotten to the world. Obscured along with the true Bikini are many other Marshallese atolls imbued also with the trauma of nuclear weapons testing. The late Pacific historian Teresia Teaiwa asserted "The sacrifice of Islanders and military personnel during nuclear testing in the Pacific cannot be represented without threatening the legitimacy of colonial power, so nuclear technology becomes gendered and domesticated. In the end the female body is appropriated by a colonial discourse to successfully disguise the horror of the bomb" (Teaiwa, 1994, p. 92). As if to emphasise the cruel irony of this fetishisation and disguise, one legacy of intense 19th century European colonisation and Christian missionary activity in the Pacific is that it is in fact socially offensive and inappropriate for Pacific Islander women to bare too much flesh in public. So, although so many tourists happily wear bikinis on their holidays in tropical Pacific destinations today, locals tend to find this indecent and rarely ever wear such swimsuits themselves.

Few Americans even realise that the US detonated not one but *67* massive atmospheric atomic weapons between 1946–1958. These "tests" impacted the lives of generations of Marshall Islanders who were either exposed to fallout or forced to migrate repeatedly and permanently away from their homelands. As Masahide Kato writes, and Marshallese survivors readily concur, "how can one deny the crude fact that nuclear war has been taking place on this earth in the name of 'nuclear testing' since the first nuclear explosion at Alamagordo in 1945?" (Kato, 1993, p. 348). There is still little awareness in the world about the Marshall Islands itself and the brave struggles of the Marshallese people, let alone the extent of nuclear testing throughout Oceania in general – such as the nearly 200 French "tests" in the Polynesian Atolls of Moruroa and Fangataufa; British "tests", including the nine detonations conducted on Aboriginal Australian land or the 24 conducted on Christmas Island; and the 12 other American "tests" conducted on the Hawaiian atoll of Kalama, known to Americans as Johnston Atoll (Kato, 1993, p. 348). Altogether, more than 2,000 nuclear weapons have been exploded all around the world, and disproportionately in places that indigenous communities live and hold sacred (Barad, 2018, p. 58).

Behind the veil of swimwear (and epic sea monster movies like *Godzilla*, inspired by the *Number 5 Lucky Dragon* fishing boat's irradiation by Bikini fallout) lie the real waters, lands and people of the Marshall Islands. The radioactive waste from these tests is still so potent that some parts of these islands will remain uninhabitable and deadly for countless future generations. The military colonialism of the Cold War nuclear complex preyed upon the marginality and perceived powerlessness of local communities like the Marshallese, allowing superpowers to contaminate Native lands without political repercussions (Johnston, 2007, p. 6). US officials exploited Marshallese generosity and trust, what they presumed to be blind naiveté and passivity, when they chose Bikini as a testing site, but as we will see, the people of the Marshall Islands were neither passive nor naïve, and to this day they are striving for justice, visibility, dignity and a healthy environment.

For world peace and the good of mankind

On the morning of Sunday, February 10, 1946, Commodore Ben H. Wyatt, the military governor of the US Navy-occupied Marshall Islands, paid a visit after local church services to Juda, one of the *irooj*, traditional chiefs of Bikini, to negotiate a special agreement on behalf of the US government. American authorities refer to Juda as "King Juda", inscribing their Western idea that there might be only one leader and bolstering Juda's authority – despite the fact that there are multiple leaders in the Marshallese system of land tenure. Alluding to America's new weapons, Wyatt asked the community for permission to use Bikini Atoll temporarily "for the good of mankind and to end all wars".

Having only begun to recover from the anxieties and mental scars of a painful war between Americans and Japanese, this proposal was strange and troubling for the Marshallese of Bikini, who were expected to make a quick decision but reluctantly debated all day (Niedenthal, 1997, p. 29). Explaining America was working to protect the people of God from evil attacks, Wyatt played upon the Marshallese Christian missionary influence, likening the plight of the Bikinians to the Biblical story of the exodus of the Israelites from Egypt, guided by God "with a pillar of smoke by day and a pillar of fire by night" (Lal and Fortune, 200, 257). Exhausted and ambivalent, Juda finally conceded that the people of Bikini would place their trust in God's hands and lend their land to the US.

One month later, Wyatt returned with a whole film crew to make a propaganda newsreel for the American populace to see. Numerous takes re-enacted the original scene of the Bikinians "agreeing" to surrender their atoll to Wyatt and his obliging translator, James Milne. Reshooting until everyone was exhausted and their faces registered no traces of resistance, the camera crew captured the scene of Juda's rehearsed compliance as he says on behalf of his people, "Emman [it is good]. Everything is good and it is in God's hands". Wyatt, smiling, stands up and addresses the crowd: "Tell them and King Juda that in everything being God's hands cannot be other than good". These tightly edited and framed black and white scenes are the first portrayal of the coming of *paijin* – the Marshallese word for the "poison" of nuclear radiation and suffering – to the Marshall Islands, and they make atomic testing seem like nothing more than a minor inconvenience. Together with footage of all 181 Islanders carrying their possessions in boxes as they trudge across the sand to board a navy ship, an upbeat voiceover narrates: "The islanders are a nomadic group and are well pleased that the Yanks are going to add a little variety to their lives" (Horowitz, 2012).

The people of Bikini were moved 200 kilometres to the east to a tiny uninhabited atoll called Rongerik. Marshall Islanders, though skilled navigators and oceanic voyagers, are *not* nomadic people, and they certainly were not seeking any "variety" in their lives. These islands had long been lands of inheritance, places for which ancestors fought and died, islands and atolls for which every centimetre of land and sea is accounted from ancient times to the present, land to which different groups of Marshallese people are uniquely affiliated through family and clan. Without one's own land affiliation, one is not considered to be a true Marshallese person. But Americans were not concerned with this, presuming there was no reason why Bikinians would want to leave Rongerik to return home (Davis, 2005, p. 607). Admiral William Blandy, who was in charge of the first atomic tests, for instance, emphasised how important it was that the indigenous populations near atomic testing sites be "small and cooperative so that they could be moved to a new location with a minimum of trouble" (Weisgall, 1994, p. 31). To make way for the Cold War, Islanders were moved repeatedly by the US military in a sort of human game of chess that has lasted, in fact, to the present day.

Aside from what American military strategists believed to be the "movability" of the Marshallese people, the Truman Administration partly chose the Marshall Islands because they were a "trophy" that had been won from Japan in World War

II. For nearly 30 years, the Marshall Islands, along with nearly all of northern Micronesia, was administered by Japan under a League of Nations Mandate and referred to as the Nanyō Guntō, much to the anxiety of the US, which wanted to secure a strong link between the US mainland, Hawai'i, Guam and East Asia. In the 1920s-30s, tens of thousands of Japanese and Okinawans migrated into the Nanyō Guntō, settling mainly in the western islands of Palau and Saipan, easily outnumbering indigenous Islanders.

Though its Japanese population was much smaller, the Marshall Islands was the far eastern frontier of the Japanese empire, and there was a complete Japanese town in the atoll of Jaluit, replete with Japanese shops and local industries. Throughout several atolls in the Marshall Islands trade in *katsuobushi* (dried skipjack) and copra (dried coconut meat) were robust, and many islands had electricity, public schools and hospitals. When Japan began to militarise the Marshall Islands in the late 1930s and early 1940s, civilians were displaced to make way for military bases, to which thousands more Japanese soldiers were dispatched. Though Bikini was only the site of a Japanese watchtower at the time of the war, US airstrikes bombarded it and most other Marshallese atolls between 1941 and 1944. During the amphibious invasions of 1944, roughly 10,000 Japanese soldiers died in the massive American assaults on Kwajalein and Enewetak Atolls, two places that would also figure prominently in the Cold War testing projects yet to come.

All these islands, strewn with war wreckage and sparsely populated by what American planners considered to be "primitive" people, were prime candidates for atomic weapons testing. Under its 1947 United Nations Trusteeship Agreement, the US gained formal strategic control over Japan's former Micronesian colonies under the condition that it nurtured the region's inhabitants toward self-determination. But as the US built up its hegemony across all of northern Oceania, its contradictory desire to use these islands for its own defensive purposes became more and more apparent. And since American militarism and weapons testing in the Marshall Islands has continued all the way to the present day, it is no wonder that most Marshall Islander elders believe that the Pacific War never actually ended (Carucci, 1989, pp. 76–77).

Several months after the Bikinians began their difficult lives at Rongerik Atoll, the US commenced its Pacific atomic tests with *Operation Crossroads*, which comprised two tests in Bikini Atoll in June and July of 1946. Each of these tests had a yield of 21 kilotons, each roughly the size of the bomb dropped on Nagasaki. Irooj (chief) Juda anxiously accepted an invitation by American officials to witness one of these tests from a naval vessel, returning later to say that although the explosion was terrifying and like nothing he had ever seen before – causing a mushroom cloud, bright lights and an incredible blast – he was relieved to see that the islands were still intact, even still roaming with pigs (Niedenthal, 2001, p. 3). His report gave his community hope that they would soon return to Bikini, a hope that soon faded.

The Bikinians' temporary home of Rongerik Atoll was in fact a restricted atoll, a place that only *irooj* were allowed to use to reward warriors for their service.

Additionally, Marshallese oral traditions referred to Rongerik as a place of great misfortune, haunted by spirits and danger. Meanwhile, the guardians of Rongerik, who resided mainly on Rongelap Atoll but were also evacuated for the duration of these very first tests, never gave their permission to American authorities to use this atoll. The rightful owners of Rongerik were upset that the Bikinians would be exploiting the natural resources of this land. But since the US Navy only left them with a few weeks of food supplies, once their rations ran out, Bikinians had no choice but to forage for even the seedlings of local plants and to eat fish that they knew might be toxic. A fire that burned much of their village in 1947 only made the situation worse. Still, American authorities made no attempts to relocate the community until they were on the brink of complete starvation in 1948, eventually moving them to the uninhabited island of Kili, where many Bikinians still live today.

In December 1947, history repeated itself when military authorities paid a visit to the people of Enewetak Atoll, 305 kilometres to the west of Bikini, to ask them also to leave their homes and their cherished lands for the good of "peace and freedom for all humankind" (Carucci, 1997, p. 3). Less than four years prior, Enewetak – also known as Brown Atoll – had been a Japanese base where over 3,300 soldiers and workers (including many from Korea) had been killed in the war, and the Marshallese population of the atoll was still reeling from the trauma of battle. More than 30 % of local Marshallese had also lost their lives, and they did not want to jeopardise the relative postwar abundance and peace that they were experiencing by angering the Americans (Carucci, 1997, p. 4). And so the people of Enewetak were relocated 209 kilometres southwest of their homeland to a desolate atoll called Ujelang, a place that they dreaded, for it was the most isolated atoll in the Marshall Islands and it had long been uninhabited due to a lack of adequate vegetation and frequent typhoons. With heavy hearts, the people of Enewetak moved to Ujelang, trusting and hoping like their counterparts in Bikini that this would only be a very short and temporary stay.

While they went on to endure the beginning of their own era of misery in exile, in April 1948 the US began its series of atmospheric tests at Enewetak, undertaking nine more massive detonations ranging in yield from 37 kilotons to the massive 10,400 kiloton "Mike" hydrogen bomb test. As the US tested its bombs in Enewetak, it was already reconfiguring its systems at Bikini for further, more dreadful experiments. It became commonplace for Marshallese living in many atolls to see distant flashes or to feel the earth vibrate like an earthquake during these tests. But it was not until 1954 that the enormity and sheer terror of these experiments became known to the world.

The day "the poison" fell from the sky

On March 1, 1954, the US Department of Energy tested its twelfth test in the Marshall Islands, its first "dry fuel" hydrogen bomb, an experiment codenamed *Bravo*. For this test, although the people of Bikini had been evacuated, their neighbours in Rongelap, Utrik, Ailuk and other atolls in the vicinity were going about life as usual, as American authorities did not consider them to be in a dangerous area. Out at sea, 23 young crewmembers aboard the Japanese fishing vessel *No. 5 Lucky Dragon* were also far outside the hazardous zone prescribed by US officials, and were getting ready to return to Japan that morning (Ōishi, 2007, p. 23). Yet, although the winds forecast for that day were shifting, threatening to put those atolls and waters in the path of whatever fallout might come from *Bravo*, no attempts were made to cancel the test, notify ships or relocate local people.

At precisely 6:45 am, *Bravo* erupted with an unexpectedly powerful force of 15 megatons, over double what it had been expected to be – the equivalent of 1,000 times the explosion at Hiroshima. Its massive energy caused blinding flashes of light to cut through the morning darkness all throughout the northern Marshall Islands, followed by a deafening roar. In what should have been a "secure" and safe place to be, the people of Rongelap Atoll awoke to discover their islands enduring hot, overpowering winds as the sky "split open", and many fainted from shock (Johnston & Barker, 2008, p. 99). From aboard the *Lucky Dragon* it looked as if the sun was rising in the West (Ōishi, 2007). Expanding out from the epicentre at Bikini Atoll, where whole islands were vaporised and craters were left in the reef, tidal waves and gigantic whirlwinds of irradiated coral dust rolled through the atmosphere, forming clouds of fallout that caught the fickle winds and were carried all throughout Northern Oceania. The radioactive dust fell particularly on Rongelap, where it stuck to everything and immediately began to sicken the people.

Though the two American meteorologists who had been stationed at Rongelap were swiftly evacuated, and the *Lucky Dragon* and its radiation-sickened crew began to race back to Japan, American authorities left the 64 residents of Rongelap, 18 of Ailinginae, and 157 of Utrik to suffer in *Bravo's* poisonous wake for a full two days, leaving them with full-blown radiation burns and various terrifying symptoms. When they finally did transport these three groups of victims to the support base at Kwajalein Atoll, Islanders were forced to leave mostly everything behind (Johnston & Barker, 2008, p. 100). Islanders on nearby atolls like Ailuk that were not as severely affected as Rongelap were not even evacuated. And at Kwajalein, these nuclear refugees were further dehumanised and humiliated over the following months, stripped naked daily and forced to stand as American soldiers hosed off their bodies and then ran Geiger counters over their bodies (Johnston & Barker, 2008, pp. 101–103). In the years that followed, anguish and trauma only deepened among the Marshallese women of Rongelap as they and their daughters had miscarriages or gave birth to babies with horrifying deformities.

A convenient "accident"

Bravo, claimed American officials, was an experiment gone awry, an "accident". Yet, documents declassified in 1994 prove that US authorities were well aware on February 28 that strong winds were heading for the northern atolls, and that not aborting the test would likely put Rongelap and nearby atolls in danger. And although the US initially claimed that *Bravo*'s 15 megaton yield was unexpected, another declassified memo discovered in 2013 proved that military testers were actually anticipating up to 20 megatons (Johnson, 2013, pp. 369–370). In November 1953, the Atomic Energy Commission had also directed that should an "accidental" exposure occur to US servicemen or local populations, medical research could yield important data. Thus began a biomedical study known as *Project 4.1*, described as a "Study of Response of Human Beings Exposed to Significant Beta and Gamma Radiation due to Fall-Out from High Yield Weapons", in which, without their consent, and often under the guise of medical treatment, Marshallese were treated as test subjects to learn about the effects of nuclear warfare. Most nuclear-affected atoll communities concur that these human experiments were continued for decades after *Bravo* as nuclear survivors developed new symptoms.

The week after *Bravo*, a delegation of Marshallese leaders, such as paramount chief Kabua, who had dominion over all of the affected islands, and Dwight Heine, who would serve as the first Marshall Islands district representative of the US Trust Territory of the Pacific Islands, tirelessly petitioned the United Nations Trusteeship council in New York to demand that nuclear testing be stopped immediately. Their request was, however, completely denied and brushed off by the UN – and it was only mentioned briefly in the press, reinforcing the narrative that Marshall Islanders were complacent about the nuclear nightmare unfolding in their homeland.

Over the next four years after *Bravo*, despite the outcry from Marshallese and Islanders from surrounding Pacific archipelagos, the US went on to conduct yet another 55 tests at Bikini and Enewetak at such a frantic pace that at one point, between the two test sites, nuclear weapons were exploded seven times in one month. Altogether, the 67 tests that the US conducted in the Marshall Islands were the equivalent of one Hiroshima atomic bomb a day between 1946 and 1958. And this was only the beginning of the age of nuclear testing in the Pacific. By the 1980s, over 200 nuclear bombs in total would be detonated in the Pacific by British and French forces, a number that does not include additional tests by France in the 1990s or the multitudes of American unarmed missile tests at Kwajalein Atoll since the 1960s (Firth, 1987, p. ix).

Despite the radioactive impact of this testing, it was not long before Marshall Islanders were returned to their land. Even while these tests were still ongoing, US officials told the people of Rongelap that it was safe to resettle and they were returned to their atoll in July, 1957. Having left their homes in a hurry several years earlier, Islanders returned to find that their land was now a dangerous place to live, and that eating local foodstuffs resulted sometimes in strange blisters in their mouths. The US Department of Energy told Islanders not to eat crabs and many fish that had previously been safe to eat were now poisonous. Indeed, the *paijin* had saturated the landscape of Rongelap and though American scientists reassured locals that the radiation would subside over time, more and more of the population developed thyroid tumours and more babies were born with birth defects, which American doctors continued to monitor closely. Marshallese leaders suggest that this, too, was in fact a continuation of *Project 4.1* (Horowitz, 2012). Concerned about the plight of the Rongelap people, in 1971, Congress of

Micronesia Marshallese representative Ataji Balos requested help from a Japanese medical team; when these doctors attempted to go to Rongelap to provide independent assessment and treatment of the resettled community they were blocked by US officials (Johnson, 2013, p. 367). Finally, after nearly 30 years, suspicion and sickness compelled the people of Rongelap to leave their homeland again in 1985, when they were rescued by the environmental group Greenpeace's ship *Rainbow Warrior* and taken to Kwajalein Atoll.

The people of Bikini and Enewetak did not fare much better. In the late 1960s, the AEC stated that well water on Bikini was safe to drink, and so an eight-year plan was drafted to repatriate people to their homeland, which involved planting coconut trees and cleaning up the land in areas that were deemed inhabitable. Despite this cleanup, the Bikini Council unanimously voted that it was too unsafe to return home, but they could not prevent some extended families from returning to live there. These families lived in Bikini until in 1978, when higher levels of radiation were detected in the water supply and in all 139 residents of the atoll, resulting in yet another evacuation. Meanwhile, in 1976, the US agreed to clean up the mess it had created with its 45 nuclear tests in Enewetak Atoll, and to build houses for resettlement. As with Bikini and Rongelap, vast parts of Enewetak also remain completely uninhabitable. And though 84,927 cubic metres of radioactive waste was cleaned from the surface of parts of Enewetak, that waste is stored in perpetuity on Runit Islet, under a massive concrete dome placed over a deep crater that was caused by the testing. This concrete dome continues to leak radioactive material into the surrounding ocean and overall environment, a problem exacerbated by the rising tides of climate change.

Re-narrating the Marshallese fight for justice

Marshall Islanders have proven repeatedly that they are not helpless, passive victims but heroic survivors who will fight injustice passionately. This is not, as it is often misunderstood, a mere fight for compensation money; it is a fight for dignity and true security. Even elderly Islander storytellers resist narratives of victimisation by crafting sarcastic but empowering stories that reclaim a sense of Marshallese pride and agency. When talking about nuclear testing, many elders speak of Etao, the legendary Marshallese omnipotent trickster god, and how his postwar journeys through the Pacific and the US led to his capture by American scientists. Imprisoning Etao in a bottle, Americans made a deal with Etao for him to teach them the secrets of nuclear weaponry in exchange for his freedom. Being a trickster, Etao is unpredictable – bringing blessings to the people sometimes and great misfortune at other times, but he is nonetheless a Marshallese god, and thus this narrative energises local communities and allows them creative and critical distance to regain a sense of agency (Carucci, 1989, p. 92). Arguably, "owning" the story of nuclear testing has helped Marshallese communities to maintain their perseverance in requesting the US for proper compensation again and again.

Compensation and reparations have never been fully granted to the survivors of the nuclear war upon the Marshall Islands; yet, Marshall Islanders continue to fight for their dignity, their land and their future. While the surviving Japanese crew members of the *Lucky Dragon* were each compensated (albeit meagrely) within a year, it would be only after numerous litigations between 1960s and 1980s, that the US created a $150 million fund in 1986 for the newly-formed Republic of the Marshall Islands to settle all past *and future* nuclear testing claims for the "exposed" four atolls of Bikini, Enewetak, Rongelap and Utrik. Yet, between 1991 and 2003 the Nuclear Claims Tribunal determined that even among survivors from those atolls, Marshall Islanders should be entitled to at least a total of over $2 billion awarded for personal injury, property loss and class action lawsuits, far exceeding the funds that were available (US Embassy Majuro, 2014).

Additionally, recently declassified documents prove that the extent of nuclear damages was far more widespread than originally thought, with data that shows exposure reaching throughout the entire Marshall Islands. For example, it has now been proven that Ailuk Atoll, to the northeast of Rongelap, was showered with almost as much fallout as Utrik, but it was never evacuated, nor were victims there entitled to any compensation or care (Johnson, 2013, p. 372). US policy since the 1950s to the present has been that most Marshallese atolls are "unexposed" except for the four atolls. Yet, based on *American standards* of exposure, *every* atoll in the Marshall Islands exceeded even the highest average exposure experienced by Americans who lived close to atomic testing sites near Nevada during the Cold War (Johnson, 2013, p. 377).

America's countless trespasses and violations of fundamental human trust and dignity have resulted in "insecurity" in every respect: high rates of cancer all throughout the Marshall Islands, shortened lifespans, birth defects, overcrowding, family divisions and ongoing mental distress. Despite clear evidence to the contrary, American officials also continue to deny that there was ever any intention to conduct medical experimentation on Marshallese people. Instead, the US maintains its position that these atomic and hydrogen tests were ultimately necessary and done with benign intentions, and claims that "misconceptions" about US nuclear testing in the Marshalls "hinder" an appreciation of how important these tests were to American national defence and studying how to rehabilitate radiation-affected land (US Embassy, Marshall Islands, 2014). Forcing its sanitised version of reconciliation upon Marshall Islanders and urging them to put these painful nuclear histories behind them as part of their "healing" process, the US still refuses to apologise, pay more in compensation or to provide basic services needed to *all* Marshallese victims.

Lejmaan Juri: resisting the tides

The Cold War was anything but "cold" in the Marshall Islands, which the US nuclear testing programme successfully transformed into one of the "hottest" nuclear spots on earth. Masquerading as benevolence "for the good of mankind", America's violence took place largely beyond the awareness of the world, invisible as the radioactive *paijin* it spawned. But Marshall Islanders experienced, witnessed and continue to remember this violence. They were never helpless victims;

they have always been resourceful and creative in their responses and resilient in their resistance. Articulate and resourceful community leaders from Bikini, Enewetak, Rongelap, Kwajalein and the other atolls most affected by the Cold War are very experienced in negotiating with Americans and they have repeatedly stood up courageously to the US. Some of these leaders went on to become prominent politicians when the independent Republic of the Marshall Islands government was formed in 1979, such as first President Amata Kabua; his cousin, second President Imata Kabua; or sixth President Christopher Loeak, all of whom also held chiefly titles over all of the affected atolls. Third President Kessai Note was also a commoner whose father had been displaced from Bikini. Ismael John of Enewetak was a teenager when he was relocated to Ujelang, and later became a frank and outspoken senator who demanded proper health care and compensation for all Marshallese nuclear survivors and urged his people not to fear the US. Foreign Minister Tony deBrum, a Marshallese senator and former government adviser who testified many times to US Congress and the United Nations, also personally researched tens of thousands of declassified documents from the US nuclear testing programme and, in the years before his death, he was nominated for a Nobel Peace Prize for his anti-nuclear activism.

Although these brave male leaders have fought hard over the decades since nuclear testing began in 1946, the most significant and enduring anti-nuclear movements have been from Marshallese women's networks all throughout the country who have united their islands in their resistance efforts. The Marshallese expression *lejmaan juuri* references the powerful role that women serve in Marshallese society as arbiters of disputes and mediators of peace. Essentially this expression means, "when the women talk, the men must stop fighting and listen". Marshallese land tenure is matrilineal, meaning it is passed through the mother line. As mothers and keepers of the land, women have always been central in the process of resolving violence and conflict. It was the women whose land of inheritance was poisoned, and who had to deal directly with the devastating trauma of stillborn babies and birth defects. And so, it was the women who most boldly stood up and began the Nuclear Free and Independent Pacific movement in the 1970s, which originated in the Marshall Islands and was swiftly joined by women's groups throughout Oceania. Unlike Louis Réard's bikini-clad imaginary women as passive playthings, the real women of Bikini and other Marshall Islanders were activists who refused to accept or forget the imperial violence wrought upon their families and their homelands.

Darlene Keju was one such Marshallese woman, an unspoken hero who was most credited for her work in alerting the world to the truth of American nuclear testing. She was a woman who embodied the principle of *lejmaan juuri* – for she stood between the different communities of nuclear-affected atolls and their male leaders, and worked to facilitate dialogue and build networks of peaceful collaboration. Since she had witnessed so many of her fellow Islanders grappling with cancer, leukemia and other diseases, she suspected that the effects of the *paijin* were far more widespread than the US was willing to admit, and began to speak publicly about these suspicions in the 1970s, long before the US Department of

Energy's documents had been declassified and proper measurements were taken to prove her assertions. She travelled to various atolls and displaced communities to interview Marshall Islanders in various places, and she meticulously documented what she found. It was through this community work that she also heard countless testimonies of Islanders who had experienced strange medical tests, thus leading her to deduce that *Project 4.1* existed as well. And her own experiences of dealing with the painful legacies of nuclear testing gave her an intimate knowledge of what was at stake; for, like many of her family members, Keju herself suffered from radiation-related cancer. She was raised in Wotje Atoll during the 1950s, a former Japanese base and Pacific war battlefield that was also irradiated by *Bravo* and other tests but never acknowledged as "exposed" by the US. She fought tirelessly for the dignity of the Marshallese people right up until her untimely death at the age of 45 in 1996.

Conscious of the need to genuinely inform and empower the Marshallese public, Keju actively advocated transparency and public health research that would not be tainted or manipulated by US government. She boldly began making numerous speeches around the US and in other countries, calling for action to the international community a full 30 years before the United Nations asked for independent studies to be conducted to ascertain the effects of the nuclear testing programme in the Marshall Islands. Speaking to 900 people at the World Council of Churches Conference in Vancouver in 1983, she was one of the first people to elucidate the history of nuclear testing in the Marshall Islands to the public, a story that was mostly unknown at that time and quickly caught the attention of peace activists worldwide. In 1979, Keju had also travelled to Japan with John Anjain and other Marshallese nuclear testing survivors at the invitation of the Japanese anti-nuclear weapons organisation Gensuikin (Johnson, 2013, p. 61). Speaking in Hiroshima and Nagasaki, she worked to build solidarity between Japanese and Marshallese organisations, as well as the survivors of the *Lucky Dragon* crew.

All of these transoceanic grassroots networks survive today, largely thanks to the collaborative efforts of Darlene Keju, other Marshallese *hibakusha* and their counterparts in the US, Japan and around the world. It is worth mentioning that the work of Keju at times went against the grain of the national interests and cosy government-to-government relations between the Marshall Islands, the US and Japan. For example, her presentation at the World Council of Churches was highly unpopular with some Marshallese leaders, because they believed her words would anger Americans and jeopardise the new Marshallese government's negotiations for more aid money from the US under the "Compact of Free Association" (eventually ratified in 1986). Keju was outraged also when her own government actually contemplated Japan and other nations' proposals for turning some of the nuclear-ravaged atolls into profit-making nuclear waste dumps in the 1990s (Johnson, 2013, p. 254).

I never knew Darlene Keju, but having grown up in Kwajalein Atoll, as a child I witnessed one of the major milestones of Marshallese resistance to Cold War militarism. Crossing the athletic fields near the air terminal one day on the main islet in 1982, I remember seeing hundreds of Marshallese women and children sitting quietly but resolutely in the hot sun. This was Operation Homecoming, a peaceful protest by the displaced landowners and residents of Kwajalein Atoll, who were demanding better living conditions, proper health support and proper compensation from the US government for the confiscation of their lands for nuclear missile testing support, a battle that continues today. Many of these women had affiliations not only to Kwajalein lands but also to Rongelap, Bikini, Enewetak and other places that had been directly influenced by atomic and hydrogen tests. They came to Kwajalein for the sake of their land and their children, many of them risking or forfeiting their jobs on the base in order to resist military colonialism and decades of nuclear testing. These fearless protests were among multiple "sail-ins" and "sit-ins", acts of civil disobedience that were modelled after Martin Luther King's March on Washington. In Marshallese these demonstrations were called *jodiks*, a word that was taken from the Japanese word *jōriku*, a term which means "to make a land invasion", as was commonly used when Americans penetrated Japanese-held islands during the Pacific War. Re-appropriating the language of the American-Japanese conflicts of wartime, Islanders confidently "invaded" and retook the land that was rightfully theirs. Since the US Army ordered a press blackout about these protests, the world would not have known what was happening if it had not been for Darlene Keju and her American journalist husband Giff Johnson, who visited Kwajalein Atoll, observed what was happening and reported it throughout the Pacific and to the international media.

On Keju's gravesite the Marshallese expression "Tuak Bwe Elimaj-nono" is inscribed, a proverb which means, "be unafraid to make your way through strong ocean currents to the next island" (Johnson, 2013, p. 365). In the Marshall Islands, where the islands of an atoll are firmly rooted to the sea floor and bridged by a deep undersea coral reef, Islanders are certain of their strong connections to each other across turbulent waters, and they are optimistic, patient and resilient in their struggles against adversity. Thus, the Islanders of these small islands have had the stamina to stand up against superpowers like the US and push against the tides. Darlene Keju is one person who set an enduring example of how to do this and she inspired generations of youth to do the same. In doing so, she also built bridges between communities all over the world and promoted the solidarity of Pacific Islanders through the Nuclear Free and Independent Pacific movement. Symbolically weaving a transoceanic *jaki* fine mat out of the threads of shared experience, Darlene Keju reminded everyone affected by nuclear testing that they were all in some way part of the same genealogy.

Gifts for a fragmented planet

As scholar Kaituu Funaki proposes, the development and stability of Pacific Island nations might better be measured not by GNP but in terms of "Gross National Giving" (GNG), which takes into consideration the Pacific way of reciprocity, generosity and trust (Funaki, 2016). This approach is mindful of multiple Pacific Island cultural frameworks, and it values a more balanced and nuanced kind of relationship between Pacific Island nations and the countries of the "Rim", in that the largeness of economy size, military power, population or amount of natural resources cease to be the metric by which a country is measured. GNG measures the health and security of a Pacific Island nation in its capacity to *give back* to the world, as opposed to how much it "takes" in aid money. Taking into consideration these relations of reciprocity between so-called "large" countries and so-called "small island states" draws attention to the many *gifts* that Marshall Islanders offer the world.

Marshallese leaders have often said that the Marshall Islands' greatest export is world peace. While some critics might dismiss this as a positive or bittersweet spin on the reality of the Republic of the Marshall Islands' dependence on America, or its exploitation by the US military as a nuclear and later ballistic missile test site for nearly 75 years, the Marshallese production, perpetuation and teaching of peace ought to be taken seriously as an important gift and as an act of resistance. Marshallese are not innocent victim bystanders – they have actively participated in ensuring this peace; nor do they simply effect peace by allowing American military manoeuvres in their territory. Not only have they suffered the consequences of decades and decades of colonisation, war, weapons testing and irradiation, they have learnt through their hardships, fought back and continued to speak up and share their stories with the world. The Marshall Islands has also been the birthplace of successive generations of people who stand up for the security and peace of the planet – not only in the pursuit of eradicating nuclear weapons but also in the promotion of climate change policy reform and caring for the environment.

Today, Marshall Islanders continue to take bold and unprecedented action to draw attention not only to their own nuclear history but to the overwhelming dangers of nuclear weapons all over the world. In 2010, Bikini Atoll, for example, was designated a World Heritage Site after a long campaign by the Bikini community. In April 2014, the Republic of the Marshall Islands initiated an unprecedented series of "Nuclear Zero" cases in the International Court of Justice to hold the nine nuclear-armed states (US, United Kingdom, France, Russia, China, India, Pakistan, North Korea and Israel) accountable for violations of international law for failing to disarm themselves in accordance with the 1968 Nuclear Non-Proliferation Treaty. Though ultimately these lawsuits failed, they received praise from leaders and citizens' groups worldwide and showed once again that the Marshallese people refuse to be coaxed into silence or amnesia about their nuclear past (Krieger, 2014).

Following in the footsteps of community leaders like Darlene Keju, a new generation of young Marshallese men and women are also fighting against global currents, navigating violent waters metaphorically like their ancestors once did in voyaging canoes to draw attention to the issues that concern not only their island homes but our entire planet. Refusing to become the unfortunate victims of imperialism, militarism and globalisation, they are choosing to use their own experiences to teach the world and affect positive change. At a time when climate change and sea-level rise threatens to swallow the entire Marshall Islands and other low-lying Pacific nations, Marshallese youth have been petitioning multinational corporations and climate-polluting nations to take action.

Poet and scholar Kathy Jetñil-Kijiner is a Marshallese woman whose words are empowering her people, uniting communities throughout Oceania and raising international awareness about nuclear and environmental issues. Having started her own Marshall Islands-based non-government organisation *Jo Jikum*, a network that empowers youth to study and engage in environmental activism, Jetñil-Kijiner has gained substantial and unprecedented international visibility for the Marshall Islands and the plight of the Marshallese people. When she was chosen to give the keynote address at the United Nations Climate Change Summit in September 2014 in front of over 100 world leaders, Jetñil-Kijiner read a moving poem dedicated to her baby daughter, promising that as a mother, together with all indigenous Pacific peoples, she would fight to make the world a safer, better place for the future (Jetñil-Kijiner, 2014). Her poem – angry but hopeful, unwavering, passionate – expressed the truth that the Marshall Islands' 3,000-year history is much bigger than its postwar woes and recent climate crises. Before receiving one of the only standing ovations ever given in the history of the United Nations, she ended her poem with simple but profound words that sum up the perseverance of generations of Marshallese people: "We deserve to do more than just survive, we deserve to thrive".

Increasingly, Jetñil-Kijiner infuses ritual into her work, to acknowledge the pain of her people and facilitate a more meaningful conversation and global understanding around nuclear colonialism and the onslaught of climate change. In 2018, she travelled by voyaging canoe to Bikini and Enewetak to produce a powerful video poem titled "Anointed", told in the ritual style of mourning for the land of Runit, where the radioactive dome is sited. The poem ends with the haunting lines:

> My belly is a crater empty of stories and answers only questions, hard as concrete.
> Who gave them this power?
> Who anointed them with the power to burn? (Jetñil-Kijiner, 2018)

As with her other work, her message is furious and defiant but also optimistic, honouring and bearing witness to the past but determined to seek a collective vision for the future. Later in 2018, she travelled to Greenland to collaborate with indigenous poet Aka Niviâna, where the two artists wrote and performed "Rise", in which both artists lament how the melting of the polar ice caps is causing Pacific islands to flood – resulting in the loss of each other's homelands. These interventions are unforgettable and influential, spread through the internet via social media, capturing the attention of ordinary citizens and policy makers around the world. In "making room to grieve", as she writes, she advocates through art and thus nurtures a deeper and more enduring sense of strength and true security through solidarity and global community (Jetñil-Kijiner, 2018).

It is in this spirit that young Marshall Islanders build true security from within, giving selflessly in the interest of future generations. And despite incredible adversity, they continue to navigate onward, from the toxic typhoons of the Cold War to the turbulent tides of globalisation and rising seas, teaching the world to work together – indeed, to thrive – in our collective humanity.

Note

1 See the highly criticised historical narrative of Alan Moorehead in his 1966 book *The Fatal Impact*, notorious for its orientalistic and idealised portrayal of pre-contact Pacific Islanders as belonging to an unspoiled eden – irrevocably ruined and corrupted as nothing more than victims of European colonisation.

References

Barad, K. (2018). Troubling time/s and ecologies of nothingness: Re-turning, re-membering, and facing the incalculable. *New Formations: A Journal of Culture/Theory/Politics*, *92*, 56–86.

Carucci, L. M. (1989). The source of the force in Marshallese cosmology. In G. M. White & L. Lindstrom (Eds.), *The Pacific theater: Island representations of World War II*. Honolulu, HI: University of Hawai'i Press.

Carucci, L. M. (1997). *Nuclear nativity: Rituals of renewal and empowerment in the Marshall Islands*. Dekalb, IL: Northern Illinois University Press.

Davis, J. S. (2005). Representing place: "Deserted Isles" and the reproduction of Bikini Atoll. *Annals of the Association of American Geographers*, *95*, 3.

Firth, S. (1987). *Nuclear playground*. Honolulu, HI: University of Hawai'i Press.

Funaki, K. (2016). New visions for international aid: Perspectives from the Pacific Islands. *Japan Society for Pacific Island Studies*, *4*, 39–62.

Hegarty, D., & Tryon, D. (Eds.). (2013). *Politics, development and security in Oceania*. Canberra: ANU Press.

Horowitz, A. J. (2012). *Nuclear savage: The islands of Secret Project 4.1*. Documentary Film. San Francisco, CA: Primordial Soup Company.

Jetñil-Kijiner, K. (2014). *Dear Matafele Peinem* (Poem read at the United Nations World Climate Summit, September 23, 2014). From *Iep Jeltok: A Basket of Poetry and Writing from Kathy Jetñil-Kijiner*. Retrieved 2015, January 24 from https://jkijiner.wordpress.com

Jetñil-Kijiner, K. (2018). *Kathy Jetñil-Kijiner*. Retrieved February 20, 2019 from kathyjetnilkijiner.com.

Johnson, G. (2013). *Don't ever whisper – Darlene Keju, Pacific health pioneer, champion for nuclear survivors*. Charleston, SC: CreateSpace Independent Publishing Platform.

Johnston, B. R. (2007). *Half lives, half-truths: Confronting the radioactive legacies of the Cold War*. Santa Fe, NM: School for Advanced Research Press.

Johnston, B. R., & Barker, H. (2008). *Consequential damages of nuclear war: The Rongelap report*. Walnut Creek, CA: Left Coast Press.

Kato, M. (1993). Nuclear globalism: Traversing rockets, satellites, and nuclear war via the strategic gaze. *Alternatives*, *18*(3), 339–360.

Krieger, D. (2014). *The mouse that roared: Stand with the Marshall Islands*. Nuclear Age Peace Foundation Blog. Retrieved October 22, 2014 from www.wagingpeace.org.

Lal, B., & Fortune, K. (2000). *The Pacific islands: An encyclopedia*. Honolulu, HI: University of Hawai'i Press.

Niedenthal, J. (1997). *For the good of mankind: A history of the people of Bikini and their islands*. Majuro: Bravo Publishers.

Ōishi, M. (2007). *Daigo Fukuryū Maru Norikumiin ga Kataru Bikini Jiken no Omote to Ura: Kore Dake wa Tsutaeteokitai* (The two sides of the Bikini Incident, told by a crew-member of the *Number 5 Lucky Dragon:* At least what I want to say). Tokyo: Kamogawa Shuppan.

Teaiwa, T. (1994). Bikinis and other s/pacific n/oceans. *The Contemporary Pacific, 6,* 1.

US Embassy, Majuro, Marshall Islands. (2014). Retrieved October 1, 2014 from majuro. usembassy.gov

Weisgall, J. M. (1994). *Operation crossroads: The atomic tests at Bikini Atoll.* Annapolis, MD: Naval Institute Press.

5 Impact of natural disasters and climate change on national security in the Pacific

Case studies of Kiribati and Tuvalu

Anand Chand and Tauisi Taupo

Introduction

Natural disasters and climate change and are two significant threats to national security in most SIDS, including PICs (United Nations, 2016; World Bank, 2013, 2014; World Bank & United Nations, 2010). There is extensive literature on natural disasters and climate change on SIDs. However, there is little literature on the impact of natural disasters and climate change in the Pacific Island Countries (PICs) (World Bank & United Nations Report, 2010; World Bank Report, 2013). Likewise, there is scant literature that links the risks of natural disasters and climate change to national security in PICs (Barnett, 2003; World Bank & United Nations, 2010; World Bank, 2013). To fill this lacuna, the chapter focusses on two phenomena, natural disasters and climate change, and how they pose a security risk for PICs, particularly Kiribati and Tuvalu. It focusses on issues such as death of and injury to individuals, economic damage and financial cost, food security, water security, human security and threats to sovereignty and nationhood.

This chapter is essential for three reasons. First, in the past two decades, the PICs have been facing the consequences of natural disasters and climate change and these raise security concerns. Second, this chapter contributes to the existing literature on natural disasters and climate change and security. Third, there is a link between these two security issues in the sense that climate change exacerbates the frequency and intensity of natural disasters such as cyclones, storms, floods and droughts. Due to climate change, natural disasters are increasing and becoming more unpredictable (Barnett, 2003; Intergovernmental Panel on Climate Change, 2018a).

This chapter has nine sections. This introductory section outlines the aim and focus of study. The next section defines the concepts of natural disaster, climate change and security. It is followed by a literature review and a background of Kiribati and Tuvalu. The chapter then presents research findings and discussion on the impact of natural disasters on PICs and specifically on Kiribati and Tuvalu, followed by the impact of climate change on Kiribati and Tuvalu. The next section examines the impact of natural disaster and climate change on various types of security. The chapter then offers some policy options for PICs' governments and overseas donor agencies and development partners. The concluding section provides a summary and future research agenda.

Definitions: natural disaster, climate change and security

UNISDR (2009, p. 9) defines a natural disaster as "a serious disruption of the functioning of a community or a society involving widespread human, material, economic or environmental losses and impacts, which exceeds the ability of the affected community or society to cope using its resources". Natural disasters include cyclones, storms, high-velocity winds, floods, landslides, droughts, wildfires floods and tsunamis (UNISDR, 2009). These natural disasters generally strike quickly and cause great harm and damage (Barnett, 2003; World Bank & United Nations, 2010; World Bank, 2013). Natural disasters and climate change have social, economic and environmental effects that can cripple and slow the economic development progress of countries.

The United Nations (1992, p. 7) define climate change as "a change of climate attributed directly or indirectly to human activity that alters the composition of the global atmosphere over comparable periods". This definition mentions that *human activities* and not *natural events* are responsible for climate change, hence outlining that human activities are drivers of environmental change such as increasing global carbon emissions and rising sea levels, which is a national security issue for small low-lying nation-states (United Nations, 1992).

Security is a broad and multifaceted concept. We define security as social, cultural, economic and political issues that threaten the survival of a nation-state. It includes issues such as death of and injury to individuals, financial cost, food security, water security and human security.

Literature review

There is abundant literature on natural disaster and climate change globally and on Small Island Developing States (SIDS), but little on PICs (Barnett, 2003; World Bank & United Nations, 2010; World Bank, 2013). The Asia-Pacific region and its people are highly exposed to natural disasters and the region has a very high level of deaths and injury compared to other regions of the world (UNESCAP & UNISDR, 2012). PICs are at the top of the United Nations (UN) World Risk Index, which measures exposure to natural hazards and coping capacity of 171 countries (United Nations, 2016). PICs frequently face extreme weather events compared to larger countries and have less capacity to respond to natural disasters and incur economic costs from natural disasters that are much higher on average (International Monetary Fund, 2016). PICs are more vulnerable because of economic resource constraints, remote geographical settings and limited capacities to respond, mitigate and adapt to natural disasters (Ahsan, 2014; Barnett & Waters, 2016).

The extreme events of natural disasters affect the lives and livelihoods of the people in the Pacific (World Bank & United Nations Report, 2010; World Bank Report, 2013). PICs are highly exposed to both natural disasters and climate change especially in densely populated coastal areas where most agricultural and marine activities take place (Govan, 2009; Foale, Cohen, Januchowski-Hartley,

Wenger, & Macintyre, 2011; Eriksson et al., 2017). Among PICs, there are smaller and low-lying atoll islands such as Tuvalu and Kiribati that are incredibly vulnerable to natural disasters and climate change with an even lower capacity to cope and respond to these (Edmonds & Noy, 2018). Besides destructive cyclones, strong winds and distant cyclones can easily affect and flood parts of these islands due to their low-lying geographical characteristics (Taupo & Noy, 2017).

With natural disasters likely to intensify in frequency and magnitude due to climate change, so are the risks to the national security of countries (Taupo & Noy, 2017). In Kiribati and Tuvalu, these phenomena threaten the long-term viability on these islands and the capacity of their people to continue living there, and they can affect the very extinction of their countries (i.e. the disappearance of their nation-states) (Nurse & Sem, 2001; Barnett & Adger, 2003). The Presidents of Kiribati, Tuvalu and the Federated States of Micronesia have put this bluntly: "sea-level rise and other related consequences of climate change are grave security threats to our very existence as homelands and nation-states" (Barnett, 2003, p. 9).

Background of case studies: Kiribati and Tuvalu

Background of Kiribati

Kiribati comprises 32 low-lying atolls and is one of three atoll nation-states ranked as a Least Developed Country (LDC) alongside Tuvalu and the Maldives (Storey & Hunter, 2010). Kiribati land area is around 800 km. Kiribati has three island groups – Gilbert, Line and Phoenix. The Gilbert group has 16 atolls and reef islands while the Line and Phoenix group each have eight atolls and reef islands. The majority of Kiribati's population of 118,000 reside in the main Tarawa island and Betio is the capital (Storey & Hunter, 2010). Twelve much smaller atolls are not permanently inhabited because of their small size and lack of freshwater. The economy of Kiribati is constrained by its geographical isolation, smallness, remoteness and lack of resources and thus imports most food from Australia. Kiribati relies on revenues from fisheries' resources and aid money from international donor agencies from countries such as Australia, New Zealand and other Asian countries (Storey & Hunter, 2010). Kiribati uses the Australian dollar as its currency.

Background of Tuvalu

Tuvalu is a small island nation located in the central Pacific with a total land area of around 26 square kilometres and an Exclusive Economic Zone (EEZ) of approximately 900,000 square kilometres (United Nations Development Programme Report, 2009). It is home to just 11,000 people, most of whom reside in the capital island of Funafuti where the narrowest point is no more than 20 metres wide (ADB, 2007; Taupo, 2018a). Like Kiribati, Tuvalu's economy is hindered by a lack of natural resources, smallness and remoteness. Tuvalu relies on its revenue from fisheries' resources and other revenue sources, and on aid from international donors and aid support from development partners such as New Zealand and Australia (ADB, 2007). Due to their proximity to the Cyclone Belt near the tectonic boundary between Australasian and the Pacific plates, Kiribati and Tuvalu are highly exposed to cyclone, storms, floods, landslides and droughts (World Bank, 2013; United Nations, 2015b; Taupo & Noy, 2017; Noy, 2017, 2016c, 2016a; Edmonds & Noy, 2018). With its highest point 3 metres above sea level, Tuvalu is one of the lowest countries in the world by ground elevation (Mortreux & Barnett, 2009). The low-lying islands of Tuvalu are incredibly vulnerable to climate change and natural disasters, hence facing an insecure future with limited options for adaptation, mitigation, relocation and migration. According to Kaly and Pratt (2000), out of the Pacific Island Countries (PICs), Tuvalu has the highest environmental vulnerability. Edmonds and Noy (2018) also pointed out that Cook Islands and Tuvalu face the highest disaster losses (in total number of lifeyears lost[1]) per person from 1980 to 2012, when compared to other PICs (see Noy [2016a] for methodology).

Research findings and discussion

Impact of natural disaster on PICs

This section looks at natural disasters in PICs as a whole before we examine the impact of natural disasters more specifically in the context of Kiribati and Tuvalu. Quantitative research methods can be used to calculate and measure the impact of natural disasters on PICs (Taupo & Noy, 2017). There are two sources of data available that keep records of natural disasters: (1) *Emergency Events Database* (EM-DAT) and (2) *Desinventar Database*. The EM-DAT data is compiled by the South Pacific Community (SPC) and relies on data provided by the national governments of PICs and the *Desinventar Database* set is provided by the United Nations Office for Disaster Risk Reduction (UNISDR).

The EM-DAT data set captures data on variables such as hydro-meteorological events, floods, wave surges, storms, droughts, landslides, avalanches, earthquakes, tsunamis, volcanic eruptions and biological epidemics and insect infestations (Taupo & Noy, 2017). It also contains data on the number of people killed, the number of people affected and the quantity of direct damages for each natural disaster. However, the EM-DAT data set does not capture some types of natural hazards like "high-frequency-low-impact disasters" and many "small and distant cyclones and storms". The EM-DAT eligibility criteria are therefore not suitable for PICs. For instance, there are many small and distant cyclones and storms that are destructive to low-lying islands, but they are not taken into account, because they do not conform to the EM-DAT criteria (Taupo & Noy, 2017). The exclusion of some natural disasters has led to an underestimation of the true impact of natural disasters in PICs. The alternative source of data set provided by Desinventar (desinventar.net) is more appropriate. The Desinventar data captures both the "high-frequency-high impact risk" and the "high-frequency-low-impact risk".

Few studies have examined the impact of different types of natural disaster on PICs (Cavallo & Noy, 2011; Noy, 2016b; Taupo & Noy, 2017; Edmonds & Noy, 2018). For instance, a study by Noy (2016b) used longitudinal data (104 years) from both EM-DAT and Desinventar databases to measure the cost of natural disasters on PICs. Figure 5.1 shows that there has been an upward trend in *occurrences* for natural disasters in PICs from 1914 to 2016 and more sharply since the year 1983 onwards. The data shows that in PICs, the incidence of storms is the highest, followed by floods and droughts.

Furthermore, EM-DAT and Desinventar databases show the direct impact of natural disasters on *people* in PICs from 1914 to 2016, as can be seen in Table 1. This table shows that 9,353 individuals in PICs lost their life, 4,663 were injured due to natural disasters, 8,540,015 were affected people requiring assistance during a disaster (e.g. requiring basic survival needs such as food, water, shelter, sanitation and immediate medical assistance), 424,526 were made homeless. Therefore, a total of 8,969,204 were affected and the financial cost was around USD 4,774 million. The large numbers of affected people suggest that some individuals may have been affected multiple times. The three major causes of death were volcanic activity, earthquakes and storms. Storms and floods are the highest cause for homeless of people in PICs. The actual financial cost would be higher, because some types of natural disasters are not captured by EM-DAT due to eligibility criteria, *de facto* excluding some events relevant to PICs as mentioned before.

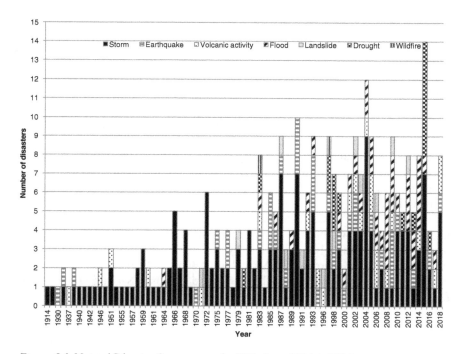

Figure 5.1 Natural Disaster Occurrences for PICs from 1914 to 2016

Table 5.1 Impact of Natural Disasters on people in PICs: 1914 to 2016

	Total Deaths	Injured	Affected	Homeless	Total Affected	Total Damage ('000 USD)
Storm	1,895	2,803	3,175,034	240,541	3,418,378	3,858,760
Earthquake	3,129	1,769	616,471	19,400	637,640	328,615
Volcanic activity	3,515	31	234,201	46,000	280,232	110,000
Flood	212	9	841,727	100,585	942,321	350,375
Landslide	518	51	1,563	18,000	19,614	NA
Drought	84	NA	3,662,019	NA	3,662,019	94,900
Wildfire	NA	NA	9,000	NA	9,000	31,650
Total	**9,353**	**4,663**	**8,540,015**	**424,526**	**8,969,204**	**4,774,300**

Source: Authors' calculations from the *Emergency Events Database* (EM-DAT)-Accessed on 14 March 2019.

Impact of natural disaster on people of PICs (including Kiribati and Tuvalu)

In recent years, the distressing impacts of droughts, cyclones and floods have resulted in massive damages and losses for the smaller islands of PICs. This section will examine the impact of natural disasters on people in PICs, including Kiribati and Tuvalu. In addition to the adverse effects of natural disasters on the economy and ecosystems, they also cause significant hardships on the population and their livelihoods and damages to physical assets (ADB, 2015).

Noy (2016b) looked at the impact of natural disasters on each PIC, showing that between 1990–2012, according to *Desinventar* database for larger PICs (e.g. PNG and Fiji), the total number of people affected by natural disasters in PICs was the highest in PNG (around 7,000,000), followed by Fiji (around 2,500,000). At the same time, Noy (2016b) also showed that the EM-DAT data underestimates the number of people affected by natural disasters in PNG (around 1,500,000) and Fiji (around 500,000). According to Noy (2016b), for Kiribati, around 85,000 people were affected by natural disasters, while for Tuvalu the number of people affected by natural disasters was around 22,000 (see both the EM-DAT and Desinventar data sets).

In addition, Noy (2016b) shows that according to the *Desinventar Database*, for larger PICs like PNG, the number of people killed was around 7,000, but the EM-DAT data shows that the figure is around 3,100. The next highest was in Samoa where around 410 died (primarily due to the 2009 tsunami) followed by the Solomon Islands (around 350) and Fiji (around 300). Noy (2016b) stressed that the death toll in Tuvalu is higher (around 20) than Kiribati (*Desinventar Database* 1990–2012).

Noy (2016b) also compiled the financial cost of damage (in USD) caused by natural disasters in the PICs, including Kiribati and Tuvalu. Between 1990–2012, the damage caused by natural disasters in the PICs was the highest in Samoa (around USD 750 million due to 2009 Tsunami-EM-DAT data), followed by Guam (around USD 730 million-EM-DAT data), American Samoa (around USD 700 million-EM-DAT data), Tuvalu (around USD 130 million-Desinventar Data) and Kiribati (around USD 10 million-Desinventar Data) (Noy, 2016b).

Natural disasters such as tropical cyclones and associated storm surge have devastating effects on the lives and livelihoods of the people of Kiribati and Tuvalu. For instance, the 1972 Tropical Cyclone *Bebe* in Tuvalu struck down 90% of the houses and killed six people (Taupo & Noy, 2017). In 2015, Tropical Cyclone Pam (TC Pam), hit Vanuatu and also caused damage to Kiribati and Tuvalu as it went close to these countries. For the affected Tuvalu islands, the estimated monetary loss and damages to households' assets was around 10% of GDP (Taupo & Noy, 2017). A survey in Tuvalu in 2015, reveals that the agriculture accounted for 5.3% of the estimated monetary value for loss and damages (Taupo & Noy, 2017). One of the affected islands was Nui, where 98% of interviewed households reported that floods from TC Pam entered their homes (Taupo & Noy, 2017). Even though TC Pam was a distant cyclone, the geographical characteristics of the low-lying islands of Tuvalu made it easier for the generated storm surge to hit the outer islands.

Impact of *climate change* on PICs: Kiribati and Tuvalu

Climate change is currently a hot topic in recent global and regional debates and is a serious issue because it poses threats to the very existence of the islands and people in SIDS, including PICs. Leaders of PICs are at the forefront of climate change and have been very vocal in the international arena in debating and advocating on the negative impacts of climate change on the islands, people, environment and future generations (World Bank, 2009; World Bank & United Nations, 2010; World Bank, 2013, 2014; United Nations, 2015a, 2015b; Noy, 2016b).

Among PICs, Tuvalu and Kiribati are the most vulnerable to the adverse effects of climate change and both countries are feeling the effects of global temperatures increase, rising sea levels and frequent and intense cyclones, floods and droughts (Food and Agriculture Organization, 2008). The rising sea level is a problem for low-lying islands like Kiribati and Tuvalu, which are not higher than 5 metres above sea level. In Kiribati and Tuvalu, even small storm surges or heavy rain floods can affect parts of the islands. Flooding is a common challenge that affects the livelihoods and agricultural activities for household consumption.

Like many other small and low-lying islands, Tuvalu and Kiribati have already felt the impacts of sea level rising through coastal erosion and flooding of low parts of the islands, especially during the highest tides of the year (i.e. king tides) (World Bank, 2009; World Bank & United Nations, 2010; World Bank, 2013, 2014; United Nations, 2015a, 2015b; Noy, 2016b). This is particularly evident in Tuvalu during high tide when seawater comes out of the ground and floods homes in low-lying parts of the islands, particularly in the capital, Funafuti (Taupo & Noy, 2017; Taupo, Cuffe, & Noy, 2018). Becker (2012) pointed out that the sea-level rise in Funafuti was three times above the global average between 1950 and

2009. Yamano et al. (2007) estimate that such consequence of climate change will likely worsen over time.

Impact of natural disasters and climate change on various types of security

This section will highlight some of the security issues that result from natural disasters and climate change in Kiribati and Tuvalu. In summary, the critical security issues relate to *food security, water security, biodiversity and ecosystems, internal relocation security* and *nationhood security and sovereignty*. Each of these security issues are discussed next.

Food security[2]

Natural disasters and climate change have devastating effects on agriculture, forestry, food production and food security. According to the FAO Report (2008), natural disasters impose severe restrictions on the economic development of PICs, the latter being in "constant mode of recovery" (Food and Agriculture Organization, 2008). Similarly, the International Panel on Climate Change (IPCC) Report (2018a) stressed that climate change would seriously threaten current food security situations in PICs and jeopardise governments' abilities to deliver on their Sustainable Development Goals (SDGs). In PICs, the majority of rural people still live and depend on subsistence food production such as taro, yams, sweet potatoes and vegetables. Both oceanic and coastal fisheries are bound to be affected by natural disasters and climate change.

Increasing coastal erosion and salinisation as a result of natural disasters and climate change will reduce food production. Furthermore, fish is a significant source of food for people in PICs and per capita consumption of fish in PICs is very high. The Food and Agriculture Organization (2008) estimated that in PICs, each person consumes on average around 70 kg of fish per year. Moreover, PICs export around USD 1.9 billion worth of fish, indicating the significance of fisheries to PICs' economies and food security (Food and Agriculture Organization, 2008). In the case of Kiribati, the Food and Agriculture Organization (2008) estimated that the cost of damages in the food sector by 2050 could represent 17–18% of Kiribati's 2002 GDP. Actions are required now to curb the ill effects of climate change and to achieve sustainable development and viable food production for PICs (Food and Agriculture Organization, 2008).

Water security

The combination of natural disasters and climate change will also affect water security in PICs. In PICs, the four primary sources of clean drinking water sources are rainwater, well water, desalinated water and imported bottled drinking water. Noy (2016c) mentioned that for clean water consumption, most people in PICs rely on rainfall and face difficulty during droughts.

PICs are increasingly facing a lack of fresh drinking water due to frequent extreme weather events. For example, in Kiribati in 1998, rainwater tanks in substantial parts dried up and people had difficulty finding clean water (World Bank, 2000). Furthermore, most people in Kiribati do not have access to clean drinking water due to the lack of rainfall during dry months and the pollution of the lagoon water. The Chinese tuna processing company also faced scarcity of water to process tuna loins and had to desalinate water from the sea from time to time (Taupo et al., 2018). In the case of the 2011 drought in Tuvalu, the government had to buy desalination units to convert seawater to freshwater to get through the water shortage problem (Taupo, 2018a).

Biodiversity and ecosystem security

Natural disasters and climate change have impacts on biodiversity and ecosystems of land and forests. Land biodiversity-related risks include forest fires and the spread of invasive species (Intergovernmental Panel on Climate Change, 2018b). Forest ecosystems are crucial to PICs' environment and they also provide sources of food, household income and traditional medicine, contributing to the food security of village people (Food and Agriculture Organization, 2008). Forests are excellent sources of edible natural fruits, nuts, plants and game meat that supplement subsistence agriculture. Natural disasters such as cyclones and storm winds have the potential to damage forest ecosystems for years, hence reducing an essential source of food for people in PICs. Furthermore, the destruction of forests, wild trees and vegetation in remote rural villages can affect people who rely on traditional medicine, which can make a difference between life and death (Food and Agriculture Organization, 2008).

There are also risks to marine biodiversity, fisheries and ecosystems, and their functions and services to humans (Intergovernmental Panel on Climate Change, 2018b). These include the potential loss of coastal resources, reduction in the productivity of fisheries and aquaculture, decline in coral reefs and impact on the growth and development of marine biodiversity. Even more threatening is the risk of irreversible loss of many marine and coastal ecosystems, which are significant sources of livelihoods.

Internal relocation security

In PICs, governments are already shifting people from low-lying coastal areas to higher ground. Similarly, both Kiribati and Tuvalu have started relocation plans (Taupo, 2018a). For example, a household survey in Tuvalu recently revealed that 41% of households have already considered moving away from their current homes to safer places away from the shoreline, while 86% of households will consider moving if they get granted permission by the government for internal relocation (Farbotko & Lazrus, 2012; Taupo, 2018a). PIC governments are using internal migration as a preferred option vis-à-vis external emigration.

Nationhood security & sovereignty

In the long-run, climate change is an existential security threat on low-lying islands like Tuvalu and Kiribati. In the worst-case scenario, if the atoll countries go under the sea due to rising sea levels, the people of Kiribati, Tuvalu and the Marshall Islands will be forced to relocate to another PIC or possibly to Australia and New Zealand. This strategy has been mooted and debated by leaders of small atoll countries in the PICs such as Kiribati, Tuvalu and the Marshall Islands. For example, on one hand, Kiribati has already bought land in Fiji, but on the other hand, Kiribati government officials claim that the land it has bought in Fiji is more for food security purposes and emigration is considered as the last option (Vaka-sukawaqa, 2016). Kiribati leaders have stressed that the option of emigration will only occur in the very drastic situation of Kiribati going under the sea. To quote Mr. Nakibae Teuatabo (Climate Change Officer in Kiribati) stressed:

> I think of emigration as being the stage where you know you're losing the battle. We're nowhere near that.
>
> (Schneider, 2009, p. 136)

The Tuvaluan government has also stressed that the relocation of its people to another country will be the last option (Roy, 2019; Stewart, 2019; Vakasukawaqa, 2016). Just like for Kiribati, Fiji has offered land to the Tuvaluan government to relocate their population, but the government has not accepted this offer so far (Roy, 2019; Stewart, 2019; Vakasukawaqa, 2016). The New Zealand government has also expressed its interest to take Tuvalu citizens (around 11,000) in case Tuvaluans are required to leave their homelands due to rising sea level and loss of their islands. The Australian government has also offered Tuvaluan people the option of relocating and offered them full Australian citizenship in exchange for their country's maritime and fisheries' rights (Stewart, 2019). The Tuvalu government also rejected the proposal and replied that it will not compromise its sovereign rights and forfeit its fisheries resources (Stewart, 2019).

There are also questions as to whether the population of these countries are willing and able to relocate and what will be the consequences of these displacements on their well-being and prosperity. PICs' peoples see relocation as a simplistic and self-defeatist approach that does not solve the problem of climate change (Roy, 2019). The people of PICs fear they will lose their identity, culture, lifestyle and traditions if they emigrate (Stewart, 2019).

Policy options

Some policy options are available that can be considered by the governments of PICs. This study argues that both *mitigation* and *adaptation* are needed to reduce the harmful impact of natural disasters and climate change.

First, with regards to *mitigation*, the Pacific Island leaders at the international level need to continue putting pressure on large developed countries to agree to reduce carbon emissions, which are detrimental to climate change. The Presidents of Kiribati, Tuvalu, the Marshall Islands and Fiji have put the dangers of climate change at the centre stage in international forums. This momentum should be intensified to protect small island countries going under the sea.

Secondly, with regards to *adaptation*, the governments of PICs should design a strategic plan and policies to assist their people to relocate to higher grounds to ease the dangers of climate change and natural disasters such as tsunamis (lessons to learn from Samoa) and flooding of coastal areas. Senior government officials in PICS need to develop a proactive strategy to address the difficulties of people living in low-lying areas.

Thirdly, both internal national funds and external overseas donor/development partner funds are needed to combat the cost of damages caused by natural disasters and climate change, and it is crucial to identify potential financial instruments that are available to facilitate both *ex-ante* and *ex-post* natural disaster risk management. Noy and Edmonds (2016) discuss risks in Pacific atoll islands and various options for financial instruments applicable to both *ex-ante* and *ex-post* natural disaster risk management such as post-natural disaster budget provisions, offshore funds, contingent credit lines, multilateral loans and grants, insurance for public assets, private insurance, sovereign insurance and regional pooling of sovereign insurance.

Another option that promotes greater financial autonomy with less reliance on foreign aid and assistance, is examined by Taupo (2018b) who looks at the financing of natural disaster risk management for the atoll islands of Tuvalu and Kiribati. Taupo (2018a) suggests that the continuous reliance on foreign aid for *ex-post* natural disaster risk management could be reduced if a country's sovereign wealth funds are used to address natural disasters. For example, under the Climate Change and Disaster Survival Fund Act 2015, the Tuvalu Climate Change and Disaster Survival Fund was established by contributions from the Government of Tuvalu as an *ex-ante* financing instrument for climate change programmes and for natural disaster response (Pacific Islands Forum Secretariat, 2018; Tuvalu Government, 2016).

Conclusion

Natural disasters affect economic security, environmental security, food security, infrastructure security and most importantly, the security of the people. PICs have been overlooked in terms of natural disasters as some of the types they face do not meet the criteria to be accepted as natural disasters in international databases. Natural disaster risks are exceptionally high in the Pacific region, with per capita impact amongst the highest in the world. Natural disaster risks for PICs should be well assessed so that policies can better reflect on pressing areas requiring the attention of the government. In order to do so, there is a need for computing risk indices and resilience indicators for PICs.

Tuvalu and Kiribati are very vocal in the international arena, raising the dangers posed by climate change, advocating for global cooperation and fighting for climate justice. For small and low-lying islands, climate change and sea-level rise are issues of national security that potentially threaten the sovereignty and survival of their nations.

Notes

1 Noy (2016b) and the United Nations (2015a) used the total number of human lifeyears lost to disasters as an aggregate measure of disaster impact using data on mortality, people affected and financial damages. Lifeyears lost is associated with differences between mortality and life expectancy, disabilities and more. This new metric provides a better representation of disaster impact (United Nations, 2015a). For details on how to calculate this index, see Noy (2016b) and the United Nations (2015a).
2 The FAO (2018) defines food security as "a condition for all people, at all times, having both physical, social and economic access to sufficient, safe and healthy variety of food, satisfying dietary needs and food preferences while having an active and healthy life in a sustainable manner".

References

ADB. (2007). *2006 Tuvalu economic report: From plan to action.* Mandaluyong City, Philippines: Asian Development Bank.

ADB. (2015). *Pacific economic monitor midyear review July.* Mandaluyong City, Philippines: Asian Development Bank. Retrieved from http://reliefweb.int/sites/reliefweb.int/files/resources/Pacific%20Economic%20Monitor_July%202015%20Midyear%20Review.pdf

Ahsan, D. A. (2014). Does natural disaster influence people's risk preference and trust? An experiment from cyclone prone coast of Bangladesh. *International Journal of Disaster Risk Reduction, 9,* 48–57. https://doi.org/10.1016/j.ijdrr.2014.02.005

Barnett, J. (2003). Security and climate change. *Global Environmental Change, 13*(1), 7–17. https://doi.org/10.1016/S0959-3780(02)00080-8

Barnett, J., & Adger, W. N. (2003). Climate dangers and atoll countries. *Climatic Change; Dordrecht, 61*(3), 321–337. http://doi.org.helicon.vuw.ac.nz/10.1023/B:CLIM.0000004559.08755.88

Barnett, J., & Waters, E. (2016). Rethinking the vulnerability of small island states: Climate change and development in the Pacific islands. In *The Palgrave handbook of international development* (pp. 731–748). https://doi.org/10.1057/978-1-137-42724-3_40

Becker, M., Meyssignac, B., Letetrel, C., Llovel, W., Cazenave, A., & Delcroix, T. (2012). Sea level variations at tropical Pacific Islands since 1950. *Global and Planetary Change, 80–81,* 85–98. https://doi.org/10.1016/j.gloplacha.2011.09.004

Cavallo, E., & Noy, I. (2011). Natural disasters and the economy: A survey. *International Review of Environmental and Resource Economics, 5*(1), 63–102. https://doi.org/10.1561/101.00000039

Edmonds, C., & Noy, I. (2018). The economics of disaster risks and impacts in the Pacific. *Disaster Prevention and Management: An International Journal, 27*(5), 478–494. https://doi.org/10.1108/DPM-02-2018-0057

Eriksson, H., Albert, J., Albert, S., Warren, R., Pakoa, K., & Andrew, N. (2017). The role of fish and fisheries in recovering from natural hazards: Lessons learned from Vanuatu. *Environmental Science & Policy, 76,* 50–58. https://doi.org/10.1016/j.envsci.2017.06.012

Farbotko, C., & Lazrus, H. (2012). The first climate refugees? Contesting global narratives of climate change in Tuvalu. *Global Environmental Change, 22*(2), 382–390. https://doi.org/10.1016/j.gloenvcha.2011.11.014

Foale, S., Cohen, P., Januchowski-Hartley, S., Wenger, A., & Macintyre, M. (2011). Tenure and taboos: Origins and implications for fisheries in the Pacific. *Fish and Fisheries, 12*(4), 357–369. https://doi.org/10.1111/j.1467-2979.2010.00395.x

Food and Agriculture Organization. (2008). *Climate change and food security in Pacific Island countries* (p. 16). Retrieved from www.fao.org/3/a-i0530e.pdf

Global Environmental Facility, Tuvalu Government, & United Nations Development Programme. (2009). *Tuvalu national biodiversity strategy and action plan: Fourth national report to the convention on biological diversity.* Retrieved from www.cbd.int/doc/world/tv/tv-nr-04-en.pdf

Govan, H. (2009). *Achieving the potential of locally managed marine areas in the South Pacific.* SPC Traditional Marine Resource. Retrieved from www.academia.edu/2230603/Achieving_the_potential_of_locally_managed_marine_areas_in_the_South_Pacific

Intergovernmental Panel on Climate Change. (2018a). Annex I: Glossary. *Global warming of 1.5°C. An IPCC special report on the impacts of global warming of 1.5°C above pre-industrial levels and related global greenhouse gas emission pathways, in the context of strengthening the global response to the threat of climate change, sustainable development, and efforts to eradicate poverty.* Retrieved from www.ipcc.ch/sr15/chapter/glossary/

Intergovernmental Panel on Climate Change. (2018b). *Global warming of 1.5°C.* Retrieved from www.ipcc.ch/report/sr15/

International Monetary Fund. (2016). *Small states' resilience to natural disasters and climate change: Role for the IMF.* Retrieved from www.imf.org/external/np/pp/eng/2016/110416.pdf

Kaly, U. L., & Pratt, C. (2000). *Environmental vulnerability index: Development and provisional indices and profiles for Fiji, Samoa, Tuvalu and Vanuatu: EVI Phase II Report.* Fiji: SOPAC.

Mortreux, C., & Barnett, J. (2009). Climate change, migration, and adaptation in Funafuti, Tuvalu. *Global Environment Change, 19*, 105–112.

Noy, I. (2016a). A global comprehensive measure of the impact of natural hazards and disasters. *Global Policy, 7*(1), 56–65. https://doi.org/10.1111/1758-5899.12272

Noy, I. (2016b). Natural disasters in the Pacific Island countries: New measurements of impacts. *Natural Hazards, 84*(S1), 7–18. https://doi.org/10.1007/s11069-015-1957-6

Noy, I. (2016c). *The economics of climate change and natural disaster risk in the Pacific island countries by 2040.* Technical Report for the World Bank.

Noy, I. (2017). To leave or not to leave? Climate change, exit, and voice on a Pacific Island. *CESifo Economic Studies, 63*(4), 403–420. https://doi.org/10.1093/cesifo/ifx004

Noy, I., & Edmonds, C. (2016). *The economic and fiscal burdens of disasters in the Pacific.* SEF Working Papers 25/2016. Victoria University of Wellington. Retrieved from http://researcharchive.vuw.ac.nz/bitstream/handle/10063/5439/Working%20Paper.pdf?sequence=1

Nurse, L., & Sem, G. (2001). Small island states. In J. McCarthy, O. Canziani, N. Leary, D. Dokken, & K. White (Eds.), *Climate change 2001: Impacts, adaptation & vulnerability* (pp. 842–875). Cambridge: Cambridge University Press.

Pacific Islands Forum Secretariat. (2018). *Pacific experiences with options relevant to climate change and disaster risk finance* (No. 3, p. 24). Retrieved from www.forumsec.org/wp-content/uploads/2019/03/PIF-Vol-3_Pacific-Experiences_FINAL.pdf

Roy, E. A. (2019, May 16). *"One day we'll disappear": Tuvalu's sinking islands.* Retrieved July 5, 2019, from Pacific Island News Association website: www.pina.com.fj/index.php?p=pacnews&m=read&o=15367796245cde3dc275d611a5e7ab

Schneider, S. H. (2009). *Climate change science and policy.* Washington, DC: Island Press.

Stewart, A. (2019, February 18). *"Imperial thinking": Tuvalu PM slams Kevin Rudd's proposal to offer Australian citizenship for Pacific resources* [Text]. Retrieved July 5, 2019, from ABC News website: www.abc.net.au/news/2019-02-18/tuvalu-pm-slams-kevin-rudd-suggestion-as-neo-colonialism/10820176

Storey, D., & Hunter, S. (2010). Kiribati: An environmental "perfect storm". *Australian Geographer, 41*(2), 167–181. https://doi.org/10.1080/00049181003742294

Taupo, T. (2018a). *Economics of disaster risk and resilience in small island developing states*. Victoria University of Wellington. Retrieved from http://researcharchive.vuw. ac.nz/handle/10063/6905

Taupo, T. (2018b). Sustainable financing for climate and disaster resilience in Atoll Islands: Evidence from Tuvalu and Kiribati. *Pacific Economic Review*. https://doi.org/10.1111/ 1468-0106.12295

Taupo, T., Cuffe, H., & Noy, I. (2018). Household vulnerability on the frontline of climate change: The Pacific atoll nation of Tuvalu. *Environmental Economics and Policy Studies*, *20*(4), 705–739. https://doi.org/10.1007/s10018-018-0212-2

Taupo, T., & Noy, I. (2017). At the very edge of a storm: The impact of a distant cyclone on Atoll Islands. *Economics of Disasters and Climate Change*, *1*(2), 143–166. https://doi. org/10.1007/s41885-017-0011-4

Tuvalu Government. (2016). *Climate change and disaster survival fund act 2015*. Tuvalu Government.

UNESCAP, & UNISDR. (2012). *Reducing vulnerability and exposure to disasters: The Asia Pacific disaster report 2012*. Retrieved from www.unisdr.org/files/29288_ apdr2012finallowres.pdf

UNISDR. (2009). *UNISDR terminology on disaster risk reduction*. Geneva, Switzerland: United Nations International Strategy for Disaster Reduction.

United Nations. (1992). *United nations framework convention on climate change*. United Nations.

United Nations. (2015a). *2015 global assessment report on disaster risk reduction*. New York: United Nations Office for Disaster Risk Reduction.

United Nations. (2015b). *Making development sustainable: The future of disaster risk management*. Geneva: United Nations.

United Nations. (2016). *World risk report 2016*. 74.

Vakasukawaqa, A. (2016, December 13). People displaced by climate change not refugees: Tuvalu PM [News]. Retrieved July 5, 2019, from Fiji Sun website: https://fijisun.com. fj/2016/12/13/people-displaced-by-climate-change-not-refugees-tuvalu-pm/

World Bank. (2000). *Cities, seas, and storms: Managing change in Pacific Island economies* (No. 1). Washington, DC: The World Bank.

World Bank. (2009). *World development report 2010: Development and climate change*. Retrieved from http://elibrary.worldbank.org/doi/book/10.1596/978-0-8213-7987-5

World Bank. (2013). *World development report 2014: Risk and opportunity – Managing risk for development*. Retrieved from http://elibrary.worldbank.org/doi/book/10.1596/ 978-0-8213-9903-3

World Bank. (2014). *Hardship and vulnerability in the Pacific Island countries*. Washington DC: The World Bank.

World Bank, & United Nations. (2010). *Natural hazards, unnatural disasters: The economics of effective prevention*. Retrieved from http://elibrary.worldbank.org/doi/book/ 10.1596/978-0-8213-8050-5

Yamano, H., Kayanne, H., Yamaguchi, T., Kuwahara, Y., Yokoki, H., Shimazaki, H., & Chikamori, M. (2007). Atoll Island vulnerability to flooding and inundation revealed by historical reconstruction: Fongafale Islet, Funafuti Atoll, Tuvalu. *Global and Planetary Change*, *57*(3–4), 407–416. https://doi.org/10.1016/j.gloplacha.2007.02.007

Part 2
Sources of gender insecurity in the Pacific

6 Human security, international agenda and responses to calls for "women's empowerment"

Penelope Schoeffel

International agendas

In this chapter I examine "security" from the perspective articulated by Chenoy (2005, p. 164) that the concept of human security:

> needs to be engendered because experience has shown that the concept of 'people'" still leaves out women, especially those at the margins. Threats from militarism, patriarchy, chauvinism, sectarianism, poverty and denial of rights affect women differently than they do men and since structures and institutions of power remain patriarchal, there is need for a gender balance as well as a feminization of security.

For the past 43 years, since the 1975 International Year for Women, the United Nations Decade for women (1976–1985), the establishment of UNIFEM (1976), there has been growing emphasis on women and gender in development. The Convention of the Elimination of All Forms of Discrimination against Women – CEDAW (1981), The Beijing Declaration and Platform for Action (1995), the Millennium Development Goals (2000–2015) and the Sustainable Development Goals (2015–2030) are just some of the instruments to which Donors and most Pacific Island States have committed. Many international agencies have also produced detailed gender implementation manuals to guide development assistance, notably the OECD Toolkit for Mainstreaming and Implementing Gender Equality. Initially international agencies and bilateral donors funded projects for women and emphasised the inclusion of women in development policy, planning, project design and assistance, but by 2000 the emphasis had shifted towards action on eliminating gender inequality, eventually reflected in the establishment and focus of the United Nations Entity for Gender Equality and the Empowerment of Women (UN WOMEN) in 2010 to replace UNIFEM.

Bilateral development assistance to the Pacific Islands appears to be on the upswing because, as Winston Peters, New Zealand Foreign Affairs Minister, put it (Lowy Institute, 2018): "the South Pacific has become an increasingly contested strategic space". Western anxiety about the rise of China and its influence in Pacific Island States appears to be driving plans for increased aid spending in Pacific Island States. The development discourse since the 1990s refers to aid donors as "development partners" encapsulating the notion that donors and recipient countries are committed to collaborative relationships based on mutuality and reciprocity, although the aid recipient seldom has an equal input in the design of development assistance programmes (Crewe & Harrison, 1998). The leading bilateral donors to the Pacific Islands are Australia, China, New Zealand and Japan. Among these, China is the odd man out (Lowy Institute, 2018). Whereas Australia and New Zealand have carefully planned aid agendas for economic development, including support for poverty alleviation, health, education and empowering women and girls, China has no development strategies for the Pacific Islands states as such. Its aid tends to be mainly infrastructure with a win-win approach in response to government requests of soft loans involving China's banks, construction companies, workers and China-sourced materials. As Dame Meg Taylor, the Secretary General of the Pacific Forum Secretariat, pointed out in her presentation to the "State of the Pacific Conference" in September 2018, while much of the commentary on China's engagement in Australia and New Zealand with the Pacific has been divisive, China is an important development partner to Pacific states, notwithstanding a number of points on which she sees a dialogue with China being of value. China's aid is popular with Pacific governments (and no doubt those of other developing countries) precisely because China has no agenda to push, such as gender equality or human rights, but only to cement friendships for its own strategic global interests

The gender agenda

In the 1970s and 80s in aid-dependent Pacific Island States, the aid focus on funding "women in development" (WID) was politically popular, building as it did on antecedent colonial welfare programmes for rural women's associations with a home economics and family health focus. In the period when WID was the agenda, considerable funding and efforts were devoted to establishing "national machineries for women" central to the integration of women in development strategies of the 1970 and 1980s (see Byrne & Laier, with Baden & Marcus, 1996). Efforts were made to establish a reciprocal linkage between non-government national councils of women (or equivalent organisations) and government departments for women's affairs. The intention was for planning and programmes to be responsive to what woman needed or wanted. In some countries funding was included for efforts to establish national and provincial councils of women as well as national councils. This tended to divide women rather than to unite them. As a gender specialist consultant since the 1980s, I observed in Papua New Guinea, for example, the tensions that sprang up between the national and provincial councils of women over access to funding and perks such as overseas travel, which the provinces considered to be monopolised by the centre. Also, in my observations, throughout the Pacific states, national women's organisations were mainly led by well-intentioned elite women who were rarely able to define women's needs in development other than to seek funding to keep themselves and their associated women's organisations afloat and for projects to justify their existence.

By the 1990s the Women in Development (WID) approach gave way to a gender and development (GAD) approach with a policy-oriented emphasis that analysed women's access to the benefits of development assistance compared to that of men. It aimed to mainstream gender considerations into development plans, programmes and projects, in keeping with neoliberal reform agendas (ADB, 2009). Its approaches included gender mainstreaming in development planning, measures to increase gender equality and actions to end violence against women, all under the rubric of "women's empowerment". While notionally attractive, "empowerment" has attracted considerable criticism of its underpinning assumption that women have individual agency when the circumstances of their inequality are structurally embedded in social and religious institutions (Schech, 1998; Rottenberg, 2014; Cornwall & Rivas, 2015).

There was considerably less enthusiasm by Pacific Island governments to apply measures such as these, as recommended by aid donors and international agencies (Schoeffel, 2018, pp. 72–73). The new emphasis on policy and planning as instruments for gender equality has generally been either ignored by Pacific island governments, or inserted into national and sector strategic plans by consultants to satisfy donor requirements. I have, on many occasions, had discussions with government officials in various Pacific Island Countries on how to mainstream gender in their strategic plans; they were mostly puzzled – "why do the aid donors want us to do this?" so that gender mainstreaming has tended to be a token effort of words rather than deeds. In my observation, the establishment of gender desks and gender focal points have largely been unsuccessful. Urged to make these appointments by the development partners, as I observed, government agencies appointed mainly young women who lack the seniority and experience to influence policy, planning and implementation.

The most recent focus on the empowerment of women is exemplified in the biggest Pacific regional gender programme *Pacific Women Shaping Pacific Development* (PWSPD), funded by Australian Aid following the 2012 Pacific Island Forum Leaders' Gender Equality Declaration; a 10-year AU $320 million commitment to "improve the political, social and economic opportunities of women living in the Pacific". The programme lines up with Australia's current neoliberal aid agenda, which ties gender inequality to economic growth:

> Gender inequality persists in our region, undermining economic growth, human development and poverty reduction. It is estimated that the Asia-Pacific region is losing up to US $47 billion annually because of women's limited access to employment opportunities, and up to US $30 billion annually due to gender gaps in education. Women in the Pacific continue to be under-represented in Parliament, comprising approximately five percent of parliamentarians compared to the global average of 21.7 %. Rates of domestic violence are alarming, with approximately one in three women in South

East Asia, and two in three women in some Pacific countries experiencing physical and/or sexual abuse by their intimate partner.

(Australian Aid, 2017a)

The PWSPD programme is headquartered in Fiji and works with Pacific governments, civil society organisations, the private sector and multilateral, regional and United Nations agencies. Its programmes and objectives (via country plans, workshops, training, support for women's organisations, etc.) are as follows:

1   **Leadership and Decision Making**

Women, and women's interests, are increasingly and effectively represented and visible through leadership at all levels of decision making.

2   **Economic Empowerment**

Women have expanded opportunities to earn an income and accumulate economic assets.

3   **Ending Violence Against Women**

Violence against women is reduced and survivors of violence have access to support services and to justice.

4   **Enhanced Agency**

Women in the Pacific will have a stronger sense of their own agency, supported by a changing legal and social environment and through increased access to the services they need. (Australian Aid, 2017b)

This programme has sponsored many well received activities. According to its report at the end of the fifth year of implementation it funded 1621 activities, of which 121 are implementation activities and 41 are strategic direction-setting and learning activities, and spent $132.41 million (Australian Aid, 2017b).

Empowerment and women's agency

The question is whether these kinds of programmes will make any difference given the structural obstacles to gender equality. These exist in all countries to a greater or lesser degree, but are particularly acute in most Pacific Island Countries. There is an assumption in this kind of programme that with opportunity and training, women, by their own agencies, will achieve advancement towards equality (Crewe & Harrison, 1998, pp. 51–55). This ignores the reality of life, particularly in rural communities where the majority of Pacific Islanders reside, where powerful social sanctions uphold the separate status and roles of men and women and the exclusion of women from leadership roles in local government and the church. The following case study offers an example of how structural barriers work in the face of well-meant aid projects.

A case study from Samoa

Many Samoan women believe that there is no gender inequality in Samoa due to the institution of *feagaiga* which honours women as sisters and as ancestors (Schoeffel, 1995). As Tcherkezoff (2017) argues, western dualistic gender concepts have no relevance to Samoa, as nearly every adult woman has two distinct gendered roles; as a sister – privileged and influential in her family and village, and as a wife – subordinate to her husband and his family. However, the privileged status of sisterhood has been severely eroded since the early 19th century. A married woman always takes her status in the village, and in the mainstream churches, from her husband. The modern way of honouring women who achieve high status in education and employment is to bestow upon them *matai* titles (chiefly titles of various ranks, previously mainly reserved for men). Of village-based *matai*, only about 5% are women and few women *matai* exercise decision-making rights (whatever the rights that are particular to their titles) in village councils (Meleisea et al., 2015).

From the time of Samoa's independence in 1962 up until to 1990 only registered holders of *matai* titles could vote in elections, but a narrow majority in a 1990 referendum supported universal suffrage. The legal provision that only holders of *matai* titles could stand for elections was unchanged. There has been no change to the pattern of outcomes since independence; the proportions of women elected to parliament have remained below the 10 % mark; a maximum of five successful candidates overall. Historically there have usually been one or two but never more than five women elected to the 49-member parliament. Ahead of the 2016 general elections, the *Increased Political Participation of Women in Samoa* (IPPWS), well-funded under the PWSPD, was launched, coordinated by UNDP and UN Women. This was in response to the legal measures put in place by for the 2016 elections by the government of Samoa (to satisfy its commitment under CEDAW) which provided that at least 10% of the members of parliament will be women. The rationale of IPPWS was that, with encouragement to stand and with campaigning know-how, more women would be elected. Many inspirational workshops were held; some led by women parliamentarians from other countries, along with funding for campaign materials and advice on campaigning.

The only measurable result of the IPPWS was that significantly more women than usual stood for 2016 election – 24 women, compared to six in the previous 2011 election. This echoed the substantial increase of women candidates who had stood in the 2006 elections, when a campaign by the Inailau Women's Leadership Network, led by the Samoa National Council of Women encouraged an unprecedented 19 women to contest the elections. However, the 2006 campaign did not result in more women being elected than in 2011 or in previous elections. Nor did the IPPWS project achieve more success in 2016. Three women who were sitting members of parliament were re-elected, plus one new woman member, and one was appointed (on the basis of the number of votes she got, although not winning the seat) under the 10% provision (Wood & Muller, 2018).

A survey of the 23 women who stood for the election found that few of them thought the IPPWS was useful (Fiti-Sinclair, Schoeffel, & Meleisea, 2017). Their responses confirmed the findings of a study of gender and local government in Samoa (Meleisea et al., 2015). This found that very few women hold the chiefly titles required to be eligible to stand for election to parliament in Samoa, and that those women who do hold chiefly titles are rarely sufficiently prominent in village, district and church decision-making processes to win political support in Samoa's village-based electoral system. These processes are characterised by a patriarchal system of community, family and religious leadership that strongly influences electoral processes and outcome (So'o, 2008; Schoeffel, Meredith, & Fiti-Sinclair, 2016). An unpublished survey of voters in the 2016 elections also found that many women thought that women should not hold chiefly titles or become members of parliament (Fiti-Sinclair, Schoeffel, & Meleisea, 2017).

Research shows that family violence is common in Samoa (Secretariat of the Pacific Community, 2006; Ministry of Women Community and Social Development, 2017). According to the 2017 Samoa Family Safety Study (Ministry of Women Community and Social Development, 2017), an estimated 60% of women between the ages of 20–49 who had ever been in a relationship had experienced spousal abuse in their lifetime, with 46% of women in this category, having been abused by their spouse in the last twelve months (Ministry of Women Community and Social Development, 2017, p. xvii). A workshop for a large rural Samoan audience showed a film that raised issues of family violence, culture and religion (Percival, 2015) followed by group discussion among audience members. The response was unexpected; the women in each discussion group took the floor to explain that it was women's fault if they were beaten by their husbands or if men were unfaithful. From their particular Christian perspective in a land where people have been Christian for over a century, Victorian ideals of Christian conjugality are now seen as customary ways to be upheld. It was the duty of a wife to submit to her husband and meet all his needs. A man should be unambiguously head of the household, his wife an obedient helpmate, gently encouraging him to curb his innate tendencies in Godly ways (Schoeffel, Percival, & Boodoosingh, 2018).

The other gender

There is a largely unspoken obstacle to the empowerment of women in leadership and the economy and to ending violence against women: the valorisation of masculinity in the traditional customs of the Pacific Islands and in conservative Christianity. As in the Pacific Women Shaping Pacific Development programme, gender-focused projects aim for what they term "women's empowerment" in education, health, employment and participation in political processes. But the emphasis has been on women and if men and masculinity are considered at all, it is mainly in the context of the problems faced by women. In development discourses gender has, until recently, almost always interpreted to mean women. As Eves pointed out:

> after decades of programming for gender equality, the belief remains widespread among development practitioners that in practice gender does not

apply to both men and women, but solely to women. At the same time, most male policy makers and theorists continue to dismiss gender as a mere women's issue. They seem not to realise that they themselves are gendered, perhaps assuming that the masculine is the standard model of human being.

(2009, p. 2)

Masculinity has been extensively documented in studies of the Pacific Islands. There are two genres of this research. The first is that of the social sciences, particularly anthropology. Hundreds of ethnographic studies since the early 20th century have addressed gendered behaviour in island cultures, mainly the behaviour of men in the rituals, political systems, status hierarchies and exchange networks in which masculinities are culturally constructed. The second genre is technical reports. Regional and country studies of gender (although mainly focussed on women) in the Pacific Islands have been sponsored by aid donors and development agencies such as the World Bank, Asian Development Bank and others (see for example ADB Country Gender Assessments for Solomon Islands, 2015; Papua New Guinea, 2011–12; Fiji, 2006; Tonga, 1989).

Concerns about the roles of men began to be aired in development contexts in the 1970s, initially about violence against women in changing and urbanising Pacific societies. There have been many discussions in both development reports and academic papers about whether such violence is aggravated by social change and whether people in this or that Pacific society believe that violence is a culturally and religiously justified male prerogative. Growing socio-economic class differences are becoming evident in Pacific urban societies, where women are increasingly as well-educated and gainfully employed as men. However, many men seem ambivalent about this trend. A man may feel diminished should other men perceive his wife to be the dominant partner (because of her superior education or job) and may vent his resentment on his wife. This is surely not just a problem in developing countries. The discomfort among both men and women with the idea of women as parliamentarians has been explored in many studies of the near absence of women from politics and parliaments of the Pacific region (Soaki, 2017; Schoeffel, Meredith, & Fiti-Sinclair, 2017; Julien & Baker, 2016; Baker, 2016; Liki, 2013; Chattier, 2015; Molotii, Baker, & Corbett, 2014). Throughout the Pacific Island States, the leadership roles of men in society are thought of as ordained by culture, nature and by God.

Gender is also about sex and reproduction and it is mainly in this context that masculinity became a much-researched development issue in the Pacific Islands. In the late 1980s concerns about women's vulnerability to violence, demonstrated in a series of studies by UNFPA and WHO, were extended to the interconnected issue of the heterosexually-transmitted spread of HIV and AIDs. This is an infection to which women are biologically more susceptible than men are and statistically more women than men are infected in Pacific Island countries (Luker, 2002). Many cross-cultural studies of the social context and increasing feminisation of HIV infection rates by anthropologists, (for example Butt & Eves, 2008; Hammar, 2010) tell us that fear of male violence deters women from refusing sexual intercourse that might infect them with HIV. Furthermore, research shows that high maternal mortality rates, especially in PNG, are associated not just with lack of antenatal services, but also with low acceptance of contraceptives. In these and other Pacific countries, birth intervals are often too short for the health of mothers and babies because old customs no longer impose post-partum taboos, as they once did, and often because husbands object to their wives using contraception.

Since the 1970s, counter measures for problematic masculinity has mainly been to remind men and women that violence is illegal, by means of advertising using posters, pamphlets, sign boards, stickers and other media. Associated with these efforts have been advertising on HIV risk and condom use targeting men, as well as community education programmes such as SPC/FSP "Stepping Stones". There have also been male advocacy groups for women's rights in some Pacific Island Countries (Commonwealth Secretariat, 2016),

Another subject that has been much researched as a development issue is the relative economic powerlessness of women compared to men. Throughout the Pacific, if not the whole world, manliness is associated with personal independence and with having command of money or its traditional equivalents. In neoliberal discourses on development, women's empowerment is proposed almost as a panacea for gender inequality. For decades we have seen study upon study asserting that more money in women's hands means more is spent on family food and on health and school expenses. Educate and employ women, it is said, and families will benefit. Although in urban settings increasing numbers of women earn money for themselves, there are still likely to be family disputes over which sex should control the spending of it. "Man the Provider" is not culturally universal in the Pacific. In many parts of rural Melanesia, "Woman the Provider" was and is expected to grow or catch at least half of a household's food and to cook it. In this cultural context men do not necessarily feel obliged to share money they earn from the sale of coffee, cocoa or oil palm fruit with their wives and children. In contrast, in Polynesian cultures such as Samoa and Tonga, men were, and in rural areas still are, the fishers and farmers, the providers for their families who cook traditional foods. In this cultural context men are perhaps more likely to share money with their wives and children (see for example Banthia, Tyroler, & Schoeffel, 2013).

Traditional and Christian values

Millennial trends towards gender flexibility and fluidity have barely touched Pacific societies. Despite the tolerance of transgender males in Polynesian societies (see for examples Besnier & Alexeyeff, 2014), people there are no more likely than those in other Pacific societies to consider the possibility of same-sex marriage. In Tonga one of the misunderstandings that prevented the government from finally ratifying CEDAW in 2017 was a public outcry that it could allow same-sex marriage, along with the claim that giving women equal rights to inherit land would undermine Tongan culture (Lee, 2017).

In Pacific islands societies, most men and women have decided views and strong opinions about what is manly and what is not. Traditional and religious values are invoked (Corbett, 2013). At many workshops and consultations sponsored by development agencies, and sometimes, more rarely by churches, Pacific Islander men and women have argued that if people would only stick to their traditional customs and to the Word of God, especially with regard to women's behaviour and clothing, there would be no problems with men. This implies that if women seem to have abandoned old cultural norms, they will bring violence of one kind or another upon themselves at the hands of men. In 2018, the Samoa Human Rights Commission heard submissions from the public on family violence. An explanation frequently offered to the Commissioners by both men and women is that wife-beating and rape occurs because women fail to behave and dress appropriately (Meleisea, personal communication 18 November, Centre for Samoan Studies, National University of Samoa, 2018). In various cultural contexts similar sentiments have documented by many anthropologists (see for example Cummings, 2008); the answer to violence against women is for women, rather than men, to return to customary ways. However, some suggest that men too, should return to old customs. A few years ago, I travelled through the highlands of PNG for an evaluation of development projects there and was told by many men that violent or dissolute male behaviour was the outcome of men living together with women (see Tuzin, 1997). They advocated the reintroduction of traditional sacrosanct men's houses as village projects. Pacific women, as well as men, tend to be ambivalent about externally sponsored efforts to promote gender equality. In the world they take for granted, in their communities and church congregations, they believe that most husbands and sons are good men, and that God and custom gave authority to men and so it is only to be expected that men may at times take advantage of it. Gender is a cultural and historical product and in Pacific societies, for thousands of years, masculine gender identity has been more elaborately and consciously cultivated than feminine gender identity, in social and economic settings that are now disappearing.

Final remarks

Development assistance has diplomatic dimensions. Targeting women with "empowerment" programmes is a more tactful option for development partners and international agencies than looking critically at men or trying to address structural issues rooted in religion and traditions. The dilemma for aid donors is, as Chiongson, Deval, Marchiori and Woolcock point out:

> 'change from the top' may achieve little when new laws championing gender equality do not consider current social values and beliefs, or when competing legal systems exist that sanction discriminatory practices. Worse, resistance, resentment and even violence against women may occur when such laws do not take into account the social and political contexts where these laws operate.
>
> (2011, p. 9)

It has not been my intention in this chapter to argue that aid should not be given to further the equality of women; I argue that it should be given with recognition that women are carrying the extra burdens of social and economic change, with associated risks to their security. As Schech points out (2008, p. 401)

> [by] failing to look critically at the ways in which the mainstream development agenda may implicitly be built on the assumption that male norms are human norms. Furthermore, it can hide 'Western' feminist biases which hold that all women are basically similar.

Aid should support activities that Pacific Island governments don't want or can't afford, such as funding research on gender issues. For example, the Centre for Samoan Studies at the National University of Samoa received a substantial grant from Australian Aid to study gender relations in village government. This produced some important evidence to counter the argument that women are separate but equal in village decision making. Aid should be given to civil society organisations that advocate for women's rights, (the long-established Fiji Women's Right Movement and Fiji Women's Crisis Centre, are examples). Although often not popular with governments, these kinds of organisations understand local contexts and issues for women's rights. Since the 1980s, aid-sponsored programmes for education, health and for strengthening institutions, especially in law and justice are having the most sustained long-term impacts to further women's equality. These include building effective police responses to family violence, along with programmes to assist strengthening family law, national commissions for human rights and especially long-term regional programmes such as the Pacific Regional Rights Resource Team (RRRT) now based in the within Secretariat of the Pacific Community.

References

Asian Development Bank. (1989–2015). *ADB country gender assessments: Solomon Islands, 2015, Papua New Guinea 2011–12; Fiji 2006, Tonga 1989*. Retrieved April 3, 2019 from www.adb.org/themes/gender/country-gender-assessments

Asian Development Bank. (2009). *ADB support for public sector reforms in the Pacific: Enhance results through ownership, capacity, and continuity*. Evaluation Study SST: REG 2009–24, Independent Evaluation Department.

Australian Aid. (2017a) *Gender equality and women's empowerment*. Strategy. Retrieved from https://dfat.gov.au/about-us/publications/Documents/gender-equality-and-womens-empowerment-strategy.pdf

Australian Aid. (2017b). *Pacific women shaping pacific development, annual progress report. 2016–2017: Supporting the Pacific leaders'gender equality declaration*. Retrieved from www.pacificwomen.org

Baker, K. (2016). Great expectations: Gender and political representation in the Pacific Islands. *Government and Opposition*, 1–27. Retrieved from www.cambridge.org/core/journals/government-and-opposition/article/great-expectations-gender-and-political-representation-in-the-pacific-islands/9B0466209F67F0336F573149B7A120F2

Banthia, A., Tyroler, C., & Schoeffel, P. (2013). *Deepening financial inclusion for women in the Pacific Islands: An assessment of the gender issues surrounding women's ability to access and control financial resources in Papua New Guinea and Samoa*. New York: Women's World Banking.

Besnier, N., & Alexeyeff, K. (Eds.). (2014). *Gender on the edge: Transgender, gay, and other Pacific Islanders*. Honolulu, HI: University of Hawai'i Press.

Butt, L., & Eves, R. (2008). *Making sense of AIDS: Culture, sexuality and power in Melanesia*. Honolulu, HI: University of Hawaii Press.

Byrne, B., & Laier, J. K. with Baden, S., & Marcus, R. (1996). *National machineries for women in development: Experiences, lessons and strategies for institutionalising gender in development policy and planning*. Report No. 36, prepared for the European Commission, Directorate General for Development.

Chan-Tung Liki, A. (2013). Leading the march for gender equality? Women leaders in the public services of Samoa and Solomon Islands. In D. Hegarty & D. Tryon (Eds.), *Politics, development and security in Oceania* (pp. 139–146). Studies in State and Society in the Pacific No. 7. Canberra: ANU E-Press.

Chattier, P. (2015) Women in the house (of parliament) in Fiji: What's gender got to do with it? *The Commonwealth Journal of International Affairs*, *104*, 177–188. Retrieved from www.tandfonline.com/toc/ctrt20/104/2

Chenoy, A. M. (2005). A plea for engendering human security. *International Studies*, *42*(2), 167–179.

Chiongson, A. R., Deval, T., Marchiori, T., & Woolcock, M. (2011). *Gender equality and development role of law and justice in achieving gender equality*. Background Paper prepared for the World Development Report, 2012. World Bank. Retrieved from https:// openknowledge.worldbank.org/handle/10986/9194

Commonwealth Secretariat. (2016). Pacific women's network male advocacy programme, Pacific Islands. In *Advancing gender equality: Case studies from across the Commonwealth*. Retrieved from https://doi.org/10.14217/9781848599451-22-en

Corbett, J. (2013). "A calling from God": Politicians and religiosity in the Pacific Islands. *Global Change, Peace and Security*, *25*(3), 283–297.

Cornwall, A., & Rivas, A. (2015). From gender equality and "women's empowerment" to global justice: Reclaiming a transformative agenda for gender and development. *Third World Quarterly*, *36*(2), 396–415,

Crewe, E., & Harrison, E. (1998). *Who's development: An ethnography of aid*. London: Zed Books.

Cummings, M. (2008). The trouble with trousers: Gossip, *kastom*, and sexual culture in Vanuatu. In L. Butt & R. Eves (Eds.), *Making sense of AIDS: Culture, sexuality and power in Melanesia* (pp. 133–149). Honolulu, HI: University of Hawaii Press.

Eves, R. (2009). *Men, masculinity and development in the Pacific*. SSGM Briefing Note No. 2, pp. 1–4.

Fiti-Sinclair, R., Schoeffel, P., & Meleisea, M. (2017). *Women and political participation: The 2016 election in Samoa*. Centre for Samoan Studies, National University of Samoa and the pacific Leadership Programme.

Hammar, L. (2010). *Sin, sex, and stigma: A Pacific response to HIV and AIDS*. London: Sean Kingston Publishing.

Julien, B., & Baker, K. (2016). *Improving the electoral chances of Pacific women through an evidence-based approach*. A Synthesis Report Prepared for the Centre for Democratic Institutions and the State Society and Governance in Melanesia Program, ANU.

Lee, H. (2017). CEDAW smokescreens: Gender politics in contemporary Tonga. *The Contemporary Pacific, 29*(1), 66–90.

Lowy Institute. (2017). *Chinese aid in the Pacific*. Retrieved from https://chineseaidmap. lowyinstitute.org/

Lowy Institute. (2017). *Pacific aid map*. Retrieved from https://pacificaidmap.lowyinstitute. org/

Lowy Institute. (2018). *Winston Peters on New Zealand in the Pacific*. Retrieved from https://www.lowyinstitute.org/publications/winston-peters-new-zealand-pacific.

Luker, V. (2002). *Gender, women and mothers: HIV/AIDS in the Pacific, gender relations center*. The Australian National University, Working Paper No. 7. Retrieved from http:// rspas.anu.edu.au/grc/publications/pdfs/LukereHIV.pdf

Meleisea, L. M., Meredith, M., Chan Mow, M. I., Schoeffel, P., Lauano, S. A., Sasa, H. . . . Boodoosingh, R. (2015). *Political representation and women's empowerment in Samoa* (Volume 1: Findings and Recommendations and Volume 2: Research Methods and Results). Centre for Samoan Studies. National University of Samoa. Retrieved from http://samoanstudies.ws/storage/2015/07/Centre-for-Samoan-Studies_Final-Report-Volume-1-English.pdf

Ministry of Women Community and Social Development. (2017). *2017 Samoa Family Safety Study*. Government of Samoa: Apia.

Molotii, A., Baker, K., & Corbett, J. (2014). *Women's representation and the question of temporary special measures in Tuvalu*. ANU In Brief No. 17. Retrieved from http:// ssgm.bellschool.anu.edu.au/

Percival, S. (2015) *Raise the Sennit sail: Exploring violence against women and girls*. Documentary film series. Tiapapata Art Centre. Retrieved from http//www.creativesamoa. com/multimedia

Rottenberg, C. (2014). The rise of neoliberal feminism. *Cultural Studies, 28*(3), 418–437.

Schech, S. (1998). Between tradition and post-coloniality: The location of gender in Australian development policy. *Australian Geographer, 29*(3), 389–404.

Schoeffel, P. (1995). The Samoan concept of Feagaiga and its transformation. In J. Huntsman (Ed.) *Tonga and Samoa: Images of gender and polity* (pp. 85–109). Christchurch: MacMillan Brown Centre for Pacific Studies.

Schoeffel, P. (2018). From women's lib to WID and to GAD: Reflections on the evolution of woman-conscious events and programmes in the Pacific Islands. In P. Thomas (Ed.), *Pacific reflections: Personal perceptions of aid and development* (pp. 71–75). Development Bulletin, No. 80. Canberra: The Australian National University.

Schoeffel, P., Meredith, M., & Fiti-Sinclair, R. (2017). Women, culture and political participation in Sāmoa. *Journal of Samoan Studies, 7*(3), 19.

Schoeffel, P., Percival, S., & Boodoosingh, R. (2018). It's all about Eve: Women's attitudes to gender-based violence in Samoa. In C. Blythe, E. Colgan, & K. B. Edwards (Eds.), *Rape culture, gender violence & religion: Interdisciplinary perspectives* (pp. 9–32). London: Palgrave Macmillan.

Soaki, P. (2017). Casting her vote: Women's political participation in Solomon Islands. In M. Macintyre & C. Spark (Eds.), *Transformations of gender in Melanesia* (pp. 95–114). Canberra: ANU Press, The Australian National University.

So'o', A. (2008). *Democracy and custom in Samoa: An uneasy alliance*. Suva: Institute of Pacific Studies.

Tcherkezoff, S. (2017). The Samoan Village, the brother sister relationship and the rule of exogamy. *The Journal of Samoan Studies, 7*, 6–36.

Tuzin, D. (1995). *The Cassowary's revenge: The life and death of masculinity in a New Guinea society*. Chicago, IL: University of Chicago Press.

Tuzin, D. (1997). *The Cassowary's revenge: The life and death of masculinity in a New Guinea society*. Chicago, IL: University of Chicago Press.

Winston Peters on New Zealand in the Pacific, Lowy Institute 2017. Retrieved from www.lowyinstitute.org/publications/winston-peters-new-zealand-pacific

Wood, T., & Muller, S. (2018). *Samoan election results: Trends and patterns 1964–2016*. Discussion Series, Development Policy Centre, Australian National University.

7 Mapping gender security–insecurity in Fiji

Rape myths and sexual prejudice

Sara N. Amin, Tanya Trussler and James Johnson

Introduction

This chapter draws on the concept of human security, which emphasises that security is "freedom from fear, freedom from want" (UNDP, 1994, pp. 23–24). Human security requires "protecting people from severe and pervasive threats, both natural and societal, and empowering individuals and communities to develop the capabilities for making informed choices and acting on their own behalf" (Ogata & Cels, 2003, p. 274). Human security is gendered in part because women's and sexual minorities' experiences of violence, threat of violence and their security needs differ in important ways from those of heterosexual men (Hoogensen & Rottem, 2004; Chenoy, 2005). Feminist theorisation and research have shown that gendered (in)security is in part produced through the normalisation and rationalisation of sexual violence and sexual prejudice in society against women and LGBQT+ groups (Lonsway & Fitzgerald, 1994; Ward, 1995; Aosved & Long, 2006; Shepherd, 2008; Merry, 2009). Globally, ideas related to sin, immorality, deserving victims, male entitlement and natural order of things have been shown to be important sources of how sexual violence and prejudice are justified. This produces a situation in which women and LGBQT+ peoples are vulnerable to aggression, violence and marginalisation, which can impact on their health, well-being and bodily integrity and reduce access to services and opportunities, thus increasing their insecurity (Richardson & May, 1999; Chenoy, 2005; Merry, 2009). Moreover, the prevalence of attitudes that normalise sexual violence or prejudice also impacts on the ability of survivors to seek redress and justice given that police, laws, judges or other actors may deny claims of violence, victimhood or discrimination (Jordan, 2004). This further increases the insecurity faced by women and LGBQT+ groups since they may be less likely to utilise formal processes to reduce their source of insecurities (Jordan, 2004; Suarez & Gadalla, 2010). Thus, mapping out rape myth acceptance (RMA) or rape-supportive attitudes and sexual prejudice is a critical step in understanding how (in)security is gendered in each context.

In the last decade there have been several large-scale national studies conducted to examine the prevalence, incidence and impact of domestic and sexual violence in the Pacific, including Fiji (WHO, 2005; FWCC, 2013), the Solomon Islands (SPC, 2009), Kiribati (SPC, 2010), Vanautu (VWC, 2011), PNG (Fulu et al., 2013) and Tonga (Ma'a Fafine mo e Famili, 2012). These studies have primarily focussed on experiences of and attitudes toward domestic violence against women and marital rape, ignoring attitudes toward sexual violence more broadly. However, there has been no systematic quantitative report on rape myths and sexual prejudice in Fiji, despite important qualitative research and activist work documenting the way these types of attitudes produce a culture of violence against women and LGBQT+ peoples in the country (George, 2008). This chapter thus provides a quantitative descriptive analysis of rape myth acceptance, rape-supportive attitudes and sexual prejudice in Fiji, based on a nationally representative sample (N=1500) from the Fijian Interpersonal Attitudes and Perceptions Assessment (FIAPA) conducted in 2017–2018.

By outlining the way RMA and sexual prejudice maps out in Fiji, this chapter points to how attitudes about sexual violence against women and sexual prejudice against gays are internalised, normalised and rationalised, thus creating a context of gendered insecurity. This initial mapping also highlights how these attitudes vary by social factors including ethnic, religious, other socio-demographic and relational variables. We conclude with implications of our findings for changing attitudes and enhancing security.

The study: key concepts, measures and data

The findings in this chapter are based on data collected from the FIAPA conducted in 2017–2018 from a sample of 1500 respondents, 746 women, 753 men and 1 respondent missing information on sex. Respondent age ranged from 18–86, with a median age of 30 and a mean age of 33. We utilised convenience sampling of Fiji citizens from the areas of: a) Nadi and Lautoka (n=500), b) Suva, Lami and Pacific Harbour (n=500), and c) Vanua Levu and Taveuni (n=500). The sampled areas covered the urban and rural areas in three of the four divisions of the country (Western, Central and Northern), with Indo-Fijian and iTaukei respondents sampled equally through each region. As such, the sample is underrepresented in terms of the iTaukei population and the population from the Central division. In reporting our analyses here, we compared both weighted and non-weighted data and since there was no substantive difference between the weighted and non-weighted analyses, we present here the findings from the weighted data, as is usually recommended in the literature (Dorofeev & Grant, 2006).

To increase diversity and representativeness of the sample, respondents were recruited from various spaces that are accessed by diverse socio-economic groups in the country: shopping areas, churches, community centres, etc. Seven research assistants were trained to administer the questionnaires and respondents were compensated with a $25 food voucher from a local grocery store. While the FIAPA questionnaire had 224 items in total, asking questions related to social distance, identity, sexual violence, sexual prejudice, mental health and other psychosocial metrics, in the following section we describe the specific measures that we use for the findings presented in this chapter.

Sexual violence acceptance measure

Rape myths are "attitudes and beliefs that are generally false but are widely and persistently held, and that serve to deny and justify male sexual aggression against women (Lonsway & Fitzgerald, 1994, p. 134)". These include, but are not limited to, ideas of "boys will be boys", "she was asking for it", "she did not fight back so it is not rape", "alcohol causes men to rape" and men's entitlement to sex from (some kinds of) women. Following the research on rape myths, in this study, we use the Illinois Rape Myth Acceptance (IRMA) Scale (McMahon & Farmer, 2011) as the measure for attitudes toward sexual violence. The scale contains 22 items that evaluates agreement with common rape myths (e.g. "When girls go to parties wearing slutty clothes, they are asking for trouble", "If a girl acts like a slut, eventually she is going to get into trouble". Each item is scored on a 5-point Likert scale (1-strongly disagree, 5-strongly agree) and the scale is constituted by 4 subscales: beliefs related to "She asked for it", beliefs related to "He didn't mean to", beliefs related to "It wasn't rape" and beliefs related to "She lied". Our scale had only 21 items of the 22 items, where the missing question was "If a girl doesn't physically resist sex – even if protesting verbally – it can't be considered rape". This item is part of subscale 3, i.e. beliefs related to "It wasn't rape". To make our data comparable to other studies using the IRMA scale, we created the scale using the 21 items that we had and then mathematically altered it to be make it comparable to those who used all 22 questions.

Sexual prejudice measures

Sexual prejudice is "a negative attitude toward an individual based on her or his membership in a group defined by its members' sexual attractions, behaviors or orientation" (Herek & McLemore, 2013, p. 311). Morrison and Morrison (2002) have suggested that given evolution of the socio-legal context in relation to norms about homosexuality, homonegative attitudes are manifest in two interrelated but statistically distinct forms. On the one hand, *Old-fashioned Sexual Prejudice* (see Herek, 1988) reflects moral (e.g. "Female homosexuality is a perversion") or religious (e.g. "Homosexuality is a sin") opposition to homosexuals and homosexual behaviours. On the other hand, the authors believe that *Modern Sexual Prejudice* reflect more contemporary concerns. Specifically, this form of bias involves feeling that homosexuals make unnecessary or illegitimate demands in an effort to change the status quo (e.g. staging Gay Pride parades). This form of bias includes the belief that discrimination against gay people is no longer an important or pervasive social issue, the belief that gays receive "too much special attention" from the media and key government institutions (e.g. funding from the government to support health care or legal protection) and finally, feelings that gay people "flaunt" their homosexuality to the point that it makes them responsible for their own problems and marginalisation (see Morrison & Morrison, 2011 for a fuller discussion).

Given this is the first national assessment of sexual prejudice in Fiji, we have used 9 of the original 10-item version of the Attitudes Towards Gays (ATG) scale

(Herek, 1988) and the Modern Homonegativity Scale (Gays) (MHS-G) (Morrison & Morrison, 2002) in our study to measure old-fashioned and modern sexual prejudice, respectively. The ATG scale measures negative attitudes toward gay men along a general condemnation/tolerance factor (e.g. "I think homosexuals are disgusting", "Homosexuality is a perversion"). Respondents were asked to rate their level of agreement on a 5-point Likert-type scale (where 1 = strongly disagree and 5 = strongly agree). Responses were summed to create an old-fashioned prejudice score (α=.91), where higher scores indicate greater prejudicial attitudes and lower scores indicate less prejudicial attitudes. Our scale only contained 9 of the 10 items of the original ATG, but was mathematically altered to contain scores in the range of 10–50 to allow for comparisons with studies that use all of the original ATG items.

The MHS-G scale (Morrison & Morrison, 2002) measures negative attitudes towards gays based on abstract/symbolic concerns (e.g. "Gays have all the rights they need"). Participants in the present study were given the 12 items from the scale. A sample item is "If gay men want to be treated like everyone else, then they need to stop making such a fuss about their sexuality/culture". All items on this scale were measured on a 5-point Likert-type scale, to which a respondent is asked to specify his/her level of agreement where 1 = strongly disagree and 5 = strongly agree. Our data is missing the item "in today's tough economic times, [our] tax dollars shouldn't be used to support gay men's/lesbian women's organizations". This item was not asked since tax dollars are not available to LGBQT+ groups in Fiji. Responses were summed to create a modern prejudice score (α=.78), where higher scores indicate more prejudicial attitudes and lower scores indicate less prejudicial attitudes toward gay men. The possible range of scores was made to be between 12–60 to allow for comparisons with studies that use all 12 items in the MHS.

Socio-demographic and relational measures

In addition, the study also included questions related to socio-demographic background, including sex, age, ethnicity, religiosity, number of children and marital status. Because research has shown that knowing someone of a stigmatised group can reduce one's bias against the group, we also had questions related to interpersonal contact (IPC) with gays. The IPC Scale (adopted from Barron, Struckman-Johnson, Quevillon, & Banka, 2008) measures the extent that the participants had made or had not made significant or meaningful contact with various groups (e.g. gay men). For example, one of the items was "I have a close friend who is gay. We spend a lot of time together". This measure consists of 7 items to which a respondent is asked to rate his/her level of agreement on a 5-point Likert-type scale, where 1 = strongly agree and 5 = strongly disagree. We summed responses to create an IPC score, where higher scores indicate greater interpersonal contact with gay individuals.

In the following section, we present findings from our study, examining these in relation to existing research on attitudes related to sexual violence and sexual prejudice. Following standard practice, we discuss findings that are significant at α=0.05.

Gendered insecurity: widespread agreement with rape myth acceptance and homonegativity

Our data indicate that insecurity in Fiji is gendered with women living in a context where most people (both men and women) normalise and rationalise violence against women, and gay men are living in a context where a majority of people oppose both their rights and their sexual identity. Table 7.1 summarises the average score and variation on each scale, while Tables 7.2 and 7.3 indicate the percentage of agreement on each item for each scale.

In Table 7.2, out of the 21 IRMA items, 50% or more of the respondents agreed or strongly agreed with 15 of the 21 rape myths, indicating that rape myth acceptance is widespread. Our finding not only confirms existing research on the Pacific, but seems to indicate that attitudes supporting and legitimising sexual violence against women are more widespread than previously documented. For example, from a national representative sample of 3186 women in Fiji, FWCC (2013) found that 33% of women agreed with the statement "It is a wife's obligation to have sex with her husband even if she does not feel like it". The percentages of women agreeing with this statement was 18% in Vanuatu (VWC, 2011), 33% in Kiribati (SPC, 2010) and 44.3% in Papua New Guinea (PNG) (Fulu et al., 2013). However, most studies on the Pacific have focussed on marital rape. Attitudes about rape beyond marriage have been researched most extensively in PNG, where Fulu et al. (2013) found that 22.1% of women and 31.1% of men agreed that a woman is to blame when rape occurs and 45% of both men and women agreed that "If a woman does not physically fight back, it's not rape". Fulu et al. (2013), who also surveyed men who had committed sexual violence, found that the most common reported motivations for rape of a partner or non-partner was sexual entitlement (71%), followed by entertainment seeking (63%) and punishment (50%). The support in our data for the "She asked for it" items and "He didn't mean to" items seem to provide additional support for previous qualitative evidence from Fiji, the Solomon Islands and Kiribati (FWCC, 2013; SPC, 2009, 2010), which also indicate that sexual violence is often motivated by sexual entitlement and using sex to punish women.

In the same way that feminist theorisations have highlighted that sexual violence against women and rape myths are embedded in cultural norms and

Table 7.1 Mean scores for rape myth acceptance and sexual prejudice in Fiji

	Minimum	*Maximum*	*Mean Score*	*Std Deviation*	*Valid Sample Size*
IRMA	22.00	110.00	70.92	13.49	1411
ATG	10.00	50.00	72.93	15.46	1357
MHS-G	12.00	60.00	42.39	8.49	1469

Table 7.2 Percentage of respondents that agree with rape myths

Item	Agree/Strongly Agree
Subscale 1: "She asked for it."	
If a girl is raped while she is drunk, she is at least somewhat responsible for letting things get out of hand	51.2
When girls go to parties wearing slutty clothes, they are asking for trouble	49.8
If a girl goes to a room alone with a guy at a party, it is her own fault if she is raped	56.4
If a girl acts like a slut, eventually she is going to get into trouble	61.6
When girls get raped, it's often because the way they said "no" was unclear	33.0
If a girl starts kissing a guy, she should not be surprised if a guy assumes she wants to have sex	62.7
Subscale 2: "He didn't mean to"	
When guys rape, it is usually because of their strong desire for sex	65.0
Guys don't usually intend to force sex on a girl, but sometimes they get too sexually carried away	64.8
Rape happens when a guy's sex drive goes out of control	62.3
If a guy is drunk, he might rape someone unintentionally	40.9
It shouldn't be considered rape if a guy is drunk and didn't realise what he was doing	30.7
If both the man and woman are drunk, it can't be rape	47.7
Subscale 3: "It wasn't rape"	
If a girl doesn't physically resist sex – even if protesting verbally – it can't be considered rape	42.7
If a girl doesn't physically fight back, you can't really say it was rape	43.4
A rape probably doesn't happen if a girl doesn't have any bruises or marks	28.2
If the accused "rapist" doesn't have a weapon, you really can't call it rape	24.0
Subscale 4: "She lied"	
If a girl doesn't say "no" she can't claim rape	50.7
A lot of times, girls who say they were raped agreed to have sex and then regret it	63.5
Rape accusations are often used as a way of getting back at guys	44.5
A lot of times, girls who say they were raped often led the guy on and then had regrets	58.4
Girls who are caught cheating on their boyfriends sometimes claim it was rape	56.6

institutions and not individual pathology, Herek (2007) has pointed to the importance of understanding sexual prejudice as a cultural phenomenon, not a psychological one. Thus, Herek (2007) argues that sexual prejudice can be understood as an internalisation of existing cultural stigma against non-heterosexual behaviours. Sexual prejudice is "a negative attitude toward an individual based on her or his membership in a group defined by its members' sexual attractions, behaviours or orientation" (Herek & McLemore, 2013, p. 311).

Table 7.3 Percentage of respondents that endorse homonegativity

	Item	Scale	Agree/Strongly Agree
1	Male Homosexual couples should not be allowed to adopt children.	ATG	63.4
2	I think Male homosexuals are disgusting.	ATG	65.3
3	Male homosexuals should not be allowed to teach in school.	ATG	46.6
4	Male homosexuality is a perversion and wrong.	ATG	64.2
5	Male homosexuality is not a natural expression of sexuality in human men.	ATG	64.3
6	If a man has homosexual feelings, he should do everything he can to overcome them.	ATG	62.3
7	I would be very upset if I learned that my son was a homosexual.	ATG	72.1
8	Homosexual behaviour between two men is just plain wrong.	ATG	73.5
9	The idea of male homosexual marriages seems ridiculous to me.	ATG	74.3
10	Many gay men use their sexual orientation so that they can obtain special privileges.	MHS	56.7
11	Gay men seem to focus on the ways in which they differ from heterosexuals, and ignore the ways in which they are the same.	MHS	56.9
12	Gay men have all the rights they need.	MHS	35.0
13	It would be ridiculous for universities in Fiji to provide students with undergraduate degrees in Gay and Lesbian Studies.	MHS	52.4
14	It is ridiculous to assume that male homosexuality should be embraced through festivals and parades.	MHS	58.6
15	Gay men do not still need to protest for equal rights.	MHS	61.3
16	Gay men should stop shoving their lifestyle down other people's throats.	MHS	68.7
17	If gay men want to be treated like everyone else, then they need to stop making such a fuss about their sexuality/culture.	MHS	71.7
18	Gay men who are open about their sexuality should not be admired for their courage.	MHS	59.1
19	Gay men should stop complaining about the way they are treated in society.	MHS	64.3
20	Gay men have become far too pushy in their demand for equal rights.	MHS	65.9
21	Gay men just can't fit into our society.	No scale	50.6
22	A man's homosexuality is a justifiable cause for job discrimination.	No scale	43.1
23	Male homosexuality is detrimental to society because it breaks down the natural divisions between the sexes.	No scale	57.8
24	State laws regulating private, consenting male homosexual behaviour should not be loosened or reduced.	No scale	51.9
25	Male homosexuality is a sin.	No scale	79.7

26	The growing number of gay men indicates a decline in Fijian morals.	No scale	65.6
27	Male homosexuality in itself is a problem for society.	No scale	63.7
28	Male homosexuality is a threat to many of our basic social institutions.	No scale	60.9
29	Male homosexuality is an inferior form of sexuality.	No scale	60.4
30	Gay men are sick.	No scale	58.0
31	The media devote far too much attention to the topic of homosexuality.	No scale	56.5
32	Gay men tend to have mental disorders.	No scale	45.6
33	Gay men should not have the same rights as straight (heterosexual) men.	No scale	53.2
34	Gay men should not be allowed to work with children.	No scale	51.0
35	Gay men are immoral.	No scale	57.9
36	Those who support the rights of gay men are probably gay themselves.	No scale	52.9
37	It's sad to know that homosexuality is now legal in Fiji since February 2010.	No scale	58.9
38	Gay men should be avoided whenever possible.	No scale	54.8

Our data indicates that endorsement of homonegative attitudes are also widespread in Fiji, with 50% or more of the respondents agreeing or strongly agreeing with 34 of the 38 items. As Table 7.3 indicates, this is true for both items that related to old-fashioned sexual prejudice (ATG) and modern sexual prejudice (MHS).

The widespread and strong agreement in our data on Fiji (Table 7.3) of both old-fashioned and modern sexual prejudice needs to be understood in Fiji's socio-legal context. In Fiji, homosexuality was constitutionally recognised in 1998 and legalised in 2010. Our data indicates that almost 60% of respondents are disappointed about this legalisation of homosexuality (Item 37, Table 7.2). Our data also challenges post-colonial research in Pacific societies, which have argued that there may be greater acceptance of culturally acceptable ways of homosexual behaviour (Aldrich, 2008; Besnier, 1994). In particular, the strength of agreement with old-fashioned sexual prejudice in the data indicates that tensions and controversies surrounding homosexuality in the Pacific is not only being produced by a demand for a specific identity based on sexual "trait" or the use of a "rights" framework. Instead, most of our respondents continue to see any form of homosexuality as "morally" wrong and that gay men should be able to, and have a responsibility to, change their behaviour in relation to their sexual identity. This supports findings in an experimental design study in Fiji, which found respondents endorsed both old fashioned and modern sexual prejudice with a proclivity to support the most blatant sexual prejudice (Johnson & Vithal, 2015).

Thus, in this section, we have seen that overall, a majority of respondents agree with attitudes that support sexual violence against women and sexual prejudice against gays. In the next section, we present findings on some of the factors by which these attitudes towards sexual violence and sexual prejudice vary.

Socio-demographic correlates of attitudes that support rape myths and homonegativity

Using the existing body of research on the correlates and predictors of RMA and homonegativity, we examined in our data to what extent attitudes varied by sex, age, ethnicity, religiosity, region, education level, having children, marital status and interpersonal contact with a gay person.

Using chi-square difference tests for each item of the scales, our data indicate that there is some small (less than 11%) but significant differences by sex and ethnicity on the specific items of the IRMA and only by ethnicity for the ATG and the MHS-G items. Specifically, women are in *greater* agreement than men on RMA items. For both RMA and sexual prejudice items, iTaukei respondents are in *greater* agreement than Indo-Fijians. When we look at summed scores on the three scales, there is on average, no significant difference by sex and ethnicity. However, there are some variations between men and women and by ethnicity in the IRMA subscales. On average, compared to men, women are more accepting (0.52) of rape myths related to "He didn't mean to" (subscale 2) (t=-2.49972, df=1460). Men, on average are more in agreement (0.46) with "She lied" items (subscale 4) (t=2.36250, df=1474). In relation to ethnicity, only for the IRMA subscale "He didn't mean to", Itaukei respondents scored slightly higher (0.44) on average than Indo-Fijian respondents (t=2.132, df=1460). The absence of over-all difference by sex for RMA and MHS-G and ATG are different from findings elsewhere (Suarez & Gadalla, 2010; Morrison & Morrison, 2011; Boakye, 2009; Emmers-Sommer, 2014). However, when gender ideologies in a particular context include ideas of men's (sexual) entitlement and privilege, previous research has shown that differences by sex can disappear (see e.g. Fakunmoju, Abrefa-Gyan, & Maphosa, 2019; Adinkrah, 2001; Nayak, Byrne, Martin, & Abraham, 2003)

Unlike sex and ethnicity, differences by religiosity and region are consistently significant in relation to support for RMA and sexual prejudice against gays. As expected by previous research, those that scored higher on the religiosity scale also scored higher on all three scales, indicating that religiosity is an important correlate of attitudes that support sexual violence against women and sexual prejudice against gay men. Both historians (Lal, 1992) and contemporary sociologists (Naidu, 2009) have documented that social relations and norms vary between the regions in Fiji, rooted in pre-colonial, colonial and post-colonial politics. On average, respondents scored strongest support of RMA in the North (mean=74.25), followed by respondents in the West (70.12) and then the Central (68.37) region. However, when looking at overall sexual prejudice scores, region seems to matter somewhat for old-fashioned sexual prejudice, but not modern sexual prejudice: while ATG scores were significantly higher in the North (38.61) compared to the Central region (36.42) there was no significant difference in ATG scores between the Western (37.12) and the Central regions. There was no difference in modern sexual prejudice (MHS-G) between the regions.

Interestingly, having children are significant correlates of attitudes towards sexual violence and prejudice among our respondents. Similar to findings by Kerry and Murray (2018) parents are more likely to be accepting of rape myths and sexual prejudice. We find that those with children on average scored higher on IRMA subscale 1 (She asked for it) (md=0.82, t=-2.918, df=1378.445), 3 (it wasn't rape) (md=0.62, t=-3.660, df=1475) and 4 (she lied) (md=0.49, t=-2.477, df=1323.166) than those without. Those with children on average score 1.64 higher (t=-3.626, df=1277.024) in modern sexual prejudice (MHS-G) and 2.52 higher (t=-5.342, df=1350) in old-fashioned sexual prejudice.

In terms of couplehood, our research found those who have ever been coupled scored, on average, higher by 1.69 (t=-3.556, df=1351) on old-fashioned sexual prejudice and by 2.49 (t=-2.486, df=1460) on modern sexual prejudice. Research completed by Abeid et al. (2015) in Tanzania, found that those who have ever been coupled score higher on average on the IRMA "She asked for it" and the "It wasn't rape" subscales than those that were single.

Unlike research on sexual violence and rape myths elsewhere, which has shown that those with more education (Boakye, 2009) and those who are younger may be less likely to endorse rape myths (Abeid et al., 2015; Anderson, Simpson-Taylor, & Hermann, 2004; Aromäki, Haebich, & Lindman, 2002; Boakye, 2009;

Emmers-Sommer, 2014), our RMA data did not vary by age, but age was positively correlated for both old-fashioned sexual prejudice (r=0.086) and modern sexual prejudice (r=0.056). Education, however, was significant for both sexual violence and sexual prejudice measures: those who have not attended university scored on average 5.23 higher (t=6.790, df=1405) on the IRMA scale compared to those who have attended university. While there was no significant difference by education level in average scores on modern sexual prejudice (MHS-G), old-fashioned sexual prejudice scores (ATG) on average were significantly higher for respondents who had not attended university (md=2.09, t=4.074, df=1352).

Thus far, we have discussed to what extent each of the various socio-demographic factors correlate with attitudes toward sexual violence and sexual prejudice. In this final section of our findings, we look at how attitudes related to rape myth acceptance and sexual prejudice vary for men and women, utilizing ordinary least squares regression (see Table 7.4).[1] For men, rape myth acceptance is predicted by religiosity, region, education level, having children and marital status. However, for women, marital status is not significant, while religiosity, region and education level are significant predictors of RMA. For both men and women, attending university reduces, on average, support for RMA and religiosity increased, on average, support for RMA. However, region seems to act very differently for women and men when it comes to RMA. While men from the Western and Northern regions have on average higher RMA scores than men from the Central region, women from the Western and Northern regions have lower RMA scores.

Table 7.4 Ordinary Least Squares Regression based predictors of rape myth acceptance and sexual prejudice, reference region Central

Independent variables	Dependent Variable					
	IRMA		ATG		MHS-G	
	Female	Male	Female	Male	Female	Male
Age	−0.980	−1.084	−0.874	0.584	−0.538	0.310
Ethnicity	−0.716	0.228	−1.834	−0.772	−0.434	−0.488
Religiosity	4.181***	2.652**	3.469**	2.059*	5.387***	2.152*
Region (Western)	−4.555***	1.438	1.692	1.382	0.558*	−0.453
Region (Northern)	−5.083***	2.649**	3.545***	1.694	2.446*	−1.545
Education level	−3.968***	−2.851**	−0.581	−1.980*	1.246	0.088
Having children	1.045	3.091**	2.908**	3.383**	3.284**	1.316
Marital status	0.333	−2.545*	−1.668	−0.687	−1.435	0.229
Interpersonal contact with gay men	−1.189	−0.380	−4.472***	−6.190***	−2.810**	−0.456
Adjusted R²	0.110	0.040	0.069	0.122	0.064	0.011
(Std Error)	(13.10)	(13.14)	(8.15)	(8.57)	(7.93)	(8.68)
F	9.805***	3.981***	6.220***	10.345***	6.131***	1.864

*** p<0.001, ** p<0.01, * p<0.05

Table 7.5 Pearson correlations between IRMA, ATG and MHS-G

	IRMA	MHS-G	ATG
IRMA	1	.322***	.284***
MHS-G		1	.739***
ATG			1

*** Correlation is significant at the 0.001 level (2-tailed).

Herek and McLemore (2013) in their review of sexual prejudice research point to the importance of examining how endorsement of homonegativity may work differently for different groups. In our study, we find that sexual prejudice is structured differently for men and women. For men, old-fashioned sexual prejudice is predicted by religiosity, having children, education level and interpersonal contact with a gay person. Men with children, those who are more religious, those who have had less interpersonal contact with a gay person, those from the Northern and the Western regions and those who did not attend university, have higher scores supporting old-fashioned (ATG) forms of sexual prejudice. However, when it comes to modern (MHS) forms of sexual prejudice, only religiosity is significant in predicting men's oppositional attitudes towards gays. In contrast, for women, religiosity, having children, IPC and region are significant predictors of both old-fashioned (ATG) and modern (MHS) forms of sexual prejudice. However, the effects of these variables on strength of support by women are smaller on modern vs. old-fashioned forms of sexual prejudice.

Finally, the three scales were significantly correlated with each other (see Table 7.5), supporting the argument that attitudes that legitimize sexual violence against women are usually part of a larger system of oppressive beliefs against non-conforming gendered behaviour (Hockett, Saucier, Hoffman, Smith, & Craig, 2009; Suarez & Gadalla, 2010; Herek & McLemore, 2013).

Implications for security

The findings above point to three key points for understanding how insecurity is gendered in Fiji and what it may mean for efforts at prevention and change. Firstly, insecurity in Fiji is gendered with women living in a context where most people (both men and women) normalise and rationalise violence against them and gay men living in a context where a majority of people oppose both their rights and their sexual identity. The general absence of gendered and ethnic difference to both attitudes related to sexual violence and sexual prejudice in Fiji may indicate the strength of patriarchal ideology, which privileges heteronormative men, male entitlement to women's bodies and gender conforming behaviour.

It is important to point out that these dominant attitudes persist in Fiji despite the presence of a strong women's rights movement and an LGBQT+ movement, both of which have impacted on positive legal changes. This leads to our second point that legal changes cannot be considered sufficient in changing attitudes that engender insecurity. When considering what is needed in changing attitudes, it will be important to consider the sites of resistance individuals and groups will face. The theoretical perspective System Justification Theory (SJT) suggests that, within any given society, individuals will be motivated to varying degrees to consciously or unconsciously support the positive components and rationalise away the various social, moral or economic failures of that society (see Jost, Banaji, & Nosek, 2004; Jost & Van der Toorn, 2011 for greater discussion). Although members of the advantaged groups within a society have a greater likelihood of endorsing system justification beliefs, there are cases in which disadvantaged groups will defend the legitimacy of the system's failure even more vigorously than the advantaged group members (Henry & Saul, 2006). The fact that among our respondent's women did not differ significantly from men in support of rape myths, and overall had a higher score than men, provides some evidence of this process. Further, SJT suggests that *some* oppressed and disadvantaged members of society have developed an internalised sense of inferiority which can lead them to support system policies and/or beliefs that may not be beneficial to them and could, in fact, harm them (see Gaucher & Jost, 2011; Jost, 1997; Major, 1994; Major, McFarlin, & Gagnon, 1984). Feminist theorisation on rape and sexual violence, as well as the work on stigma of sexual minorities, further support the importance of paying attention to how the work for changing attitudes needs to occur with members of all groups – the marginalised as well as the dominant.

Finally, we would suggest that efforts to change these attitudes will require paying attention to how support for sexual violence and prejudice are structured in Fiji. This is where our findings are particularly important. Prevention, awareness and consciousness raising efforts will need to be gendered (given the variation by sex in predictors of support for these attitudes), contextualised by region (given the variation in RMA and homophobia by region), by paying attention to how parenting influences these attitudes and in dialogue with religious stakeholders (given the importance of religiosity as a correlate).

In sum, the current analysis has shed light upon both the incidence and facilitators of problematic attitudes associated with rape and homosexuality in Fiji. This examination has been long overdue and it is hoped that it will ultimately play a role in providing greater security to those women and homosexual individuals who have suffered much too long.

Acknowledgements

The funding for administering the FIAPA was provided through the Strategic Research Themes grants at the University of the South Pacific (USP). Dr. Asenati Chan Tung (Australian National University) and Dr. Yoko Kanemasu (USP) are co-investigators of the grant and the FIAPA study, without whom this study would not have been possible.

Note

1 We conducted a multicollinearity test for all factors in the regression and the Variance Inflation Factor was between 1–2.9, indicating that multicollinearity is not a problem.

References

Abeid, M., Muganyizi, P., Massawe, S., Mpembeni, R., Darj, E., & Axemo, P. (2015). Knowledge and attitude towards rape and child sexual abuse: A community-based cross-sectional study in Rural Tanzania. *BMC Public Health, 15,* 428–441.

Adinkrah, M. (2001). Patriarchal family ideology and female homicide victimization in Fiji. *Journal of Comparative Family Studies, 32*(2), 283–301.

Aldrich, R. (2008). *Colonialism and homosexuality.* London: Routledge.

Anderson, V. N., Simpson-Taylor, D., & Hermann, D. J. (2004). Gender, age and rape-supportive rules. *Sex Roles, 55,* 77–90.

Aosved, A. C., & Long, P. J. (2006). Co-occurrence of rape myth acceptance, sexism, racism, homophobia, ageism, classism, and religious intolerance. *Sex Roles, 55*(7), 481–492.

Aromäki, A. S., Haebich, K., & Lindman, R. E. (2002). Age as a modifier of sexually aggressive attitudes in men. *Scandinavian Journal of Psychology, 43*(5), 419–423.

Barron, J., Struckman-Johnson, C., Quevillon, R., & Banka, S. (2008). Heterosexual men's attitudes toward gay men: A hierarchical model including masculinity, openness, and theoretical explanations. *Psychology of Men & Masculinity, 9*(3), 154–166.

Besnier, N. (1994). Polynesian gender liminality through time and space. In G. Herdt (Ed.), *Ritualized homosexuality in Melanesia* (pp. 285–328). Berkeley, CA: University of California Press.

Boakye, K. E. (2009). Attitudes toward rape and victims of rape: A test of the feminist theory in Ghana. *Journal of Interpersonal Violence, 24*(10), 1633–1651.

Chenoy, A. M. (2005). A plea for engendering human security. *International Studies, 42*(2), 167–179.

Dorofeev, S., & Grant, P. (2006). *Statistics for real-life sample surveys: Non-simple-random samples and weighted data.* Cambridge: Cambridge University Press.

Emmers-Sommer, T. (2014). Adversarial sexual attitudes toward women: The relationships with gender and traditionalism. *Sexuality and Culture, 18,* 804–817.

Fakunmoju, S. B., Abrefa-Gyan, T., & Maphosa, N. (2019). Confirmatory factor analysis and gender invariance of the revised IRMA scale in Nigeria. *Journal of Women and Social Work, 34*(1), 83–98.

Fiji Women's Crisis Centre (FWCC). (2013). *Somebody's life, everybody's business! National research on women's health and life experiences in Fiji (2010/2011): A survey exploring the prevalence, incidence and attitudes to intimate partner violence in Fiji.* Suva: Fiji Women's Crisis Centre.

Fulu, E., Warner, X., Miedema, S., Jewkes, R., Roselli, T., & Lang, J. (2013). *Why do some men use violence against women and how can we prevent it? Quantitative findings from the United Nations multi-country study on men and violence in Asia and the Pacific.* Bangkok: UNDP, UNFPA, UN Women and UNV.

Gaucher, D., & Jost, J. T. (2011). Difficulties awakening the sense of injustice and overcoming oppression: On the soporific effects of system justification. In *Conflict, interdependence, and justice* (pp. 227–246). New York: Springer.

George, N. (2008). Contending masculinities and the limits of tolerance: Sexual minorities in Fiji. *The Contemporary Pacific,* 163–189.

Henry, P. J., & Saul, A. (2006). The development of system justification in the developing world. *Social Justice Research, 19*(3), 365–378.

Herek, G. M. (1988). Heterosexuals' attitudes toward lesbians and gay men: Correlates and gender differences. *Journal of Sex Research, 25,* 451–477.

Herek, G. M. (2000). Sexual prejudice and gender: Do heterosexuals' attitudes toward lesbians and gay men differ? *Journal of Social Issues, 56*(2), 251–266.

Herek, G. M. (2007). Confronting sexual stigma and prejudice: Theory and practice. *Journal of Social Issues*, *63*(4), 905–925.

Herek, G. M., & McLemore, K. A. (2013). Sexual prejudice. *Annual Review of Psychology*, *64*, 309–333.

Hockett, J., Saucier, D. A., Hoffman, B. H., Smith, S. J., & Craig, A. W. (2009). Oppression through acceptance? Predicting rape myth acceptance and attitudes toward rape victims. *Violence Against Women*, *15*(8), 877–897.

Hoogensen, G., & Rottem, S. V. (2004). Gender identity and the subject of security. *Security Dialogue*, *35*(2), 155–171.

Johnson, J., & Vithal, P. (2015). *Bias in paradise: Examining factors that influence modern and old fashioned sexual prejudice in the Pacific Region*. Unpublished manuscript. The University of the South Pacific.

Jordan, J. (2004). Beyond belief? Police, rape and women's credibility. *Criminal Justice*, *4*(1), 29–59.

Jost, J. T. (1997). An experimental replication of the depressed-entitlement effect among women. *Psychology of Women Quarterly*, *21*, 387–393.

Jost, J. T., Banaji, M. R., & Nosek, B. A. (2004). A decade of system justification theory: Accumulated evidence of conscious and unconscious bolstering of the status quo. *Political Psychology*, *25*, 881–920.

Jost, J. T., & Van der Toorn, J. (2011). System justification theory. In P. A. M. van Lange, A. W. Kruglanski, & E. T. Higgins (Eds.), *Handbook of theories of social psychology*. London: Sage.

Kerry, N., & Murray, D. R. (2018). Conservative parenting: Investigating the relationships between parenthood, moral judgment, and social conservatism. *Personality and Individual Differences*, *134*, 88–96.

Lal, B. V. (1992). *Broken waves: A history of the Fiji Islands in the twentieth century* (Vol. 11). Honolulu, HI: University of Hawaii Press.

Lonsway, K., & Fitzgerald. L. (1994). Rape myths: In review. *Psychology of Women Quarterly*, *18*, 133–164.

Ma'a Fafine mo e Famili. (2012). *National study on domestic violence against women in Tonga*. Nuku'alofa: Ma'a Fafine mo e Famili.

Major, B. (1994). From social inequality to personal entitlement: The role of social comparisons, legitimacy appraisals, and group memberships. *Advances in Experimental Social Psychology*, *26*, 293–355.

Major, B., McFarlin, D., & Gagnon, D. (1984). Overworked and underpaid. *Journal of Personality and Social Psychology*, *47*, 1399–1412.

McMahon, S., & Farmer, G. L. (2011). An updated measure for assessing subtle rape myths. *Social Work Research*, *35*(2), 71–81.

Merry, S. (2009). *Gender violence: A cultural perspective*. Oxford: Wiley-Blackwell.

Morrison, M. A., & Morrison, T. G. (2002). Development and validation of a scale measuring modern prejudice toward gay men and lesbian women. *Journal of Homosexuality*, *43*, 15–37.

Morrison, M. A., & Morrison, T. G. (2011). Sexual orientation bias toward gay men and lesbian women: Modern homonegative attitudes and their association with discriminatory behavioral intentions. *Journal of Applied Social Psychology*, *41*(11), 2573–2599.

Naidu, V. (2009). *Draft report Fiji Islands country profile on excluded groups*. Unpublished Report for UNESCAP, Suva.

Nayak, M. B., Byrne, C. A., Martin, M. K., & Abraham, A. G. (2003). Attitudes toward violence against women: A cross-nation study. *Sex Roles*, *49*(7/8), 333–342.

Ogata, S., & Cels, J. (2003). Human security: Protecting and empowering the people. *Global Governance*, *9*(3), 273–322.

Richardson, D., & May, H. (1999). Deserving victims? Sexual status and the social construction of violence. *The Sociological Review*, *47*(3), 308–331.

Shepherd, L. (2008). *Gender, violence and security*. London: Zed Books.

SPC. (2003). *The Samoa family health and safety study*. Noumea: SPC and the United Nations Population Fund.

SPC. (2009). *Solomon islands family health and safety study: A study on violence against women and children*. Report prepared by the Secretariat of the Pacific Community for the Solomon Islands Ministry of Women, Youth and Children's Affairs, and the National Statistics Office, Ministry of Finance and Treasury, National Reform and Planning. Noumea: SPC.

SPC. (2010). *Kiribati family health and support study: A study on violence against women and children*. Report prepared by the Secretariat of the Pacific Community for the Ministry of Internal and Social Affairs, and the Statistics Division, Ministry of Finance and Economic Development, Republic of Kiribati. Noumea: SPC.

Suarez, E., & Gadalla, T. M. (2010). Stop blaming the victim: A meta-analysis on rape myths. *Journal of Interpersonal Violence*, *25*(11), 2010–2035.

United Nations Development Programme (UNDP). (1994). *Human development report 1994*. New York and Oxford: Oxford University Press. Retrieved February 19, 2019 from http://hdr.undp.org/en/content/human-development-report-1994

Vanuatu Women's Centre (VWC). (2011). *Vanuatu national survey on women's lives and family relationships*. Port Vila: Vanuatu Women's Center.

Ward, C. A. (1995). *Attitudes toward rape: Feminist and social psychological perspectives*. London: Sage Publications.

WHO. (2005). *WHO Multi-country study on women's health and domestic violence against women: Initial results on prevalence, health outcomes and women's responses*. By Claudia García-Moreno, Henrica A.F.M. Jansen, Mary Ellsberg, Lori Heise and Charlotte.

8 Gender and post-conflict security sector reform

Experiences from Bougainville and Solomon Islands

Nicole George

Introduction

Although male recruitment has been the norm within the security agencies of Pacific Islands states for a much of their post-colonial history, increased effort to recruit and promote women into this sector has recently become evident. In this chapter, I reflect on the impact of efforts to include a gender focus in programmes of security sector reform (SSR) in two conflict affected states of the Western Pacific, Bougainville, an autonomous territory of Papua New Guinea (PNG) and Solomon Islands (SI). Both of these states have been subject to peacebuilding processes that have sought, in varying degrees, to restore political and economic institutions so that these will function in line with liberal, democratic and free-market principles. The Regional Assistance Mission to the Solomon Islands (RAMSI) is one such intervention. It was launched in 2003 in SI to bring an end to a damaging inter-tribal conflict that had raged on the central island of Guadalcanal in the preceding years accounting for some deaths as well as widespread violence, lawlessness and displacement. Many accounts of the conflict identify the sectional capture of state security forces as a factor contributing to the unrest (Braithwaite et al., 2010; Dinnen, McLeod, & Peake, 2006; Peake & Studdard Brown, 2005). Peacebuilding efforts here have placed a heavy emphasis upon the restoration of law and order institutions generally, including measures to rebuild popular trust in state security agencies (Dinnen et al., 2006). Over time, and reflecting the growing traction of international policy frameworks such as the United Nations Security Council's Women Peace and Security policy agenda (WPS), SSR reform in SI has also sought to increase recruitment of women into policing and correctional agencies as well as enhancing security agencies' responsiveness to security issues impacting on women such as gender violence (George, 2018a).

Interesting regional comparisons can be drawn between SI and Bougainville, where a devastating conflict also occurred, lasting from the late 1980s until the late 1990s. In contrast to Solomon Islands, peacebuilding on Bougainville has occurred in a way that recognises the sovereignty ambitions of Bougainvilleans and the majority desire for institutions and processes of post-conflict governance to give adequate recognition both to the territory's distinctive cultural and political traditions as well as liberal principles of statehood (Wallis, 2012; Boege, 2009).

Security sector reform is underway in this context also, and a "home grown" police force has been established to replace the compromised PNG policing presence active on the territory prior to, and during, the conflict. As in SI, there has been considerable effort lately put into improving women's participation within this sector (Dinnen & Peake, 2013, p. 579; George, 2018a).

On the surface these gains seem positive, but deeper investigation of the gendered experience of security sector reform in both cases reveal significant challenges that are yet to be surmounted. It is certainly true that women can derive critical benefits as individuals working within state security agencies, and as members of communities where the safety of women is regulated in gender sensitive ways. Nonetheless, my analysis also reveals the informally institutionalised gendered logics that facilitate discrimination against women at a range of levels are not easily overturned even when gender becomes a focus of SSR and that this factor helps to constrain the transformational potential of reform efforts.

To develop this argument, I draw on interviews conducted in each country's capital city with women who have been recruited to security agencies, with advisory partners from regional agencies assisting the implementation of reform, and with representatives of women's organisations in the broader community, to consider where and how women have been able to capitalise on the possibilities that SSR has offered them, as well as to identify the gendered obstacles that remain in place.[1] I triangulate these observations with documentary and secondary source analysis and passive observation of everyday security sector practice. My analysis has focussed on where and how women's presence within these agencies contributes to the progression of gendered reform. My conclusions are that long-lasting gender reform of state security agencies is currently hampered by an "add women and stir approach" that fails to disrupt the deeper gendered logics that structure everyday, informal operations within these institutions and within the broader pluralised regulatory environment in each context. Without this, gender reform within these agencies amounts to tantalising promise without being substantively transformational.

I begin this chapter by locating this research in broader academic debates about the process of security sector reform as part of the liberal peacebuilding. From here, I discuss literature examining the gendered experience of security sector reform in post-conflict contexts and set out the analytical directions that guide my own study. In the final two sections, I discuss findings from my study of women's participation in security sector reform in Bougainville and Solomon Islands. I show that while there is a great deal of enthusiasm for the incorporation of women in each context, as well as for a more responsive security sector response to questions of women's safety, the gendered logics described in earlier sections of the discussion are powerful and in each case function in ways that do not erase gender discriminatory practices. The fact that these logics function informally and often feature as a shadowy presence in narrative and observations of practice make them difficult to tackle. Nonetheless my effort is to both identify them and show how they can function to undermine the rhetoric of women's advancement that has become strongly attached to programmes of SSR in each case.

Liberal peacebuilding and security sector reform

Beyond the containment of violence and the restoration of order, peacebuilding missions of the late 20th and early 21st century have increasingly taken a "state-building" orientation. This involves the re-constitution of regulatory, governance and economic institutions in accordance with liberal democratic principles (de Coning, 2018). These activities are critical to the "technical and programmatic" blueprint for peacebuilding that privileges the development of liberal market and governance institutions as critical to the restoration of order (de Coning, 2018, p. 303). Security sector reform has also become a central plank of these conflict stabilisation efforts (Riis Andersen, 2011), contributing to a strengthened system of law and order but also occurring as part of a broader state institution-building process that aims to insure that public agencies generally are adequately equipped and operate in line with standards of accountability (Bastick, 2019, p. 360). As I will make clear in the sections below, in Bougainville and Solomon Islands, seeds of discontent over the intimidation, corruption and indiscriminate exercise of force allegedly perpetrated by state security agencies were factors that fuelled the escalation of conflict in both cases and so efforts to improve the reputation and standing of these institutions has been locally welcomed (Braithwaite et al., 2010; Dinnen & Peake, 2013; Kokiai Tunum, 2003, pp. 7–11).

In general terms, SSR processes occurring in post-conflict contexts, place a strong emphasis upon building security agencies' governance culture so that it accords with international principles of good governance, rule of law and respect for human rights. In this vein, enforcement agencies are encouraged to conceptualise their contribution to the law and justice sector as partial rather than predominant and to recognise that their authority is negotiated and perhaps limited by a range of other actors also operating within that sector including government ministries, parliaments, ombudsmen, the judiciary and civil society (Bastick, 2019, p. 360).

Of course, the liberal peace presupposes a pre-existing understanding and acceptance of liberal democratic ideals as the most appropriate basis upon which systems of social and political regulation and authority should be modelled. Yet, as a great many critical observers have demonstrated in recent years, acceptance of liberal models of state regulation is far from universal. Indeed commentary on security provision in post-colonial states dealing with the legacies of conflict is strongly informed by the idea that a sole reliance upon state agencies as sources of order and security may be both inefficient and unsustainable (Baker & Scheye, 2007; Dinnen & McLeod, 2009; Mac Ginty, 2008). This contention is particularly pertinent in Pacific Islands contexts such as Solomon Islands or Papua New Guinea where some observers argue that the state has never had enough influence to "displace" or weaken the "resilient local cultures derived from the small-scale, self-regulating societies" (Dinnen & McLeod, 2009, p. 334).

These accounts contend that efforts to better accommodate "local" systems of justice would greatly assist justice outcomes for local populations. However, as I have argued elsewhere, while the general tenet of this position is sensible, recognition needs also to be given to the gender discriminatory ways that hybridised systems of regulatory authority consolidate order in an everyday sense and dispense justice to women (George, 2017; Bull, George, & Curth-Bibb, 2017). Communal and customary principles of order centering on the restoration of communal relationships, rather than protections of the rights of women are often allowed to take precedence within these forums (Zorn, 2010; Salomon, 2003). Such scenarios may be acceptable to women as a rightful form of justice, but there are also documented cases where this has not been the case (Salomon, 2003) and where women express enormous frustration over the way their demands for justice are treated within customary fora.[2] This indicates the importance of allowing women a choice to access state-based sites of regulatory justice sites if that is their wish or to consider where and how plural regulatory environments might be beneficial. It is thus important to give critical consideration to the ways SSR programmes give recognition to, and intersect with other, pre-existing sites of regulatory authority, rather than simply assuming the regulatory environment is a blank slate to be "filled" (Riis Andersen, 2011).

Security sector reform and the policing of gender

The idea that a "reformed" security sector should be able to more sensitively and effectively police gender is a powerful theme in the policy on security sector reform. The aim is to rebuild state security agencies so that they present a more friendly and protective face to women. In addition, United Nations Security Council resolutions on Women Peace and Security call attention to the need for critical vetting of state security forces in order to exclude those members who have committed sexual and gender-based violence (Bastick, 2019, p. 365).

The ambition to reform the security sector so that women can find a more sensitive response to their experiences of gendered crime may appear deceptively simple to achieve in principle. When reforms are seen to challenge longstanding informal institutional rules, what I refer to from here-on as institutional logics, the effort to implement gender-sensitive change can become more challenging. In post-conflict contexts where communities fear that their identity, culture and sense of well-being and safety has become degraded or remains in threat, state security agencies' may, in collaboration with other religious and customary/cultural leaders, engage in a restrictive policing of women's activities as a matter of course (de Alwis, Mertus, & Sajjad, 2013, p. 178). This means that when women's comportment is understood to breach communal understandings of what is appropriate or rightful, they may incur heavy discipline from their own communities but also from members of security agencies too (George, 2017).

For example, in some conflict transition contexts, new policy provisions providing women with new rights and or protections may be written into constitutions and legal codes. However, even while SSR programmes may aim to ensure these provisions are respected and implemented, studies of policing reform have shown how individual personnel may be heavily resistant to these provisions in everyday practise. In line with the argument developed above, these provisions may be ignored because policing personnel interpret them to be at odds with the gendered "logics" in the form of "familiar taken-for-granted rules and norms" (Chappell, 2014, p. 574) that have hitherto guided policing work. Thus, these provisions may be rejected by individual officers in everyday security agency operations because they are understood to threaten longstanding principles about the "rightful" place of women within the communal order (George, 2017). Alternatively, they may be resisted or resented because they are not considered a "rightful" focus of police authority or a prestigious area of policing activity (Bull et al., 2017).

Recruitment of women: gendering the ranks of the security sector

A second focus of SSR involves efforts to recruit more women into this sector. Indeed, improving the participation of women in state security agencies is some-times proposed as a reform measure that will also produce improved policing responsiveness to particular sorts of gendered crimes such as gender violence and sexual assault. The idea being that when women are a more visible presence in the police force, women in the community are more inclined to bring counts of gendered assault and abuse to police attention (Bastick, 2019, p. 365). This may be particularly important in sites where police or other state regulatory authorities have been compromised in the conflict period.

Improving women's participation in state security agencies is often encouraged as part of efforts to demonstrate state commitments to the progression of women's equality and empowerment. Indeed, improved numbers of women within these agencies is frequently identified by decision makers as a key indicator of state or multilateral agencies' efforts to implement the women, peace and security agenda as well as to demonstrate their commitments to progression on gender equality goals. The idea here is that by bringing women into occupation areas that are traditionally associated with men, or where men have been dominant, women are being supported to breakdown gendered barriers and benefit from the opening up of new employment and economic opportunities.

But neither an increased number of women recruited by security agencies, nor increased commitments to effectively "police" gender, by themselves, ensure the success of widespread gender reform within this sector. Extant studies have shown that a broader institutional culture that devalues the presence of women, or that restricts women's roles to particular areas, for example the policing of violence against women (VAW) as compared to other "high prestige" areas of work, can be detrimental to women's standing (Nelson, 1996, p. 140). Likewise, research on the introduction of women's policing units designed to improve responses to women complainants has found that these are often poorly integrated into the broader police force, under-resourced or managed by disinterested officers who fear their career progression is harmed by this type of policing, all of which under-mines the benefits that women might draw from this type of initiative (Pancha-nadeswaran & Koverola, 2005; Mobekk, 2014).

These considerations indicate the difficulty of making gender a transformational focus of SSR programmes. Going beyond the "add women and stir" approach to gender reform[3] requires tackling longstanding gender prejudicial logics shaping how norms of gender appropriate behaviour for women and men are understood and what legitimate security sector activity should be. If this is not done, and reform is conceptualised rather more superficially, as simply requiring greater inclusion of women and tougher policing policy on issues of gendered security, then the overall progress of gender reform will be more circumscribed.

The following section now demonstrates how the principles outlined above are helpful for analysis of efforts to progress security sector reform as part of broader conflict transition processes in Bougainville and Solomon Islands. Gender has become a more central focus of SSR programmes as each state transitions from conflict but this has not necessarily overturned the persistent gendered logics that are institutionalised within the broader society, and within security agencies themselves. Instead, this has constrained the gender transformative impact of the SSR agenda in both contexts.

Security sector reform in post-conflict Bougainville

Strong commitments to uphold Bougainville's customary distinctiveness have guided the design of the territory's post-conflict governance framework. As a result, peacebuilding and statebuilding have followed a hybridised liberal-local design interweaving the authority of state and customary systems of regulatory authority (Wallis, 2012; Boege, 2009). The effort to rebuild state institutions has aimed to decentralise authority, particularly systems of regulatory authority so that alongside state security agencies, constitutional recognition is designated to the regulatory powers of customary institutions such as "village assemblies, councils of chiefs, councils of elders and customary law" (Boege, 2009, p. 35) The effort to develop a system of regulatory authority that reflects the "grain of local beliefs" was deemed particularly important given the tarnished reputation of the PNG state police force and its history of punitive action and indiscriminate force against Bougainvilleans during the conflict period (Dinnen & Peake, 2013, p. 572). In addition to recognition of customary authority, the system of regulatory authority has also included the development of an auxiliary police force. This force of 350 personnel deployed in 196 rural locations aims to extend the reach of policing authority into more remote areas of territory beyond the largely urban focus of the Bougainville Police Force (Dinnen & Peak, 2013, p. 575). The BPS itself, numbers only roughly 200 officers and faces severe resourcing constraints and resistance to its authority in some central and southern districts of the territory where former conflict protagonists retain a distrust of the ABG and its leadership and have established "no-go" zones to hold off external influence (Dinnen & Peake, 2013, pp. 575–576). The auxiliary police officers or CAPs (Community Auxiliary Police), as they are locally known, are understood to offer a more trusted law enforcement role in the eyes of the community than the regular police force because they operate sensitively alongside "local leadership and governance structures, including dispute resolution practices" (Dinnen & Peak, 2013, pp. 576–577). It has been argued that CAPs enjoy strong community relationships and have even succeeded in extending the jurisdiction of the police into parts of the "no-go zones" as a result of the trust they garner (Dinnen & Peake, 2013, p. 578). Others contend, however, that CAP officers are considered very much the "second tier" of policing by regulars in the BPS and may struggle to liaise effectively with BPS officers who are reluctant to recognise their authority (anonymised communication, external support agency, January 2018).

Gender and security sector reform in Bougainville

Bougainville's peace agreement, signed in 2000 included only one reference to women, an omission that was rectified to some degree in the later constitution that guaranteed women participation, albeit at minority levels, in structures of parliamentary decision making (George, 2018a). In the years since, there has been a concerted effort to lift women's participation in other sectors including improving women's access to high level bureaucratic posts and their participation in local government. As part of this effort, greater effort has been devoted to the recruitment of women into the security sector and particularly the territory's policing institutions. This means that presently the BPS is aiming to achieve a target of 25% participation of women. For the CAP programme, international support partners have established a more ambitious target for a 50% intake of women. At present this seems a rather distant proposition with female CAPS numbering only 66 of the 350 officers appointed and only two women holding the CAP equivalent of sergeant ranking.[4]

There is some evidence to suggest that the introduction of the CAP policing presence has been beneficial to women in other ways however. Recent research into community perceptions of this policing structure has found that women in jurisdictions with CAP officers are more likely to take grievances to those officers than other sites authority (both chiefly and regular police) and that they tend to articulate an increased sense of general security (Cooper, 2017). New Zealand police assisting with the implementation of the CAP programme in Bougainville, and who have observed developments within this programme over a sustained period of time, are less optimistic about these sorts of gains however. They contend that CAP performance is generally dependent upon the type of rapport individual officers are able to build within the community, and with other the sources of local authority that may be required to assist them. The authority of CAPs and especially female CAPs may also be diminished in some circumstances particularly if they are confronted with village assemblies comprised solely of men, which might undermine their ability to bring matters such as experiences of gendered violence to the attention of other village authorities.

Interviews with agencies assisting the SSR process in Bougainville also revealed how ongoing gender discriminatory practise within this sector can impede women's career progress as well as the gender justice outcomes secured by women more generally outside the force. This is particularly apparent if we enquire about women's exposure to violence from family members or intimate partners, a phenomenon that has become particularly urgent in the post-conflict context. Recent studies have shown that up to 80% of men admitted to the perpetration of physical or sexual violence against their female partners in their lifetime, as well as escalating rates of violent assault against women brought to the attention of police and medical authorities (ABG, 2016). The adoption of the PNG Family Protection Act should improve policing of violence against women in Bougainville. It establishes a system of interim protection orders, enables neighbours, relatives and children to report cases of violence, and provides police with the capacity to remove violent offenders from their homes in order to protect victims. Full implementation of the law has been impeded however because the ABG has committed to the development of an implementation plan that has suffered unexplained but significant delays (ABG, 2016). This local policy "lag" means that while Bougainvillean women's rights to security are protected in law, the security sector is currently hamstrung in its capacity to police violence against women in accordance with the most current legal provisions. This, and other challenges undermining the legitimacy of state policing authority in this context, make it probable that even those cases that are brought to police attention are far outweighed by those that are unreported.

Of course, women may choose, or may be pressured to choose, to have their experiences of violence be regulated within customary tribunals under the authority of customary leaders or village elders. These systems of justice may be more accessible sites of authority to which women can take complaints of violence, but they are not always the most effective in meeting women's expectations for justice. In cases of sexual violence for example, research conducted on Bougainville has found that women are often required to marry their assailants to ensure the preservation of communal or kin-based relations (Howley, 2002). Women who persist with a desire to take their cases to the attention of police, may face censure from their communities, or the family of their assailant, for exposing them to state scrutiny. This kind of backlash is not necessarily taken fully into account by the various providers of support services for women exposed to violence in Bougainville, who subscribe strongly to a "rights based approach for clients, and state that they are unable to provide ongoing protection to women who refuse to progress their cases through the court system" (Garasu, personal communication 3 February, Chabbai, 2018).

These challenges are not necessarily easily resolved even when complaints of violence are brought to police attention however. Evidence on the policing of gender violence across the Pacific Islands region generally suggests that women are frequently counselled by state and non-state authorities to avoid acting in ways that could potentially jeopardise their marriages and household security and often advised to return home to a violent environment (Bull et al., 2017). Interviews with representatives of international policing agencies assisting the BPS revealed that while this challenge is also evident in Bougainville, women BPS and CAP officers often face the same barriers that everyday Bougainvillean women outside the force confront when it comes to managing or reporting experiences of violence in the family or community. One interlocutor explained for example that in her 8-month period of deployment she had encountered five cases where women in the regular force had been subjected to serious incidents of violence perpetrated by their husbands, two of whom were also were serving in the regular force, one at CID level. In a number of these cases the women involved where deterred by their superiors from pressing charges against their partners.

These scenarios demonstrate how informal gendered logics shape SSR processes in ways that undermine the implementation of laws and policies that, on paper at least, offer women protection from physical insecurity. The fact that even women working within this sector face barriers in their ability to mobilise the law to achieve justice, indicate the depth of the effort required to promote change in this context. Anecdotally it was clear that women from international police forces that have been deployed in Bougainville are interested to support and mentor young local women officers, and to ensure that women share in the career building opportunities that male officers are often able to access more easily. It is certainly true that women's participation in the security sector sends important messages to the community about the acceptability of women in non-traditional employment sectors. Nonetheless, efforts to mentor and support local women within the BPS will also need to be attentive to the gendered logics inside and outside the profession that structure and potentially constrain women's work-lives and their eventual career progression.

SSR in post-conflict Solomon Islands

SSR in SI has been a priority within the peacebuilding and conflict transition intervention that commenced in the country in 2003 and that was known as the Regional Assistance Mission to SI or (RAMSI). As in Bougainville, conflict dynamics in this location also undermined the legitimacy of state policing and corrections agencies that frequently operated in partisan and unaccountable ways that fuelled further grievance and violence. In addition to other statebuilding activities, the mission placed a heavy focus on the restoration of security, law and order across the country and the establishment of a heavy "command and control" presence (Braithwaite et al., 2010; Whalan, 2010, p. 633).

SSR was a central pillar of the RAMSI approach to peacebuilding, and aimed to rebuild and strengthen the Royal Solomon Islands Police Force (RSIPF) and national department of corrections, today known as Correction Services Solomon Islands (CSSI) (Peake & Studdard Brown, 2005). This central focus on state security has, however, been heavily criticised for being overly blunt and for failing to recognise other sites of customary and religious regulatory authority as also critical to the restoration of order in this context (Braithwaite et al., 2010).

In later years, these criticisms became more pointed and RAMSI programmers sought to focus more attention upon questions of gender and the challenges undermining peace for SI women (George, 2019). Yet these efforts have generally reinforced, rather than challenged, the broader security focus of the RAMSI intervention and are yet to translate in ways that have dramatically altered the subordinate standing of women within or outside SI security agencies.

Women's recruitment to security agencies

Efforts to recruit women into state policing and corrections have been successful with women numbering 84 out of the 443 officers within Corrections Services Solomon Islands (CSSI) and 200 of the 1500 active personnel within the Royal SI Police Force (RSIPF). Women are also working at high levels in both these institutions. The Deputy Police Commissioner is currently a female officer and within CSSI, a woman now holds the executive level position of Director of Strategic Planning, although she is the only woman to hold a position at this level within the ministry (George, 2018b).

Women's advances within CSSI, are particularly notable and commonly celebrated as a site where gender commitments have produced positive outcomes. Individual women officers are also keen to recount positive stories of their career progress in recent years. Interviews with two women officers holding middle level positions within CSSI revealed the high value that women place on building their careers within these institutions and the new opportunities they have accessed as a result of reform (Personal communication Honiara 17 August 2018). My interlocutors were enthusiastic about the fact that reforms within the ministry now allowed women to work both in women's and men's prisons, and in high risk areas, overturning a previous stipulation that female officers work only in the women's prison. They argued that the previous policy restricting women's work in men's prisons had long prevented female officers from accessing training opportunities or promotions and impeded their career advancement. They also described a suite of new gender polices adopted by CSSI on discrimination, harassment and flexible rostering for women. They were also proud of the professional network called "women in corrections" that they had been involved with since 2006 and the fact that they had more opportunities for professional education and training.

In comparison with SSR in Bougainville, the broad "security first" ethos (George, 2018a) of peacebuilding in Solomon Islands has meant a reduced emphasis placed on informal customary and religious peacebuilding institutions as complementary to conflict stabilisation processes in Solomon Island. Commitments to the development of community policing programmes have also been weak generally and rarely focussed specifically upon the recruitment of women. For example, a pilot community policing programme that ran from late 2009 through until the last months of 2010 created just under 30 posts in three different provinces of the Island and saw only one woman nominated by local leaders as a programme participant (Dinnen & Hayley, 2012). Echoing research findings from Bougainville, evaluation studies conducted in SI have also indicated that women would generally value greater access to female community police officers, particularly in cases when they seek support due to their exposure to marital or familial violence. Yet it was also found that processes of mediation either through custom or the church are often preferred to other state-based forms of regulatory intervention, even where these usually result in women being told to return to their husbands and endure the violence (Dinnen & Hayley, 2012) (see further discussion on this point below).

SSR and gendered institutions

Women's contributions as regular police within the RSIPF are often showcased in RAMSI publicity, and drawn upon to demonstrate how SSR has produced outcomes that are beneficial to local women (Australian Government, 2017). Yet passive observation of the ways that male and female police undertook duties on the streets of Honiara, the capital city of SI, in 2017 indicated to me that gender may influence how superior officers allocate duties to women.

I frequently observed, for example, that when police were on duty to manage traffic congestion, a particular problem that plagues Honiara in early morning and late afternoon, the job of directing vehicles more usually fell to female officers than their male counterparts. Hence, it was women in police uniforms who stood for hours in searingly hot, dusty and diesel-fumed conditions, unravelling inevitable traffic snarls while their male colleagues, upwards of three or four in number, waited inside an air-conditioned vehicle parked to one side of the road. This pattern suggests the presence of informal gendered logics reinforcing women's subordinate standing within policing agencies and naturalising their capacity to perform the most dirty, uncomfortable and tedious policing duties.

Similar gendered logics are evident within CSSI too. My interlocutors were generally enthusiastic about their increasing visibility in this sector arguing that they were "doing something for our nation" and that their work was about more than "keys, locks and bars". They went on to explain the particular influence women can have upon prisoners, who, they argued, often saw them as mothers. "We are like cooling tablets, like Panedol" they explained. "We can calm the prisoners and meditate tensions if they are on the verge of a riot". This narrative has become widely repeated in local debate about the roles of women in CSSI and was recounted to me by representatives of Australian Department of Foreign Affairs and Trade personnel working in Honiara and has even been used as the title of a locally published report on the subject (CSSI, 2012).

Yet, although, this attention and valuing of women officers' work is welcomed by the women themselves, the security officer "as mother" framing might also be more critically apprehended for the ways in which it upholds longstanding gendered norms reinforcing women's "natural" capacity for conflict mediation and peacebuilding work. Within many cultures of the Pacific, women's standing within society as mothers is depicted as providing them with a particular kind of gendered moral authority that is influential when they seek to intervene to reduce violent forms of masculine aggression. These same ideas are clearly in evidence when women's work within the CSSI is appraised. But constructions of female officers (maternal) authority within the agency, may also be invoked and understood by prisoners, fellow officers and superiors as a norm by which to assess the "appropriateness" of women's conduct and to undermine those women who do not adhere to this informally institutionalised "standard". This informal standard may also result in a scenario whereby women's capacities in managing inmate behaviours are assessed as an innate capacity or reflex rather than a professional skill and thus valued differently to the work undertaken by men in the same roles.[5]

As in Bougainville, efforts to improve the law and order response to VAW in SI have been amplified as part of the peacebuilding intervention with a new family protection law established in 2014 to confront the extreme levels of violence against women that were documented in a national study on the incidence rates of family violence in 2009 (SPC, 2009, p. 3).[6] There is also a national mandatory reporting policy framework in place, established to assist women suspected of exposure to violence when they come into contact with health or law and order professionals (MWYCFA SI Government, 2016, p. 24). However, the concrete effectiveness of this law is far from clear. Since its formalisation, only 18 people had been convicted of family violence offences and only one person had received a custodial sentence, suggesting weak institutionalisation in everyday practice and the persistence of strong gendered logics within the law and justice sector that privilege the integrity of the family unit over the security of individual women exposed to violence.

Conclusion

This chapter has shown that even though security sector reform has followed different patterns in Bougainville and SI, and has been shaped in differing ways by the distinctive trajectories of post-conflict transition in each context, similar gendered challenges can be identified in each site. Programmes of security sector reform have focussed on increasing women's representation as regular officers in state policing and corrections agencies, and in Bougainville, also within that country's community policing programme. These programmes have been complimented by efforts to improve the policing of gendered security so that women might have access to more effective state protections from phenomena such as familial and conjugal violence.

While all of this seems to promise a great deal for women, the analysis presented here also shows the persistence of discriminatory gender logics within security and regulatory institutions in each context which undermine the transformative content of these reforms. Perhaps surprisingly, even where customary practices uphold women's standing and their roles as mediators and arbiters of disputes, as occurs in Bougainville, these gendered logics persist. Certainly, programmes lifting women's participation in security agencies enable women to access new employment possibilities and career trajectories. But unless attention is also focussed on the gender discriminatory norms and logics that operate within these institutions, and perhaps outside them, there will remain powerful constraints shaping women's experiences as security officers within these agencies too.

Analysis of interlocutors' testimony and observations of everyday regulatory practice demonstrates that female officers' gender is not obscured by their uniform and that informal gendered logics are not overturned simply by policy innovation.

Rather, gendered logics can operate in ways that legitimate discriminatory practices both in the ways female officers' contributions to security are assessed and in the ways their workloads are allocated. Likewise, while programmes of legal reform promise, on paper at least, greater protections for women when they are exposed to phenomena such as familial or conjugal violence, the transformative impact of these policies is hard to identify in practice.

In post-conflict environments, SSR programmes constitute an important focus of the broader effort to restore rule of law and to ensure citizens have access to justice. Commitments to making gender a focus of the reform agenda are important, but do not, of themselves, usher in a new area of gender-inclusive state security. Beneath the effort to make the SSR agenda gender responsive, a range of informal and discriminatory institutional logics persist. If these remain unacknowledged and thus unaddressed, the gender-just quality of the post-conflict peace will be a tantalising but illusive promise at best.

Notes

1 This research was conducted as part of an Australian Research Council Funded Linkage Project partnered by the Australian Department of Foreign Affairs and Trade. Fieldwork was conducted in SI in August 2017 and Bougainville in February 2018.
2 In the course of my research on gender politics in the region I have encountered many cases where women have complained to me about the contemporary leniency of customary punishments, or the ways in which they, as complainants or witnesses can be deemed liable according to custom when they present testimony that is considered to damaging to male figures of authority in their families or their community.
3 A reference to the idea that simply bringing women into masculinised environments will automatically make those environments gender equal.
4 Figures supplied by in-country representative of the New Zealand Police Force International Support Group, 31 January 2018.
5 I have shown elsewhere how the idea that Bougainville's women have a natural affinity for peacebuilding has been invoked by masculine political opponents in ways that delegitimize women's claims that they have a right to participate in decision-making (George 2016).
6 This study showed that nearly two in three (ever-partnered) women (aged 15–49) have experienced physical or sexual violence, or both, inflicted by their partner – with sexual violence more common than physical violence, and incidents of severe violence also highly prevalent.

References

ABG (Autonomous Government of Bougainville). (2016, August). *Policy for women's empowerment, gender equality, peace and security*. Buka: Department of Community Development and Women's Affairs.

Australian Government. (2017). *Foreign policy white paper*. Canberra. Retrieved January 22, 2019 from www.fpwhitepaper.gov.au/foreign-policy-white-paper/chapter-seven-shared-agenda-security-and-prosperity/stepping-our

Baker, B., & Scheye, E. (2007). Multi-layered justice and security delivery in post-conflict and fragile states. *Conflict, Security and Development*, 7(4), 503–528. https://doi.org/10.1080/14678800701692944

Bastick, M. (2019). Gender and security sector reform. In Gentry, C. E., Shepherd, L., & Sjoberg, L. (Eds.), *The Routledge handbook of gender and security* (pp. 359–372). Abingdon Oxon; New York, Routledge.

Braithwaite, J., Dinnen, S., Allen, M., Braithwaite, V., & Charlesworth, H. (2010). *Pillars and shadows: Statebuilding as peacebuilding in Solomon Islands*. Canberra: ANU Press.

Boege, V. (2009). Peacebuilding and state formation in post-conflict Bougainville. *Peace Review*, *21*(1), 29–37.

Bull, M., George, N., & Curth-Bibb, J. (2019). The virtues of strangers? Policing gender violence in Pacific Island countries. *Policing and Society*, *29*(2), 155–170. https://doi.org/10.1080/10439463.2017.1311894

Chappell, L. (2014). "New," "old," and "nested" institutions and gender justice outcomes: A view from the international criminal court. *Politics & Gender*, *10*(4), 572–594.

Cooper, J. (2017, July 23). *Expanding at the margins of the state: A field experiment on community policing in Papua New Guinea*. Paper Presented at European Political Science European Political Science Association 7th Annual General Conference.

CSSI (Correctional Services Solomon Islands). (2012). *Cooling agents and Panadol: The CSSI gender audit report*. Regional Assistance Mission to Solomon Islands (RAMSI), Honiara. Unpublished; available upon request.

de Alwis, M., Mertus, J., & Sajjad, T. (2013). Women and peace processes. In C. Cohn (Ed.), *Women and wars* (pp. 169–193). Cambridge: Polity Press.

de Coning, C. (2018). Adaptive peacebuilding. *International Affairs*, *94*(2), 301–317.

Dinnen, S., & McLeod, A. (2009). Policing Melanesia: International expectations and local realities. *Policing and Society*, *19*(4), 333–353.

Dinnen, S., McLeod, A., & Peake, G. (2006). Police-building in weak states: Australian Approaches in Papua New Guinea and Solomon Islands. *Civil Wars*, *8*(2), 87–108, https://doi.org/10.1080/13698240600877221

Dinnen, S. & Haley, N. (2012). *Evaluation of the Community Officer Project in Solomon Islands (English)*. Justice for the poor research report; J4P. Washington, DC: World Bank. Retrieved from http://documents.worldbank.org/curated/en/409581468303004515/Evaluation-of-the-Community-Officer-Project-in-Solomon-Islands

Dinnen, S., & Peake, G. (2013). More than just policing: Police reform in post-conflict Bougainville. *International Peacekeeping*, *20*(5), 570–584. https://doi.org/10.1080/13533312.2013.853961

George, N. (2016). Light heat and shadows: Women's reflection on peacebuilding in post-conflict Bougainville. *Peacebuilding*, *4*(2), 166–179.

George, N. (2017). Policing "conjugal order": Gender, hybridity and vernacular security in Fiji. *International Feminist Journal of Politics*, *19*(1), 55–70. https://doi.org/10.1080/14616742.2017.1283248

George, N. (2018a). Liberal–local peacebuilding in Solomon Islands and Bougainville: Advancing a gender-just peace? *International Affairs*, *94*(6), 1329–1348.

George, N. (2018b). *Solomon Islands: A situational analysis of women's participation in peace processes* (pp. 1–12). *Monash GPS Mapping Peace project*. Retrieved from http://mappingpeace.monashgps.org/situational-analysis/solomon-islands/

George, N. (2019). Gender, security and Australia's 2018 Pacific Pivot: Stalled impetus and shallow roots. *Australian Journal of International Affairs*, *73*(3), 213–218. https://doi.org/10.1080/10357718.2019.1584155

Howley, P. (2002). *Breaking spears and mending hearts: Peacemakers and restorative justice in Bougainville*. Annandale, NSW: Federation Press.

Kokiai Tunum, M. (2003). Where is Kaea? In J. Tankunani Sirivi & M. Taleo Havini (Eds.), *As mothers of the land: The birth of the Bougainville women for peace and freedom* (pp. 7–11). Acton: ANU Press.

Mac Ginty, R. (2008). Indigenous peace-making versus the liberal peace. *Cooperation and Conflict: Journal of the Nordic International Studies Association, 43*(2), 139–163.

Mobekk, E. (2014). Gender, women and security sector reform. *International Peacekeeping 17*(2), 278–291. https://doi.org/10.1080/13533311003625142

Nelson, S. (1996). Constructing and negotiating gender in women's police stations in Brazil. *Latin American Perspectives, 23*(1), 131–148.

Panchanadeswaran, S., & Koverola, C. (2005). The voices of battered women in India. *Violence Against Women, 11*(6), 736–758.

Peake, G., & Studdard Brown, K. (2005) Policebuilding: The international deployment group in the Solomon Islands. *International Peacekeeping, 12*(4), 520–532.

Riis Andersen, L. (2011). *Security sector reform and the dilemmas of liberal peacebuilding.* DIIS Working Paper 2011:31. Danish Institute for International Studies, Copenhagen. Retrieved from http://hdl.handle.net/10419/122261

SPC (Secretariat of the Pacific Community). (2009). *Solomon Islands family health and safety study: A study of violence against women and children.* SPC, Noumea. Retrieved from https://pacific.unfpa.org/sites/default/files/pub-pdf/SolomonIslandsFamilyHealth andSafetyStudy.pdf

Salomon, C. (2003). Quand les filles ne se taisent plus: Un aspect du changement postcolonial en Nouvelle Calédonie. *Terrain: Revue d'ethnologie de l'Europe, 40*, 1–17.

Wallis, J. (2012). Building a liberal-local hybrid peace and state in Bougainville. *The Pacific Review, 25*(5), 613–635.

Whalan, J. (2010). The power of friends: The regional assistance mission to Solomon Islands. *Journal of Peace Research, 47*(5), 627–637.

Zorn, J. G. (2010). The paradoxes of sexism: Proving rape in the New Guinea courts. *Lawasia Journal*, 17–58.

9 Gender vulnerability to climate change and natural hazards

The case of Tropical Cyclone Winston, Fiji

Andreas Kopf, Michael Fink and Eberhard Weber

Introduction

Climate change and amplified natural hazards put Pacific Island Countries (PICs) particularly at risk. Even though climate change is a global issue, its impacts vary between and even within countries. In particular, many scholars as well as policy makers see women in these societies amongst the most vulnerable groups due to gender-specific roles, unequal power relations in (household) decision making and lack of access and control over resources and information (Arora-Jonsson, 2011; Denton, 2002; Kaijser & Kronsell, 2014; Terry, 2009).

Gender vulnerability to climate change and related hazards is a relatively new policy topic, both globally and locally in the South Pacific. In Fiji, local women organisations such as the Fiji Women's Crisis Centre (FWCC) or Fiji Women's Rights Movement (FWRM) have demanded gender mainstreaming into climate change policy for many years (FWRM, 2018). However, national and regional policy frameworks and guidelines only recently acknowledged the need to include climate change as an emerging issue for achieving gender equality (Government of Fiji, 2017). This lack of analytical focus on gendered vulnerabilities to climate change and related hazards in Fiji is also found in academic research. Adequate support to eliminate or reduce gendered vulnerability requires a deeper understanding of the multiple causes and factors that contribute to women's structural vulnerability in the first place and how these may affect women in the wake of climate change and natural hazards. In this chapter, we aim to contribute to closing this gap and explore the gender disparity in vulnerability to climate change-related hazards and risks in Fiji.

We approach this by relating gender as a distinct category of social differentiation to the field of climate change vulnerability and adaptation through a social vulnerability and human security lens. We argue that climate change and related impacts undermine the human security of certain socially disadvantaged groups, such as women and girls, whose capacity to cope with and adapt to such impacts is constrained by their social positioning within society. Social vulnerability here refers to the inability of specific groups of people in societies to withstand the negative effects of climate change they are exposed to (Kelly & Adger, 2000) and can therefore be seen as the antonym of human security (Watts & Bohle, 1993).

In a next step, we identify gender inequalities within the Fijian society as a baseline of vulnerability, i.e. the conditions that prevailed before Tropical Cyclone (TC) Winston struck Fiji, the focus of our case study. We focus on inequalities in socio-cultural, political and economic spheres and give special attention to gender-based violence (GBV). The TC Winston is used as an example to show gender-specific vulnerabilities to climate-induced natural hazards and to highlight the untapped potential of women for adaptation.

Methodologically, this chapter is based on a desk review of existing literature and secondary data to gain a broader understanding of the gender dimension of vulnerability and human security in Fiji. Specific information on the gendered impact of TC Winston comes from special reports from relief agencies and media. The findings are backed through vast and longstanding research activities of the authors on vulnerability and climate change adaptation in Fiji (Fink, 2010, 2016; Weber, 2012, 2014; Neef et al., 2018). This chapter concludes by considering the importance of social change to achieve gender mainstreaming into areas of climate change vulnerability and adaptation.

Social vulnerability, human security and gender

Although climate change is a global phenomenon, the countries of the Global South such as those in the Pacific are likely to be more affected due to their high exposure to its impacts and the damage these can entail. Changes in rainfall patterns and rising temperatures and sea levels expose coastal communities to climate-related hazards like coastal erosion, the salinisation of soils and freshwater sources, as well as extreme precipitation and periods of droughts. Climate-related natural hazards, such as severe TCs, have regularly caused serious socio-ecological disruptions in Fiji in the past, putting livelihoods, health and well-being of the local populations at stake. As a result of climate change, these trends are likely to become worse in the future (Mataki, Koshy, & Nair, 2008).

Over the past few decades, many academic and policy publications have highlighted that women and girls in particular are disproportionally affected by the impacts of climate hazards and change (MacGregor, 2010). The reasons for such gender-differentiated perspective on climate change are many, and reflect partly the outcome of broader social scientific discourses of the 1980s and 1990s, when gender concerns and gender mainstreaming became recognised as an important and distinct aspect of the human development agenda (Denton, 2004). Therefore, it is important to understand how women are specifically affected by climate change, as well as the conditions and processes that affect their vulnerability prior to, during and after natural hazards.

Vulnerability is a relatively old concept and has different meanings across various disciplines. In a climate change and natural hazards context, the concept of vulnerability is meant to identify those factors which lead to the susceptibility of a system to external shocks and stresses, as well as a range of options, means and capacities to cope with and adapt to any perturbations (Füssel & Klein, 2006). Chambers (1989) differentiates between the internal and external dimensions of vulnerability: the external dimension refers to the exposure of individuals and groups to external hazards and shocks, while the internal dimension refers to the means these affected populations have to respond and cope with these events and stresses. Social vulnerability is determined by the different economic, social, political, institutional and cultural contexts and conditions of groups and individuals, leading to different baseline vulnerabilities to mitigate the effects of climate hazards and change (Füssel & Klein, 2006; Gallopín, 2006).

Previous studies have shown that gender inequality is a significant dimension of social vulnerability because of its high intersectionality with other socio-structural disadvantageous factors that give rise to inequalities (Neumayer & Plümper, 2007; Enarson, 2000). For instance, women often do not have access to land, property, education and formal work, they are often excluded from decision making in many societies, and are disproportionally affected by poverty, which all limit their capacity to successfully deal with climate shocks and stresses without suffering physical and/or psychological harm (Kaijser & Kronsell, 2014). Gender inequalities result from socially and culturally constructed gendered power structures and gender-specific roles as reproducers and care takers, that tend to subjugate women to men's control or authority (Thompson-Hall, Carr, & Pascual, 2016; Alston, 2014; Denton, 2002). Such patriarchal ideas and values imply that "men hold power in all the important institutions of society", whereas "women are deprived of access to such power" (Lerner, 1986, p. 239). Nevertheless, differences exist among women as they are not a homogenous social group.

The concept of social vulnerability leads us to question the apparent social neutrality of climate change, as suggested by descriptions such as "climate change as a problem of mankind". Women's vulnerability to climate change and natural hazards is influenced by their social positioning in a male-dominated society. In order to understand their particular vulnerability, it is thus necessary to look at general gender inequalities within a society as inequalities produce socially-differentiated vulnerability. Empowerment, equal participation and decision making in public and private environments can contribute to overcome/challenge patriarchy and gender-discriminating power relations.

Human security is tied to social vulnerability. It can be conceptualised as the combination of three dimensions of freedom (Ogata & Sen, 2003). First, vulnerable people require "freedom from want", which refers to the fulfilment of basic needs. The potential negative impacts of climate change and natural hazards threaten basic means for a life in dignity. Second, human security entails "freedom from fear", i.e. to ensure people's protection from harm and violence. In the context of this study, gender-based violence (GBV) against women is a central concern (Fisher, 2010). GBV refers to acts that inflict physical, mental or sexual harm or to threats of such acts, coercion or other deprivations of freedom on the basis of gender (Chikwiri & Lemmer, 2014). Third, these freedoms must be combined with the "freedom to act on one's own behalf" (Ogata & Sen, 2003). This last freedom corresponds to the idea of (women's) empowerment, where one's agency is recognised for personal and societal fulfilments and where there is equal (or at least improved) access to assets and decision making.

Therefore, for social adaptation to climate change and hazards to be achieved, gender inequalities and vulnerability need to be addressed, also contributing to increased human security. We apply these ideas to the following case of climate-induced natural hazards in Fiji. We first look into the structural gender inequalities in the country to provide/create a gendered social vulnerability baseline, and we then explore the impacts of climate change-related natural hazards on gender inequalities.

Gender baseline vulnerability in Fiji

Despite the fact that gender inequalities are widespread worldwide, global reports on the gender gap and disparities reveal that most Pacific Island countries including Fiji rank particularly low. Key figures of the *Global Gender Gap Report* (World Economic Forum, 2018) highlight that gender inequalities in Fiji (ranked No. 125 in 2017 and 106 in 2018) remain a huge societal challenge, despite the government's commitment and actions to mainstream gender equality across various sectors and levels of policy.[1]

In this section, we look into structural gender vulnerabilities in Fiji through the lens of human security. The right of freedom to act on one's own behalf will be regarded as women's power in decision-making processes and control over resources. Freedom from want is translated here into access to resources. Women's freedom from fear is looked at in relation to GBV.

Women's limited power in decision making

As in most countries of the South Pacific, social and political organisation in Fiji is dominated by institutionalised patriarchal structures (Ravuvu, 1983). Power-based, hierarchical gender relations continue to curtail gender equality at many levels of decision making. From the national political level to the community and to the household level, women are often excluded and have less freedom to participate in decision making and leadership than men (ADB, 2016; Chattier, 2015). The community and family are among the most important social institutions within the Fijian culture and both are socially organised along traditional patriarchal norms (Chattier, 2012; Harrington, 2004). Women have traditionally little say in neither village meetings nor other community decision-making processes. Patriarchal decision making is also common practice within households, although women often have the best chance to have an influence on decisions at this level (Harrington, 2004).

Rapid modernisation and urbanisation slowly pave the way to a pervasiveness of modern Western ways of life into the traditional social fabric, which slowly contributes to a softening of traditional lifestyles (Naidu, 2003, 2006). Nonetheless, the culturally-normed division of gender roles and duties have been quite static, particularly in traditional social settings like villages (Becker, 1995; Charan, Kaur, & Singh, 2016). Women's customary roles are closely linked to reproductive and domestic duties, such as bearing and raising children, preparing meals and taking care of elders. This position constrains their public presence and impedes access to information. Traditional social perceptions of women's subordination are widespread in society. Women are expected to oblige to the decisions of men (Bolabola, 1986), which curtails women's rights to self-determination.

The unequal power distribution in terms of governance at community and household levels contribute to a large extent to the marginalisation of women in climate change adaptation and disaster risk reduction decision making as well (Charan et al., 2016). As such, women's vulnerability to climate change and hazards depends to a large extent on good decision making of men in the process of defining, planning and implementing community and household-based adaptation and coping activities and projects. As economic empowerment and the rights of women to act on their own behalf are constrained, women's human insecurity and vulnerability can increase.

Women's constrained access to resources

Women's vulnerability is further exacerbated by gender-specific disadvantages in accessing and controlling resources that affect their capacity to cope with and adapt to climate change and hazards. In this context, we will have a closer look at financial income and access to land.

Although women's participation in the labour market is increasing in Fiji, they are still underrepresented compared to men. Less than half of women's population of working age participate in the labour market, often due to prevailing gender norms, compared to 81% of men's population (Narsey, 2011). While the informal sector appears to offer the majority of employment opportunities (60%) for both men and women in Fiji, relatively more women than men are employed in the precarious and low-paid informal sector. In 2013, women's gross national income per capita (FJ\$4,100) was roughly 60% lower than those of men (FJ\$10,214) (Live and Learn & CARE, 2016). These economic trends leave women disproportionally and more frequently in economically insecure and unstable living conditions, particularly female-headed households who share a double burden of paid work and unpaid domestic care work (Government of Fiji, 2016; Live and Learn & CARE, 2016).

Women's labour market participation is significantly higher in rural than in urban areas (ADB, 2016). A gendered division of labour is common in the more agriculture and subsistence-based rural settings, with both gender groups contributing to households' income generation. Men are commonly responsible for the physically challenging work, including plantation farming, construction work, logging and fishing offshore. Women are mostly responsible for the housework including food security, though they are quite active in subsistence food production (home gardening, inshore fishing), selling of agricultural produce and the production of handicrafts. For example, the weaving of traditional mats out of pandana leaves is one common practice in rural Fiji to earn a relatively stable household income, as these mats do not easily perish and are less affected by market price fluctuations (Fink, 2016). Even though rural women contribute much to earning income, this does not necessarily translate into access and control over financial income and capital as decision making is done at the household level.

In addition to unequal access and control over financial means and decisions, land issues are of major relevance for adaptation to climate change and natural hazards. In an unmitigated climate change future, rising tides and amplified natural hazards will increase the pressure on agricultural and subsistence land (Barnett, 2011). The native Fijians, which make up the large majority of the agriculture-dependent rural population, benefit from a legal land tenure system that assigns almost 88% of the overall land to them as customary land (Prasad & Tisdell, 2006). This circumstance is a key asset for coping and adapting to environmental changes since measures for self-protection and adaptation can be implemented with a higher degree of autonomy. For instance, access and control over land makes it easier to implement the creation of new farming plots in more secure areas and even allows households and communities exposed to environmental hazards to plan and resettle to safer areas within community boundaries (Gharbaoui & Blocher, 2016; McNamara & Des Combes, 2015).

However, gender differences in land rights are often overlooked in this context. Customary land is owned by the *mataqali* (clan), who controls and allocates land parcels across *mataqali* members. The inherent land tenure system theoretically gives both male and female descendants equal access to land (Ravuvu, 1983; Bolabola, 1986). Culturally, however, women have *de facto* little say in decisions on land issues within their *mataqali* (Bolabola, 1986; Nayacakalou, 1978, p. 111). As a result of culturally constructed gender norms and power gaps, unequal access and control over resources remains a common obstacle to gender equality and women's agency in the light of climate change and related extreme events across Fiji.

Gender-Based Violence (GBV)

The Government of Fiji addresses GBV against women in many ways. For example, it issued the Domestic Violence Decree (2009) and the Child Welfare Decree (2010), it included sexual harassment in the Employment Regulation Decree, and for more than 20 years gender awareness training has been compulsory for new police recruits (Live and Learn & CARE, 2016). Nevertheless, GBV is still commonplace today for many women in Fiji. A study conducted by the FWCC (2011) reveals that 72% of all interviewed women stated that they have been victims of domestic violence. Almost two-thirds (61%) of the 3193 interviewed women have experienced physical violence, more than half (58%) have been victims of emotional violence and one-third (34%) have been sexually abused at least once in their lives, mostly by their husbands or partners. In the majority of cases, women have experienced such forms of violence more than once. Sexual violence against children is very high as well. Every one in six women (16%) was sexually abused before the age of 15, in most cases by a male family member or a friend of the family. Incidences of all forms of domestic violence appear to be higher in rural areas than in urban centres. The health effects of domestic violence are diverse, and range from serious bodily injuries to psychological complaints. In the following section we will have a closer look on how a severe cyclone impacted on the vulnerability of women.

Gender-specific impacts of cyclone Winston in Fiji

In order to gain an understanding of the gender dimensions of vulnerability to natural hazards, we analyse the post-disaster situation of TC Winston in 2016. We first provide an overview of the overall impacts of TC Winston. This is followed by an analysis of gender-specific impacts on the use of material resources, GBV and decision making.

TC Winston hit the Fijian archipelago in February 2016. This cyclone was one of the strongest recorded in the southern hemisphere. TC Winston swept with maximum average wind speeds of up to 233 km/h and wind gusts of 306 km/h across the eastern, northern and western parts of the island group (Government of Fiji, 2016). Suva, the capital of Fiji, was hardly affected. Instead, the path of TC Winston went mostly through rural areas. Overall, 350,000 people or 40% of Fiji's total population were severely affected, many of them in multiple ways and 44 fatalities were confirmed. The estimated total loss and damage was FJ$ 1.99 billion or roughly 20% of the country's gross domestic product, excluding environmental impacts on forests, mangroves and corals (ibid., 2016). More than 30,000 houses were damaged or destroyed leaving 150,000 people in need of assistance. More than 50,000 people sought shelter in roughly 1,000 formal and informal evacuation centres. Extreme wind speeds and heavy precipitation affected around 60 % of Fiji's farms. Areas close to the path of TC Winston lost up to 100 % of crops and 164,000 people needed food assistance. 250,000 people had no access to safe drinking water or sanitation.

The UN Office for the Coordination of Humanitarian Affairs (UNOCHA) coordinated the official recovery process in collaboration with humanitarian partner organisations in support of the national government (UNOCHA, 2016a). The disaster relief assistance was organised in clusters such as protection and shelter, health, food, water, sanitation and hygiene and education. Gender concerns had been a cross-cutting topic in all clusters.

Within the first few weeks, 370,000 people were provided food and emergency rations (UNOCHA, 2016b). Nevertheless, cases of severe acute malnutrition have been reported as feeding of infants and young children did not reach minimum standards (UNICEF, 2016). Relief workers distributed new seedlings in several rounds. The first round took only a few weeks and consisted of one million sweet potato seedlings, which can be ready for harvest within three months' time and was distributed to more than 45,000 families (UNOCHA, 2016b). Meanwhile, the prices of staple food like cassava doubled all over the country, which had a profound effect on the food security and livelihoods of both women and men. However, cyclone-affected households suffered the most from rising food prices. Having their basis for food and income destroyed, food scarcity has particularly caused women to suffer psychosocial stress due to their prescribed roles as food provider (Live and Learn & CARE, 2016; Kiran & Hawea, 2016).

Under the general social and economic conditions that favour men, women's labour market participation declined. Due to the destruction of plantations, it appears that men sought increased involvement in the informal sector as a coping strategy to generate income. More involved in informal employment, women were likely to be the first to be forced out (Government of Fiji, 2016). Moreover, due to the traditional gender norms and roles, women were particularly burdened with securing food and water in times of scarcity for their families and to supervise children. As a result, women had little time to engage themselves in income generating activities. The dearth of alternative coping strategies within the society led to an economic widening of the gender gap.

Regarding food insecurity, the government recognised that "anecdotal reports suggest that women and girls are offering sex in exchange for food" (Government of Fiji, 2016, p. 102). In the post-disaster assessment, the government further mentioned reports on sexual harassment, domestic violence and "requests from men for sexual favours in exchange for food" (ibid., p. 103), but no details were provided to indicate the severity, quantity and nature of sexualised GBV. There is also a lack of information from which areas in Fiji the issues were put forward and by whom. It appears that these reported issues have not been taken further up by any officials. Given the lack of reliable data, it remains unclear whether these acts of violence occurred frequently or rather exceptionally or if the reports were accurate.

Nonetheless, there was some awareness that unsafe shelter increases risks of GBV.

There are urgent concerns for women, children, the elderly and the disabled, who are often at increased risk of sexual and physical violence in such centres. [. . .] A lack of privacy, overcrowding, a lack of police presence and oversight of centres, a lack of safe water and access to hygiene materials are critical issues that need immediate action. Access to privacy and safe spaces is also needed, as well as access to information about basic services including psychosocial support. [. . .] Immediate actions [should be to] conduct protection monitoring and oversight of centres to reduce risks of harassment, physical and sexual violence. WASH [water, sanitation and hygiene] facilities in and around evacuation centres need to be safe, well lit, with separate latrines for men and women.

(GenCap & UN WOMEN, 2016, p. 2)

As a result of the growing awareness of unsafe shelter, national guidelines were produced in March 2016 to pay attention to and at least to some extent handle referrals of GBV survivors (FIJI National GBV Sub Cluster, 2016) and to furthermore identify and prioritise most vulnerable individuals such as lesbian, gay, bisexual, transgender/transsexual and intersexed (LGBTI) individuals, single woman headed households and pregnant or breastfeeding women (MWCPA, 2016). In that regard, the priority of relief workers was to distribute tarpaulins and tents as quickly as possible so that target groups could leave the centres.

Taking into account the massive destruction that took place, it can be seen as a huge success that within five weeks the number of people in evacuation centres were reduced to 300 (NDMO, 2016). The employed strategies aimed to minimise length of time spent in centres and prioritise the most vulnerable. However, immediate concerns over GBV within these centres were not addressed.

Whereas evacuation centres closed quickly, the restoration of water and sanitation infrastructure took longer. After ten weeks, some 50,000 people still had no access to safe water and 184,000 people lacked sanitation and hygiene products. By that time, all schools had started operating again; yet, many without proper shelter or sanitary facilities. Tents were used as temporary learning spaces for more than 7,700 children (UNICEF, 2016). Getting schools to start operating quickly (even in temporary settings) may have helped ease the burden of women responsible for domestic chores and childcare, as it leaves more time to women while children are attending school. Many dignity kits for girls and women were distributed through schools in order to reach the most vulnerable. These were designed to support women's self-esteem, confidence and safety as they did not only include hygiene items, but also culturally-appropriate garments, torches and whistles for protection (Inter-Agency Standing Committee, 2015). Nevertheless, the lack of sanitary school facilities might have impeded girls' attendance, and thus reduced their visibility for relief workers. Such risks have been mentioned (Live and Learn & CARE, 2016), but once again no numbers are available.

It remains uncertain if women benefitted equally from the packets households received, and to what extent the most vulnerable groups of women – single mothers, poor, pregnant, ill and elderly – have been taken special care of. For example, available data on the distribution of seedlings and other rations do not give a clear picture of gender (in)equalities. Hence, Live and Learn & CARE (2016) state the need to disaggregate beneficiaries by sex, age and household composition and to include women and minority groups in food assistance and decision-making processes for sustainable livelihoods.

Traditionally, women usually take care of household chores and raise children, thereby staying out of public affairs. The main idea to overcome the post-disaster phase was then again that women stay at home, do the household chores, cook the food and look after the children while men handled public affairs. Such task sharing might not have meant to be against women but for their safety, as villagers associate public spaces as potentially harmful (Kiran & Hawea, 2016). Yet, these are typical patterns which restrain empowerment, as it keeps women out of public and decision-making processes. Women's potentials to overcome the disaster were largely ignored and hampered. Specific knowledge women have was hardly acknowledged and utilised, neither by community leaders nor humanitarian workers (Loy, 2019), for example, on how to preserve, store and ration food.

Despite social environments that constrain their actions, women played a major role in the recovery process as it were mainly them who sought safe places for their children and grandchildren, prevented them from panicking during the event and eased post-traumatic suffering (Kiran & Hawea, 2016). Women not only share knowledge on food preservation, but women cook communally and regularly share the food they have. Additionally, women helped identifying the most vulnerable within their community (Loy, 2019). In Fiji, women build strong networks within and beyond village communities. Wives conventionally move to their husbands' villages, but they stay in touch with their kinship (Fink, 2016), they requested help from people who had not been affected. Women's skills, knowledge and networks can therefore be a key source for disaster risk reduction and climate change adaptation, which could be considered to be integrated in future institutional post-disaster relief work.

Ways forward to lower gender vulnerability in Fiji

In this chapter we have presented an explorative analysis of the gender disparity in relation to vulnerability to climate change-related hazards in Fiji. Our discussion has focussed on the nexus between gender vulnerabilities, human security and climate change. In Fiji, the security of women is undermined by their lack of power in decision making, their limited access to and control over resources and the fact that they often experience violence. This gender dynamic results in a high level of social vulnerability that has implications during natural hazards. The recovery process of TC Winston served as a case to explore how socially ascribed gender roles and norms that tend to constrain women's agency play out during natural hazards and post-disaster recovery.

From the existing documentation and secondary data that our analysis builds on, we can first of all attest that the stakeholders involved in the recovery process have done an incredible job in view of the enormous destruction caused by the cyclone. The handling of the post-disaster situation was effective as the greatest needs, such as food and shelter, were quickly addressed in the areas most affected. Moreover, awareness about gender inequality has been mainstreamed in Fiji's disaster relief work. However, we found little evidence that awareness of gender issues has also been translated into a priority area of relief work. The disaster response reports suggest that existing gender norms mainly reduced and limited women's agency to the role of food provider and caregiver during the recovery process. Women's ascribed focus and burden of being responsible for their families' food security in times of scarcity not only caused psychosocial stress among women, but also hindered them to resume or engage in income generating activities and left them out of decision-making processes. Unfortunately, the existing reports only mention these issues without giving a clear picture of the extent to which these happened and the implications for the recovery process. We thus acknowledge and recommend that much more qualitative and quantitative research be carried out to fully understand the interplay between gender norms and unequal power relations in household and community decision making and the implications of these social structures for women's social vulnerability and human (in)security during and after disasters in Fiji. Disaster relief organisations can play a role here too by ensuring that their relief work is socially inclusive and transparent and provide participation opportunities to all gender and all age groups.

Although no reliable numbers about cases of GBV during and after TC Winston exist, reports provided anecdotal evidence which suggest that sexual abuse of women has been taking place. This highlights women's specific vulnerability to violence during and after disasters. Consequently, awareness about such risks for women needs to be further increased in local communities, disaster relief and humanitarian agencies and concerns of GBV addressed and integrated into disaster preparedness, response and recovery strategies at all levels. This process could be facilitated by further research into the issue, and disaster relief organisations could work together with women affected by violence in the wake of TC Winston towards guidelines and strategies to reduce these risks in the future. This might include improved guidelines for evacuation centres to increase security of all genders against acts of violence, the reduction of overcrowding in these centres and emergency shelters, the quick installation of safe sanitary facilities and training of community members to observe and safeguard vulnerable people. Probably more important is to raise awareness in the Fijian society about the fact that issues of GBV are not the product of disasters, but are already largely existent in the society. Efforts to overcome these issues require an open, honest and critically reflective public dialogue. Such social dialogue can expand and further include general debates about issues of gender inequality in the Fijian society with the aim of a social reconfiguration and reconstruction of gender relations to build up a less vulnerable and more gender equitable society.

Note

1 For example, Fiji has ratified the Convention on the Elimination of all Forms of Discrimination Against Women (CEDAW) in 1979, and signed up to the implementation of the UN Beijing Platform for Action in 1995 at the Fourth UN Women's Conference as well as the Revised Pacific Platform for Action (RPPA) on Advancement of Women and Gender Equality (2005 to 2015) and subsequent programmes.

References

Alston, M. (2014). Gender mainstreaming and climate change. *Women's Studies International Forum, 47*, 287–294.

Arora-Jonsson, S. (2011). Virtue and vulnerability: Discourses on women, gender and climate change. *Global Environmental Change, 21*(2), 744–751.

Asian Development Bank. (2016). *Fiji country gender assessment 2015*. Mandaluyong City, Philippines: Asian Development Bank.

Barnett, J. (2011). Dangerous climate change in the Pacific Islands: Food production and food security. *Regional Environmental Change, 11*(1), 229–237.

Becker, A. E. (1995). *Body, self, and society: The view from Fiji*. Philadelphia, PA: University of Pennsylvania Press.

Bolabola, C. (1986). Fiji: Customary constraints and legal process. In *Land rights of Pacific women* (pp. 1–67). Suva: Institute of Pacific Studies.

Chambers, R. (1989). Editorial introduction: Vulnerability, coping and policy. *IDS Bulletin, 20*(2), 1–7.

Charan, D., Kaur, M., & Singh, P. (2016). Indigenous Fijian women's role in disaster risk management and climate change adaptation. *Pacific Asia Inquiry*, 7(1), 106–122.

Chattier, P. (2012). Exploring the capability approach to conceptualize gender inequality and poverty in Fiji. *Journal of Poverty*, 16(1), 72–95.

Chattier, P. (2015). Women in the house (of parliament) in Fiji: What's gender got to do with it? *The Round Table*, 104(2), 177–188.

Chikwiri, E., & Lemmer, E. M. (2014). Gender-based violence in primary schools in the Harare and Marondera Districts of Zimbabwe. *Journal of Sociology and Social Anthropology*, 5(1), 95–107.

Denton, F. (2002). Climate change vulnerability, impacts, and adaptation: Why does gender matter?. *Gender & Development*, 10(2), 10–20.

Denton, F. (2004). Gender and climate change: Giving the "latecomer" a head start. *IDS Bulletin*, 35(3), 42–49.

Enarson, E. (2000). *Gender and natural disasters*. Geneva: International Labour Organisation, Recovery and Reconstruction Department. Working Paper No. 1, Infocus Programme on Crisis Response and Reconstruction.

FIJI National GBV Sub Cluster. (2016). *Guidance on GBV case referral*. Guide for Referrals of GBV Survivors – TC Winston. Retrieved from https://gbvguidelines.org/wp/wp-content/uploads/2018/05/Fiji-National-GBV-Sub-Cluter-Guidance-on-GBV-Case-Referral.pdf

Fink, M. (2010). *Vulnerability of small islands coastal villagers to natural hazards: Participatory livelihood analysis of Malawai village, Gau Island, Fiji*. Vulnerability Mapping Working Paper No. 2, Bonn.

Fink, M. (2016). *Soziale Sicherung im Spannungsfeld gesellschaftlicher Transformation – Eine partizipative Studie in Küstendörfern der Fidschi-Inseln*. Doctoral dissertation. Goettingen: Goettingen University Press.

Fisher, S. (2010). Violence against women and natural disasters: Findings from post-tsunami Sri Lanka. *Violence Against Women*, 16(8), 902–918.

Füssel, H. M., & Klein, R. J. (2006). Climate change vulnerability assessments: An evolution of conceptual thinking. *Climatic Change*, 75(3), 301–329.

FWRM. (2018). *Submission on National Disaster Management Act (1998) and Plan (1995)*. Retrieved from www.fwrm.org.fj/images/FWRM_National-Disaster-Plan_Submisison-.pdf

Gallopín, G. C. (2006). Linkages between vulnerability, resilience, and adaptive capacity. *Global Environmental Change*, 16(3), 293–303.

GenCap & UN WOMEN. (2016, February). *TC Winston: Gender snapshot no. 129*. Suva. Retrieved from https://reliefweb.int/report/fiji/tc-winston-gender-snapshot-no-1

Gharbaoui, D., & Blocher, J. (2016). The reason land matters: Relocation as adaptation to climate change in Fiji Islands. In *Migration, risk management and climate change: Evidence and policy responses* (pp. 149–173). Cham, Switzerland: Springer.

Government of Fiji. (2016, February 20). *Fiji: Post-disaster needs assessment*. Tropical Cyclone Winston. Retrieved May 2016 from https://reliefweb.int/report/fiji/fiji-post-disaster-needs-assessment-may-2016-tropical-cyclone-winston-february-20-2016

Government of Fiji. (2017). *National adaptation plan framework*. Retrieved from https://cop23.com.fj/wp-content/uploads/2018/03/NAP-Framework-Fiji.pdf

Harrington, C. (2004). "Marriage" to capital: The fallback positions of Fiji's women garment workers. *Development in Practice*, 14(4), 495–507.

Inter-Agency Standing Committee. (2015). *Guidelines for integrating gender-based violence interventions in humanitarian action: Reducing risk, promoting resilience and aiding recovery*. Retrieved from https://gbvguidelines.org/wp/wp-content/uploads/2015/09/2015-IASC-Gender-based-Violence-Guidelines_lo-res.pdf

Kaijser, A., & Kronsell, A. (2014). Climate change through the lens of intersectionality. *Environmental Politics, 23*(3), 417–433.

Kelly, P. M., & Adger, W. N. (2000). Theory and practice in assessing vulnerability to climate change and facilitating adaptation. *Climatic Change, 47*(4), 325–352.

Kiran, S., & Hawea, J. (2016). *Voices from ground zero; A FRIEND experience post TC Winston in Ra province, Fiji: Foundation for Rural Integrated Enterprises & Development (FRIEND)*. Retrieved from http://friendfiji.com/wp-content/uploads/2016/07/Voices-from-Ground-Zero-a-FRIEND-experience-post-TC-Winston-in-Ra-province-Fiji.pdf

Lerner, G. (1986). *The creation of patriarchy*. Oxford: Oxford University Press.

Live and Learn & CARE. (2016). *Rapid Gender Analysis – TC Winston, Fiji*. Retrieved from www.sheltercluster.org/sites/default/files/docs/ll-care_tcwinston_rapidgenderanalysis.pdf

Loy, I. (2019, January 30). *Fiji's unheralded frontline disaster responders: Women*. The New Humanitarian. Retrieved from www.thenewhumanitarian.org/interview/2019/01/09/qa-how-include-more-local-women-emergency-response

MacGregor, S. (2010). "Gender and climate change": From impacts to discourses. *Journal of the Indian Ocean Region, 6*(2), 223–238.

Mataki, M., Koshy, K., & Nair, V. (2008). Top-down, bottom-up: Mainstreaming adaptation in Pacific island townships. *Climate Change and Adaptation*, 264–277.

McNamara, K. E., & Des Combes, H. J. (2015). Planning for community relocations due to climate change in Fiji. *International Journal of Disaster Risk Science, 6*(3), 315–319.

MWCPA. (2016, March 31). *Fiji Tropical Cyclone Winston: Safety & protection: Identifying and prioritising vulnerable populations for humanitarian and recovery*. Ministry of Women, Children and Poverty Alleviation: Safety and Protection Cluster, Suva. Retrieved from https://reliefweb.int/report/fiji/safety-protection-identifying-and-prioritising-vulnerable-populations-humanitarian-and

Naidu, V. (2003). Modernization and development in the South Pacific. In A. Jowitt & T. N. Cain (Eds.), *Passage of change: Law, society and governance in the Pacific* (pp. 7–31). Canberra: ANU Press.

Naidu, V. (2006). The state of the state in Fiji: Some failings in the periphery. In S. Firth (Ed.), *Globalisation and governance in the Pacific Islands* (pp. 297–316). Canberra: ANU Press.

Narsey, W. (2011). *Report on the 2008–09 household income and expenditure survey*. Suva: Fiji Bureau of Statistics.

National Disaster Management Office (NDMO). (2016). *National Emergency Operations Centre. Tropical Cyclone Winston*. Situation Report 122 of 28/03/2016: National Disaster Management Office. Retrieved from ttps://reliefweb.int/report/fiji/national-emergency-operation-center-tropical-cyclone-winston-situation-report-122

Nayacakalou, R. R. (1978). *Tradition and change in the Fijian village*. Suva: South Pacific Social Sciences Association.

Neef, A., Benge, L., Boruff, B., Pauli, N., Weber, E., & Varea, R. (2018). Climate adaptation strategies in Fiji: The role of social norms and cultural values. *World Development, 107*, 125–137.

Neumayer, E., & Plümper, T. (2007). The gendered nature of natural disasters: The impact of catastrophic events on the gender gap in life expectancy, 1981–2002. *Annals of the Association of American Geographers, 97*(3), 551–566.

OCHA. (2016a). *Fiji: Severe Tropical Cyclone Winston.* Situation Report No. 20 (as of 31 March 2016). Retrieved from https://reliefweb.int/report/fiji/fiji-severe-tropical-cyclone-winston-situation-report-no-20-31-march-2016

OCHA. (2016b, April 22). *Humanitarian Bulletin. Cyclone Winston – Fiji.* Retrieved from https://reliefweb.int/sites/reliefweb.int/files/resources/220416_humanitarian_bulletin.pdf

Ogata, S., & Sen, A. (2003). *Human security now.* Final Report of the Commission on Human Security, Japanese Government and UNDP, Tokyo, Japan.

Prasad, B. C., & Tisdell, C. A. (2006). *Institutions, economic performance and sustainable development: A case study of the Fiji islands.* New York: Nova Publishers.

Ravuvu, A. (1983). *Vaka i Taukei: The Fijian way of life.* Suva: Institute of Pacific Studies of the University of the South Pacific.

Terry, G. (2009). No climate justice without gender justice: An overview of the issues. *Gender & Development, 17*(1), 5–18.

Thompson-Hall, M., Carr, E. R., & Pascual, U. (2016). Enhancing and expanding inter-sectional research for climate change adaptation in agrarian settings. *Ambio, 45*(3), 373–382.

UNICEF. (2016). *Partner update.* Cyclone Winston in Fiji & News from the Pacific. Retrieved from https://reliefweb.int/report/fiji/unicef-pacific-partner-update-cyclone-winston-fiji-and-news-pacific-1-april-30-april.

Watts, M. J., & Bohle, H. G. (1993). The space of vulnerability: The causal structure of hunger and famine. *Progress in Human Geography, 17*(1), 43–67.

Weber, E. (2012). Climate and environmental change and food security. *Journal of Pacific Studies, 32*, 99–110.

Weber, E. (2014). Environmental change and (Im)mobility in the South. In *A new perspective on human mobility in the south* (pp. 119–148). Global Migration Issues, 3. Dordrecht: Springer.

World Economic Forum. (2018). *The global gender gap report 2018.* Geneva: Switzerland. Retrieved from http://www3.weforum.org/docs/WEF_GGGR_2018.pdf

10 Can theology contribute to the security of women in the Pacific household?

Richard A. Davis

Introduction

Many women in the Pacific find their personal security most at risk at home, with wife-beating at epidemic proportions in Pacific Island Countries (PICs) with up to two-thirds of women being beaten or sexually violated by their intimate partner (UNFPA, 2019). These same nations have very high rates of Christian adherence and church attendance. In this context, individuals and organisations are increasingly realising that churches and Christian theology have an important part to play in reducing rates of violence against women and increasing the personal security of women. This chapter will consider proposals from three organisations who, in wishing to eliminate or reduce rates of violence against women, have tried to apply Christian teachings or theology to this problem. First, the Pacific Community, in promoting the human rights of women, have sought help from theologians in understanding and overcoming religious and cultural objections to human rights. Second, UnitingWorld, the Uniting Church of Australia's development agency, has developed a theological framework to promote gender equality. Third, the Fiji Council of Churches has promoted 16 Days of Activism in Fiji suggesting that "Gender Based Violence is a Sin". This chapter will consider these proposals in brief, and then discuss how a focus on human security and its concern with fear can help assist theology make an important complementary contribution to improving the situation of battered women in PICs.

This paper is about "wife-beating". The term has been selected with care. Today we are faced with an ever-expanding range of euphemistic terms to describe this topic: "gender-based violence", "intimate partner violence", "spouse assault", "violence against women" and "family violence". Some of these terms can diminish the impact of actual violence or make it appear that men and women suffer in the same way to the same extent (Dobash & Dobash, 1979, pp. 11–12; cf. UNFPA, 2016). Some of these terms are wider, encompassing any violence against women in society, including that which takes place in public. I want to be specific and focus on wife-beating, meaning the violence of a husband against his wife in the home. My focus on wife-beating is also because this is a common form of violence against women in PICs and also because this is where the church has a lot to repent of in its patriarchal theology and where it can challenge patriarchal theology. While this might not be inclusive of other cohabitating couples in PICs, heterosexual marriage remains the norm for most family households.

The Pacific Community and human rights

The Pacific Community or PC (formerly the Secretariat of the Pacific Community) is the scientific and technical agency of 26 member countries and territories in the South Pacific. The Pacific Community's Regional Rights Resource Team (RRRT) has a mandate to promote human rights and has a programme to encourage PICs to eliminate violence against women through human rights legislation and other legal instruments (Regional Rights Resource Team). On 25 April 2016 I received an invitation from the director of the RRRT that included these words: "RRRT recognises the crucial role religion plays in Pacific society and the role churches have to play in assisting the pursuit of human rights. All too often human rights are seen as an opposing force to the church or contradict religious or cultural beliefs and practices. RRRT hopes that with support from Pacific theologians will work with churches primarily through regional networking bodies to develop tools for pastors, priests, church leaders in finding resonation between human rights and scriptures" (letter to author, 2016). Accepting the invitation, I agreed to address the RRRT on the topic of "Human Rights and Christianity from a Theologian's Perspective" on 29 April 2016.

The human rights approach is one way to promote the security of women in the Pacific. In this context, such an approach will require overcoming objections to human rights as unchristian and as Western impositions. What can theology add to this? To many Pacific Christians, human rights are viewed with deep suspicion. Among other factors, this is due to the fear that parental control of children will be eroded and that human rights are opposed to the cultures of PICs. Could a theology of human rights address these concerns? This is not as straightforward as the RRRT wishes it to be. There are theologians who support human rights (Bird, 2018; Maritain, 1944; Moltmann, 1984, 1999; Wolterstorff, 2008) and there are theological opponents of human rights (Hauerwas, 1986; MacIntyre, 1984; Milbank, 2012; O. O'Donovan, 2009; J. L. O'Donovan, 1996, 1997), with varying degrees of sophistication in their argumentation. In PICs, human rights are rightly perceived as a threat to patriarchal cultures and theologies, which explains some of the resistance to this human rights agenda in the Pacific. Overall the promotion of human rights in the Pacific will involve long-term cultural change, with theology able to play a part in that through education about rights and the equality of women with men. The RRRT may be disappointed, however, to find that theology does not universally or uncritically support human rights and therefore cannot uncritically support their human rights agenda.

Uniting World's framework paper

In an attempt for the church to make a difference to gender-based violence, UnitingWorld developed a "Framework Paper on Human Dignity and Gender

Equity from a Biblical-Theological Perspective" (Bird, 2016). Prepared by theologian Rev. Dr. Cliff Bird from the Solomon Islands, the Framework paper is not focussed primarily on the issue of violence, but patriarchy in general. It states: "gender-based violence, violence against women and children and domestic violence are too frequently the outplaying reality of such unequal gender roles and relationships" (Bird, 2016, p. 3). In short, the Framework Paper deals with violence secondarily, as deriving from the secondary status women have in the Pacific region. What difference can this paper and its focus on gender inequality make to wife-beating?

According to Bird, patriarchy, the main target of his paper, stems from three sources. These are Western (or Aristotelian) philosophy, theology and biblical interpretation and the cultures and traditions of PICs (Bird, 2016, p. 15). To avoid any blame for patriarchy accruing to Christianity, Bird makes the point that patriarchy pre-existed Judaism and Christianity, neither of which "introduced patriarchy into the world" (Bird, 2016, p. 11). He goes on to state that: "Patriarchy is a very ancient and widespread system of male domination, and both Judaism and Christianity proved incapable of successfully opposing this system" (Bird, 2016, p. 11). While patriarchy is indeed found in Judaism and Christianity, this is a troubling statement for Christians, since it implies that Christianity *could not*, or even *cannot*, resist patriarchy, and is therefore an intrinsic part of the problem. Indeed, there are feminists, such as Daphne Hampson and Mary Daly, who declared as much in their leaving the Christian faith for this reason. On the positive side, Bird does believe that the Bible can impact patriarchy by promoting a biblically-based advocacy of gender equality. This document, therefore, has the advantage of striking at what many scholars and activists see as the source of gender-based violence – patriarchy (Dobash & Dobash, 1979, p. ix). It is also based on the Bible, which holds great authority in PICs, even beyond churches. This is important, but it is not the only place one can make inroads into the issue. Despite this positive teaching, Bird fails to confront how the very Bible he uses to promote gender equality has been used to promote patriarchal domination and fear (for instance he does not confront Ephesians 5:33, discussed below). It is not simply that his presentation of the issue is one-sided, it is that it does not challenge prevailing patriarchal interpretation head-on. Overall the paper can make a positive impact, but this is an indirect response to the problem of wife-beating and one that does not deal solidly with the reasons or theological justifications for entrenched wife-beating in PICs.

16 Days of activism

A final church intervention is worth mentioning. The Fiji Council of Churches have given prominence to the issue of gender-based violence during the annual 16 days of activism that occurs between the International Day for the Elimination of Violence against Women (25 November) and Human Rights Day (10 December). In 2017, the campaign featured photographs of church leaders under the heading "Gender Based Violence is a Sin". Using the language of "sin" makes it clear to the Christians of Fiji that gender-based violence is prohibited. However, questions can be raised over what exactly is the sin being committed and by whom. My concern here is that "gender based violence" is an abstract sociological term that covers several forms of violence based on the idea that gender is the basis for the violence. Neither does the term highlight the predominant forms of violence that are being committed and by men against women in the home. What should have been condemned more clearly by the churches is wife-beating. The slogan "Hitting Your Wife is a Sin" would, I believe, have had more impact.

Recent attempts to bring theology and church into the issue of violence against women in PICs are be applauded. Much of the contribution of theology and the churches has been in the field of prevention of violence against women. This is important, as it attempts to cut off violence and its justifications at their origins. It is hoped that these initiatives are making a difference. Yet achieving gender equality and the improving situation of women does not automatically decrease their chance of being victims of violence. In a paper from the Solomon Islands, Asenati Liki reports that women who rise into leadership positions in PICs can still be victims of domestic violence (2013). She writes that a broader approach is needed: "Attention must therefore be paid also to other areas or groups that work on increasing awareness campaign on gender equality. These include local women's church or village groups and NGOs" (Liki, 2013, p. 143). Others have questioned the focus on patriarchy being the sole source of domestic violence (Tracy, 2007). In short, the issue of wife-beating needs a multifaceted approach.

With the aim of extending the scope of theological and church-based contributions to the issue, I will now consider what bringing a security focus to the issue of gender-based violence can contribute to the churches' action and theological reflection on this issue.

A security framework

There are many ways the plight of battered women can be described. Are these women victims of violent crimes? Have their human rights been violated? Another way of looking at them is through the focus of "human security". In applying the framework of security to this issue, it should be noted that the notion of security has taken a non-statist turn in recent times (Tadjbakhsh & Chenoy, 2007). Security is no longer just about international borders and threats to the state, but includes persons, households and communities (Ogata & Cels, 2003). This development is based on belief that the security of the state is meaningless if people do not also experience the security of their bodily person. The remainder of this paper will explore the human security of battered women and how theology, or Christian teachings, can have a positive impact on the security of women in the Pacific household.

The notion of "human security" was given prominence through the Human Development Report of 1994, subtitled "New Dimensions of Human Security". The report divides human security into several dimensions. The relevant one here is the notion of "personal security", which lists different ways "human life is increasingly threatened by sudden, unpredictable violence" including "threats directed against women (rape, domestic violence)" (UNDP, 1994, p. 30). Elaborating on this theme, the report goes on to say: "Among the worst personal threats are those to women. In no society are women secure or treated equally to men. Personal insecurity shadows them from cradle to grave. . . . And from childhood through adulthood, they are abused because of their gender. . . . It was recently estimated that one-third of wives in developing countries are physically battered" (UNDP, 1994, p. 31).

Elaborating on the issue of human security, the United Nations (UN) General Assembly made a resolution in 2012 (66/290) which included this clause:

(a) The right of people to live in freedom and dignity, free from poverty and despair. All individuals, in particular vulnerable people, are entitled to freedom from fear and freedom from want, with an equal opportunity to enjoy all their rights and fully develop their human potential;

Women, therefore, according to the UN, have a right to live free from want and from fear, including fear of violence in the home. In cases of wife-beating, these factors are interrelated; escaping one's violent husband is one way to escape violence, but this action can bring the fear of losing one's means of subsistence or can lead to the wife staying in a violent relationship for their own financial security and the sake of her children.

What does personal security look like theologically? The rest of this paper is concerned with how in the context of the Pacific, the church and its theology can contribute positively to the promotion of the personal security of women in the home. As I will show, theology can contribute in both negative and positive ways. Theology must identify and confess those ways in which the church and its theology have a negative influence and how they might contribute more positively.

Freedom from fear

In recent years the theme of fear and wife-beating, seems to be getting more attention (e.g. Gill, 2004; Van Hightower, Gorton, & DeMoss, 2000; Pain, 2012; Brysk, 2018). There are, however, few theological studies of fear and wife-beating. Recent theological studies of fear appear to fall into one of two categories, either fear of the stranger, such as immigrants (e.g. Willimon, 2016) or anxiety-inducing fear of the future (e.g. Bader-Saye, 2007). Collectively such books suggest that fear is a sign of spiritual weakness. Christians should be welcoming the stranger, not fearing them (e.g. Leviticus 19:33–34; Hebrews 13:1–2) and they should be fearing the providing God alone, not an uncertain future (Luke 12:4–6). Fear is also an important factor in atheist objections to Christian faith. Consider Bertrand Russell's view that religion is based on "fear of the mysterious, fear of defeat, fear of death" (Russell, 1957, p. 22). To Russell, fear demonstrates intellectual weakness and lack of courage to face a godless world. Overall the messages from Christian theologians and atheist philosophers are similar: fear is something to be ashamed of because it is a product of dehumanising xenophobia, lack of trust in

God and a lack of courage. In short, for the Christian, fear of the unknown demonstrates lack of faith in God; only fear of God can be spoken about favourably.

There are many verses in scripture which extort us not to be afraid. Take John 14:27, as just one example: "Do not let your hearts be troubled, and do not let them be afraid" (New Revised Standard Version). This may be a comforting verse for those with anxiety and fear of an unknown future, but in the case of a wife's fear of her husband, such verses are of limited use. It is a stereotype that women should fear the unknown rapist or mugger encountered in public after dark. In fact, women have more legitimate fears from intimate partners at home (Schüssler Fiorenza, 1994, pp. viii–ix). This is not fear of the stranger, or fear of the unknown, this is fear of the known and even fear of the beloved, a fear little known in scripture or to the theological tradition.

Although fear is rarely discussed by theologians, they could make a major contribution to its understanding. As an emotion or affection, fear is well known to theologians and biblical scholars as a central theme in the Bible. It is first mentioned when Adam and Eve feared God after eating the forbidden fruit (Genesis 3:10). Elsewhere in scripture, the fear of God is promoted as the beginning of wisdom (e.g. Job 28:28; Proverbs 9:10). More relevant is the fear between men and women, which can be examined through two New Testament texts, in Paul's letter to the Ephesians and in the story of Mary's pregnancy.

The first biblical text I wish to explore comes from Saint Paul's letter to the Ephesians, where wives are commanded to fear their husband (at least according to some translations of the Greek word *phobeō* in Ephesians 5:33). In many modern translations (e.g. New International Version, New Revised Standard Version) this verse reads that wives should "respect" their husbands. In some other, still used, translations (e.g. Douay-Rheims, American Standard Version) this reads that wives must "fear" their husbands. The full verse in the New Revised Standard Version translation reads: "Each of you, however, should love his wife as himself, and a wife should respect her husband". We should not be too comforted by the exhortation for men to love their wives and for modern replacement of "respect" for "fear". In practice, these more appealing wordings make little difference in PICs, where respect may be encouraged through generating fear in the other.

Wifely fear is not only promoted by the Bible; it is also promoted by patriarchal theological traditions. Not untypical is the work of the Englishman John Dod (*c.* 1549–1645), a widely-read Puritan clergyman, also known as "Decalogue Dod", who wrote in the book that earned him this nickname of the particular duties of wives in his exposition of the Fifth Commandment:

> And first, the wife must fear her husband; as is commanded in Ephes. 5.33. Let the wife see that she fear her husband. . . . So, if ever the wife will be comfortable, and profitable to her husband, and do any good in the family, she must have a care of her heart, and look that she carry an inward fear to her husband. For, the husband is the wives [sic] head, even as Christ is the head of the Church: and even as the Church must fear Christ Jesus, so must the wives also fear their husbands. And this inward fear, must be shewed by

an outward meekness, and lowliness in her speeches, and carriage to her husband. . . . For if there be not fear and reverence in the inferior, there can be no sound nor constant honour yielded to the superior.

(Dod, 1622, p. 217)

In addition to fear is the exoneration for wives to obey their husbands. This is related to fear, for fear encourages obedience, as every lawmaker knows. When consequences of disobedience are pain or suffering, obedience is encouraged. To contribute to the reduction of fear in Pacific households, the churches need to find ways to talk about this text of terror for women in order to lessen the harm literal patriarchal readings of scripture do.

I now turn to a more helpful text, the narrative of Mary's pregnancy. The biblical story of the birth of Christ relates the fear of both Mary and Joseph at the news of her virginal pregnancy. Luke's gospel records that Mary's only fear appears to be of the angel who announces her pregnancy (Luke 1:26–38). Yet culturally she must have known how her culture might judge her as an unmarried pregnant woman. According to Elizabeth Johnson (2003), before receiving Joseph's final acceptance (Matthew 1:18–25) Mary was faced with "nothing but public disgrace, endless shame, perhaps a life of begging, perhaps even death looked before her" (p. 230).

It is only Matthew's gospel that mentions Joseph's fears on hearing the news of Mary's pregnancy:

Her husband Joseph, being a righteous man and unwilling to expose her to public disgrace, planned to dismiss her quietly. But just when he had resolved to do this, an angel of the Lord appeared to him in a dream and said, 'Joseph, son of David, do not be afraid to take Mary as your wife, for the child conceived in her is from the Holy Spirit.

(Matthew 1:19–20, New Revised Standard Version)

In the end, Joseph and Mary overcame their fears and were married and Mary gave birth to Jesus. There is no mention of violence here; Joseph planned to slip away quietly, even though, in the words of Augustine, "he could draw no other conclusion than that she was an adulteress" (2001, p. 76). In similar situations, a woman who gets pregnant from a source other than their partner could well fear violence from their male partner. In PICs both men and women believe that men are justified in beating their wives who are suspected adulterers (Pacific Community, 2016, p. 2; UNIFEM, 2010, pp. 14, 16).

Can this story offer any hope or comfort to women fearing rage and violence from husbands who suspect that their wife has been unfaithful? If biblical scholars and theologians, following Augustine's lead, are able to highlight the possibility that Joseph suspected that Mary was unfaithful to him and yet was not violent, then men can be encouraged to be gracious to those suspected of adultery, as Jesus's example shows in the case of the women accused of adultery (John 7:53–8:11). Pacific men, following the example of Joseph and Jesus, can help to eliminate fear at such situations, rather than threaten violence.

Freedom from want

While not as important here as freedom from fear, we should not ignore the other significant part of human security, freedom from want. This does not simply mean meeting one's basic human needs for food, water, shelter and clothing. Too often women must balance these two freedoms and many abused women have little option to stay living in fear of violence because they have nowhere to go where they are free from both fear and want. So while want may be a threat women face in addition to fear, here it may be a competing concern. In their study of violence against wives, Dobash and Dobash asked a woman who had left her violent husband why she stayed with him as long as she did. Her reply was: "Fear, I think. Fear of going, fear of staying" (Dobash & Dobash, 1979, p. 147). Women in PICs, as in other places, might have to decide between living in fear in their own home or facing poverty and disgrace when they leave that home (Ferraro & Johnson, 1983, p. 331). As I will show below, the church has a role to play in addressing this fear in PICs.

What can theology offer to the security of women?

Given this mixed record of the Christian scripture and tradition, what can theology contribute? The contribution of theology to the personal security of women in PICs will be in its own area of expertise that is in the promotion of Christian living, based on Christian teachings and practices. When thinking of theology, it is more accurate to think about theologies in the plural. Without wishing to reinforce the problematic modern division of public and private spheres, I wish to consider domestic and public theologies.

A helpful indigenous theology from the Pacific could be the "domestic theology" promoted by Tongan feminist theologian Keiti Ann Kanongata'a in a brief 1996 article in the *Pacific Journal of Theology*. Domestic theology offers a way of reflecting theologically on the domestic sphere largely occupied by women. Kanongata'a asks: "where is God in our domestic lives? What is God saying to us in our homes?" (1996, pp. 73–74). These are good questions to develop a contextual theology based on women's experience. Responses to Kanongata'a published alongside her brief article were appreciative, but cautious. Respondents expressed justified fears that domestic theology could perpetuate household hierarchies, patriarchy and the marginalisation of mothering (Lisa Meo & Ranjini Rebera in Kanongata'a, 1996, p. 75). Yet Kanongata'a's domestic theology was not some romantic notion that could be controlled by men. Kanongata'a wrote that domestic theology "will involve marriage, family, relationships, culture, sexuality and – violence, violence, violence" (1996, p. 74). Attention to violence in the domestic setting could be a constructive contribution of feminist theological reflection.

A turn to "domestic theology" should not diminish the contribution of public theological reflection to the issue of wife-beating. Public theology, with its focus on offering theological reflections on public issues, along with activist and feminist scholars, has brought to light the public nature of domestic violence.

It is notable that in 2017 the Centre of Theology and Public Issues at the University of Otago initiated the New Zealand Institute for Pacific Research funded research project "Tatala le ta'ui a le Atua: Rolling Out the Fine Mat of Scripture", which investigated the question of "How can the churches offer effective leadership in response to violence against women in Samoa?" (New Zealand Institute for Pacific Research, 2018). This project included conferences held at the Pacific Theological College, the University of Auckland and Piula Theological College. An emphasis of this work has been that wife-beating is no longer a purely private affair; being brought into the open, it is becoming a concern of the church and the public.

This public theological response is important since "domestic violence" could be a preferred name for the wife-beating that takes place in the private household and beyond the interest or expertise of clergy. The churches' reluctance in intervening in the family can make the church a fearful thing for the fearful wife. The fear of the wife toward her husband might be a private, even personal, thing. The fear that an abused wife has of the church and society that may condemn her, is a public indictment on the church and society and a matter of urgent importance for the churches to address.

Applying a security framework with its emphasis on fear to the work done on reducing violence against women in the Pacific reveals several things. It would be fair to say that most work by theologians has been done on reducing the underlying causes of violence in seeking gender equality. While this is important, this is not enough to increase the security of women. Likewise, improving the human rights frameworks are also important to preventing violence and to reporting of perpetrators, but they only go so far.

A focus on fear, as the concern of human security, adds something to these approaches – it addresses the non-violent control created and sustained by fear of violence, even if no physical violence takes place. It also highlights how women are caught between competing fears. They fear for their lives in staying with a domineering intimate partner; they fear for themselves and their children if they leave their home. This might be a freedom of want by leaving their primary income earning husband. It might be fear of the shame brought on their family by such an action. It might cause problems with the church, family, employers and other social factors. Taking this security focus on fear seriously, how might the church responds to these fears? There are several practical things that can be done by the Pacific churches and theologians to provide ways for women to leave their homes to escape dangerous fear-filled situations.

First, the church can preach mutual respect for husband and wife (Bird, 2016, p. 32), and oppose the notion that a wife should fear her husband, or that a husband can expect fear from his wife as a part of respect. The same goes for obedience and the fear of the consequences of disobedience (Davis, 2018).

Secondly, the church can teach that it is not a sin for the wife to leave her husband under certain circumstances. To paraphrase Christ, marriage was made for couples, not couples for marriage. Any separation or divorce is lamentable, but better than ongoing physical violence or even the murder of a wife by her husband.

Thirdly, the church, in addressing freedom from both fear and want, can create or assist places of sanctuary for women who have to leave their homes to escape dangerous fear-filled situations. This is not some liberal undermining of marriage, but is the protection of life itself, which is more important than marriage. Can the church become a refuge for women of the kind that Psalm 55:8 might inspire: "I would hurry to find a shelter for myself from the raging wind and tempest." In practice, can churches help women who wish to leave their abusive husbands in practical ways? In Fiji there are the beginnings of such moves, with the Salvation Army operating three safe houses for "vulnerable women and children" (The Salvation Army New Zealand, Fiji, Tonga and Samoa Territory). In 2019 the Catholic Church in Fiji announced plans to build a safe house for "Women and Girls who need love and protection" (Fiji Roman Catholic Archdiocese of Suva, 2019). Such leadership from the churches can encourage Pacific communities and families who traditionally support their members to do so in times of wife-beating too. In such cases, women may need to know that such help will be forthcoming should the occasion arise. If villagers and family are encouraged to do so by the church, this could reinforce the idea that such help is justified and warranted.

Fourthly, the churches can promote legislation to protect women from the perpetrators of violence. Here engaging with the RRRT in dialogue is one way forward to greater understanding of their human rights agenda, replacing outright dismissal of human rights and the need for family protection legislation. Moves to protect women might include finding ways to remove violent men from communities where they have committed violent crimes against women.

Fifthly, the church can work on its own teachings and practices and become places that are not feared by women who are seeking help and support. The church could become a place of welcome and help, not a place of judgment and condemnation. Ideally, women should not fear revealing to clergy or church officers that they are being beaten at home or fear that they will be blamed for doing so.

Finally, theology can help in showing that feminism is not just some "Western" agenda. Contrary to patriarchal forces in the Pacific that seek to contain the progress of women, the Pacific has produced many women who have stood for the rights of women and promoted equality. For instance, the inaugural Pacific Feminist Forum in November 2016, which brought together more than 100 feminists from across the Pacific region, issued the Pacific Feminist Charter (Pacific Feminist Forum, 2016). These and other women from around the non-Western world have advocated for their full inclusion in society and protection from violence. Within theological circles, the Weavers programme of the South Pacific Association of Theological Schools has also advocated for women in theology and has published Pacific feminist theology (SPATS; Johnson & Filemoni-Tofaeono, 2003). Overall, however, Pacific feminist theologies and voices have a precarious minority existence. Hopefully the churches of PICs can begin to teach the truth that the feminist view that women are fully human and deserve their full humanity is also fully compatible with Christian teaching, biblical interpretation and being a Pacific Islander.

Conclusion

In this chapter I have applied the notion of personal security to the problem of wife-beating in PICs and discussed what theology can do to promote the security of women. Practically theology and Christian practice has had an ambiguous record in helping women. In the heavily patriarchal cultures of PICs it is no surprise that biblical interpretation and theology can harm women and not liberate them. Yet theology has several resources to help women affirm their security. Adding a security focus to the issue of wife-beating draws our attention to the some of the specific things the church and its theology can do to address the fears Pacific women have of violence and want. This focus on fear makes us alert to the issues of biblical interpretation and the necessity of separating women from situations of violence.

References

Augustine. (2001). Letter 153: Augustine to Macedonius. In E. M. Atkins & R. J. Dodaro (Eds.), *Augustine: Political writings* (pp. 71–88). Cambridge: Cambridge University Press.

Bader-Saye, S. (2007). *Following Jesus in a culture of fear*. Grand Rapids, MI: Brazos Press.

Bird, C. (2016). *Framework paper on human dignity and gender equity from a biblical-theological perspective*. Sydney: UnitingWorld.

Bird, C. (2018, April 12). *Responding to domestic violence: An ecumenical voice to broken families*. A Public Lecture at Pacific Theological College, Suva, Fiji Islands.

Brysk, A. (2018). *The struggle for freedom from fear: Contesting violence against women at the frontiers of globalization*. New York: Oxford University Press.

Davis, R. (2018). Domestic violence in Oceania: The sin of disobedience and the violence of obedience. In C. Blyth, E. Colgan, & K. B. Edwards (Eds.), *Rape culture, Gender violence, and religion: Christian perspectives* (pp. 143–158). Cham, Switzerland: Palgrave Macmillan.

Dobash, R., & Dobash, R. (1979). *Violence against wives: A case against the patriarchy*. New York: Free Press.

Dod, J. (1622). *A plaine and familiar exposition of the Ten commandements. With a methodicall short catechisme, containing briefly the principall grounds of Christian religion* (The fifteenth ed., newly corr. and amended by the author). London: Printed by Richard Field, for Thomas Man, dwelling in Pater-Noster row, at the signe of the Talbot. Retrieved from https://catalog.hathitrust.org/Record/012454029

Ferraro, K. J., & Johnson, J. M. (1983). How women experience battering: The process of victimization. *Social Problems, 30*(3), 325–339.

Fiji Roman Catholic Archdiocese of Suva. (2019). *'God created women and children' 2019 lenten appeal*. Retrieved from www.archdioceseofsuva.org/news-&-events-march-2019-05.html

Gill, A. (2004). Voicing the silent fear: South Asian women's experiences of domestic violence. *The Howard Journal of Criminal Justice, 43*(5), 465–483.

Hauerwas, S. (1986). *Suffering presence: Theological reflections on medicine, the mentally handicapped and the church*. Notre Dame, IN: University of Notre Dame Press.

Johnson, E. A. (2003). *Truly our sister: A theology of Mary in the communion of saints*. New York: Continuum.

Johnson, L., & Filemoni-Tofaeono, J. (Eds.). (2003). *Weavings: Women doing theology in Oceania*. Suva: Institute of Pacific Studies.

Kanongata'a, K. A. (1996). Domestic theology. *The Pacific Journal of Theology Series II*, *15*, 73–75.

Liki, A. (2013). Leading the march for gender equality? women leaders in the public services of Samoa and Solomon islands. In D. Hegarty & D. Tryon (Eds.), *Politics, development and security in Oceania* (pp. 139–145). Canberra: ANU Press.

MacIntyre, A. (1984). *After virtue: A study in moral theory* (2nd ed.). Notre Dame, IN: University of Notre Dame Press.

Maritain, J. (1944). *The rights of man and natural law*. London: Geoffrey Bles: The Centenary Press.

Milbank, J. (2012). Against human rights: Liberty in the Western tradition. *Oxford Journal of Law and Religion*, *1*(2012), 203–234.

Moltmann, J. (1984). *On human dignity: Political theology and ethics* (M. Douglas Meeks, trans.). London: SCM Press.

Moltmann, J. (1999). *God for a secular society: The public relevance of theology*. Minneapolis, MN: Fortress Press.

New Zealand Institute for Pacific Research. (2018). *Tatala le ta'ui a le Atua: Rolling out the fine mat of scripture*. Retrieved from web.archive.org/web/20190126121000/https://www.nzipr.ac.nz/2018/07/04/tatala-le-taui-a-le-atua-rolling-out-the-fine-mat-of-scripture/

O'Donovan, J. L. (1996). Historical prolegomena to the theological review of human rights. *Studies in Christian Ethics*, *9*, 52–65.

O'Donovan, J. L. (1997). The concept of rights in Christian moral discourse. In M. Cromartie (Ed.), *A preserving grace: Protestants, Catholics, and natural law* (pp. 143–156). Grand Rapids, MI: Eerdmans.

O'Donovan, O. (2009). The language of rights and conceptual history. *Journal of Religious Ethics*, *37*, 193–207.

Ogata, S., & Cels, J. (2003). Human security: Protecting and empowering the people. *Global Governance*, *9*(3), 273–282.

Pacific Community. (2016). *Transforming power relations: Equal status of women and men at the family level in the Pacific*. Suva: Pacific Community.

Pacific Feminist Forum. (2016). *Pacific feminist charter*. Retrieved from www.fwrm.org.fj/images/PFF/PFF-Charter-Final-2Dec2016.pdf

Pain, R. (2012). *Everyday terrorism: How fear works in domestic abuse*. Centre for Social Justice and Community Action. Durham University and Scottish Women's Aid.

Regional Rights Resource Team. (n.d.). *About the Regional Rights Resource Team*. Retrieved from https://rrrt.spc.int/about

Russell, B. (1957). *Why I am not a Christian, and other essays on religion and related topics*. New York: Simon and Schuster.

The Salvation Army New Zealand, Fiji, Tonga and Samoa Territory. (n.d.). *The Salvation Army in Fiji*. Retrieved from www.salvationarmy.org.nz/fijicyclechallenge/salvation-army-in-fiji

Schüssler Fiorenza, E. (1994). Introduction. In E. Schüssler Fiorenza & M. S. Copeland (Eds.), *Violence against women* (Concilium) (pp. vii–xxiv). London: SCM Press.

Tadjbakhsh, S., & Chenoy, A. M. (2007). *Human security: Concepts and implications*. London and New York: Routledge.

Tracy, S. R. (2007). Patriarchy and domestic violence: Challenging common misconceptions. *Journal of the Evangelical Theological Society*, *50*(3), 573–594.

UNDP. (1994). *Human development report 1994: New dimensions of human security*. New York: Oxford University Press.

UNFPA. (2016). *Measuring prevalence of violence against women: Key terminology.* Bangkok: United Nations Population Fund, Asia and the Pacific Regional Office. Retrieved from https://asiapacific.unfpa.org/en/publications/violence-against-women-key-terminology-knowvawdata

UNFPA. (2019). *Violence against women – Regional snapshot (2019) – kNOwVAWdata.* Retrieved from https://asiapacific.unfpa.org/en/resources/violence-against-women-regional-snapshot-2019-knowvawdata

UNIFEM. (2010). *Ending violence against women & girls: Evidence, data and knowledge in the Pacific Island countries, literature review and annotated bibliography.* Suva: UNIFEM Pacific Sub-Regional Office. Retrieved from https://www.unicef.org/evaw.pdf

Van Hightower, N. R., Gorton, J., & DeMoss, C. L. (2000). Predictive models of domestic violence and fear of intimate partners among migrant and seasonal farm worker women. *Journal of Family Violence, 15*(2), 137–154.

Willimon, W. H. (2016). *Fear of the other: No fear in love*. Nashville, TN: Abingdon Press.

Wolterstorff, N. (2008). *Justice: Rights and wrongs*. Princeton, NJ: Princeton University Press.

11 Insecurities and strategies of the leiti (transgender) community in Tonga and the role of businesses and indigenous reconciliation practices

Sara N. Amin and Christian Girard

Background

Gender non-conformity is regulated through three systems in the Kingdom of Tonga: 1) a legal system that draws on traditional English common law in which homosexuality and cross-dressing are criminalised and are punishable by imprisonment up to ten years under Section 136 of the Criminal Offences Act; 2) a firmly rooted Christianity introduced in the mid-19th century and currently characterised by multiple denominations and interdenominational mobility; and 3) Tongan indigenous culture (Besnier, 1997). In the context of rapid social change since the 1980s, the market economy, migration and transnationalism have also impacted on the multiple dimensions of insecurities faced by gender and sexual minorities in Tonga. While there has been no enforcement of the laws against homosexuality and cross-dressing, gender and sexual minorities are subject to psychological, sexual and physical violence, as well as economic insecurities produced through discrimination in schools and families that lead to high levels of unemployment, precarity and poverty (Ministry of Internal Affairs, Women's Affairs Division, 2019).

An important category and identifier among gender and sexual minorities in Tonga is *fakaleiti*, who are recognised to be biologically male but whose gender performance is associated with women. Among gender liminal men, the preferred term is *leiti*. Anthropologist Nico Besnier explains the complexity of the category and identity of *leiti* in Tonga as follows:

> Defining a leitī is no simple task, as the category is heterogeneous. However, a number of tendencies can be identified. . . . Fakaleitī frequently engage in work activities normally associated with women: in rural contexts, mat weaving, tapa-cloth beating, and keeping house; in capitalist contexts, they are employed in sweat shops, offices, the hotel industry, in the entertainment of tourists, and primary education. Many engage in some transvestism to various degrees, and have sex with 'straight' men (never with each other), taking a 'female' role, i.e., as recipient rather than inserter. . . . Like women, fakaleitī are stereotypically associated with domestic social spheres, socialising in

the home rather than away, for example, and generally choose their friends among women, in contrast to 'straight' men who seek the company of Tongans routinely recognise a man as a fakaleitī if his demeanour exhibits certain qualities stereotypically identified as feminine, such as a swishy gait, an animated face, a highly emotional comportment, a fast speaking tempo, and a tendency to be verbose, in contrast to the stereotypically masculine impassiveness and sangfroid that mainstream Tongan men cultivate. However, while it contrasts with that of 'straight' men, the fakaleitī's demeanour is not mimetic of the average Tongan middle-age village woman. . . . Fakaleitī are a named category for mainstream Tongans, who describe them in unproblematic terms: 'men who are like women', or '50–50' (i.e., 50% woman, 50% man). In practice, fakaleitī identity is considerably more complex, fluid, and difficult to pinpoint than this checklist makes it out to be. In particular, this list is made up of possible features, none of which are necessary or sufficient conditions under which someone is identified as a fakaleitī. . . . The practice of being a fakaleiti can generate varied experiences and different positioning vis-à-vis mainstream society. Fluidity, permeability, and multi-layering are thus fundamental aspects of what it means to be a fakaleitī.

(1997, pp. 9–11)

The institutions and processes that produce insecurities have been creatively resisted and co-opted, in particular by the work of the Tonga Leitis Association (TLA), founded by Joey Joleen Mataele in 1992. According to their website (Tonga Leitis Association, 2019), TLA's mission is focused on "improving the rights and celebrating the contribution of Leitis in Tonga". While running a range of activities related to creating awareness, providing vocational training, building self-confidence and a safe space for and empowering leitis, the TLA has worked to build relationships with government, businesses, communities and churches to "make a significant difference in the lives of people with diverse sexual orientations, gender identities and expressions". Below, Joleen describes their journey of resisting and changing the conditions that produce the insecurities faced by leitis in Tonga.

THE INTERVIEW

Journey into activism

INTERVIEWER: How did you become an activist for transgender rights in Tonga?

JJM: I became a transgender rights or human rights defender, here in Tonga, when I was 14 years old. When I started just acting like myself, you know, as a trans person. Especially wearing a dress in public and of all the places that I first decided to wear a dress to, was straight to church, which is the biggest no-no here in the Kingdom. I could remember that very day when I walked in with my pleated blue dress, escorting my grandmother in. But the funny thing is my grandmother already forewarned me when we were still making our way to the church, and she said: "you know you are going to be stirring up something, right?" And I said: "I think so". But she didn't worry – as long as I was with her to Church, that was all she was worried about. I think she was more worried about my soul instead of worried about what I was wearing. So, to me, if I had that acceptance from her, I couldn't care less about what others say. So I stood up. Since then, I stood up for myself . . . and I wanted to be who I was since then.

INTERVIEWER: What made you decide at that point to do it?

JJM: Growing up, I've always known that I was more into feminine side. I recalled my doctor saying when I went for my first ever health check-up in New Zealand, that my female hormone was stronger than my male hormone. My grandmother always told me that I always liked to go to my sister's room or her jewelry, or her clothes or her shoes. I used to go and drag them down the hallway of our house and they'll find me in our bedroom sitting in front of the mirror putting on earrings and things like that, you know, feminine things. . . . But she never hit me or harass me on that, because I think she thought that I was just going through a phase. Until I grew up a bit older, then she could understand, when I started going to school, that I was always taking the female lead role on any play we had at school. Then she realised that I was different, and was totally into what I'd like to be. Always female clothes, always making sure that I take the female lead role that I had at school or anything feminine really. So, when I grew up, I knew that I was who I was then. I didn't want to continue wearing men's clothes when I wasn't comfortable with it. Every single time I put a woman's dress or dressed in a woman's way, I feel more confident, I feel good about myself. I tried wearing suits and all that to some of the events that we had, but I was very uncomfortable. . . . I felt as if I'm lying to myself.

INTERVIEWER: You are a very visible part of transgender rights in Tonga. How would you say you got there since choosing to stand up for who you are at church to now, speaking for others as well?

JJM: I left school when I was 14 years old. And then I finally found and started working as a maid cleaning up the bathrooms and all that at the International Dateline Hotel. But then I pushed my way through my music, my talent, because I love singing. I come from a musical family. I started using the music, my voice, to advocate and stand up for myself, and I started singing at the International Dateline Hotel about 40 years ago! I got a chance to sing with the band. The man who owned the band at the Dateline hotel was from town, and he knew that I had gone to school with one of his daughters. He knew I was always singing at school. By chance, the general manager just passed and saw me singing and that's when he offered me a job to sing. From there, I went into the entertainment arena, and then, went from there to where I started teaching dancing. After a couple of years I [had] taught quite a few – about 50 or 60 students and those parents trusted me with their children as I taught them Polynesian music. . . . So I used those talents to gain trust from people and stand up for myself.

When we talk about social justice here, it's an act between individual responsibility, society and others, which can balance between access to power and responsibility. Sometimes I think it's why social justice is appealed to today by debating about differences among human beings and efforts for gender and social equality. But the way I went about it is using the talent that I had, that I was gifted by God, and used it to advocate. And through fasting and prayers. I mean even though, I am LGBT, but it doesn't change the fact that I believe in my faith and my religion. I grew up in two founding families of two churches, which is the Latter-Day Saints (LDS) and the Catholic Church. I grew up with the great grandparents from both founding families. But my grandmother was always a very, very strong Catholic and my grandfather was a very strong Mormon. But between them, there was never any time that I would hear them arguing about which church or which gospel is true and which is wrong. They both agreed they'd get married and they had their children and they lived together until they died in their old age. And that, to me, was my foundation. If I can live with those two strong churches, without being discriminated [for] being who I was, and what I was, then I can withstand any discrimination.

Insecurities and challenges

INTERVIEWER: Compared to when you started working at that hotel, would you say leitis face similar opportunities and challenges to find work?

JJM: Well, what has changed is the attitudes of people towards leitis, towards trans people. Now, for working uniforms and all that, it's different. A lot of places, the private sector – not the government – it's easy for any trans to get a job now, because we have a better relationship with a lot of businesses. Some of these businesses are the ones that are actually supporting us during our Miss Galaxy Pageant. As soon as we have graduates from the scholarships that we provide, then we find them jobs and even if we don't find it for them, they find it themselves.

When I first started actually, I wasn't really allowed to wear women's clothes to work. I was always in uniforms and it was men's style uniforms. Until when I started singing, and then I started wearing what I wanted to wear and they came to understand and allowed me to do that. So, even when I attended some of the cocktail parties that I was invited to, I definitely would go dressed up. It was more like dressing up to kill! (laughter) Every single time there's a big function going on, some of them always said: "I wonder what she's going to turn up in". But it's been pretty good – it's a lot better now than those years. Leitis are much [more] comfortable finding jobs and wearing what they want to wear now than before.

At the same time, we're still facing a lot of negativity from social media, from people that have left Tonga and lived overseas. And some of them are just spewing things that they don't know anything about. I mean, they comment on a lot of positive things that we do and they all translate it into something that is so different from what we do and our targets. But it doesn't really bother us, because I hardly go – I try to avoid all of those negativities, because I know for sure that that's not going [to] solve anything if I, if we turn around and argue back. Most of the time, I say to the girls: Avoid being on social media, and avoid answering back to any of those negativities.

INTERVIEWER: What are the kinds of insecurities you think leitis face in Tonga?

Some of the things they face, some of the discrimination they face is being on the street. Some of them will just be walking down the road and some will tease them or . . . I mean, when I grew up, I used to be very aggressive about people throwing anything at me or swearing at me on the street. I'm always fighting back. I'm no longer a fist-fighter. I used to fight every single person who would say anything bad about me. Nowadays, we do face discrimination on the street and all that, but majority of what we're facing now is on social media and this type of bullying is horrific.

We try and tell, our members, not to fight back, because it gets a bit vulgar – the sort of words that they use, and now girls get so angry. I'm a bit worried, because some of the leitis might turn around and say something about someone or some of those people that they know very well who is a known person in those communities, you know, some kind of sexual experience with one of the leitis, and that will be the worst-thing scenario – to find out that that person that's being negative on us is actually one of those people.

We try our best to advise our girls, our trans community not to bother with all the negativity. I keep saying to them: "The more you get angry and the more you say all those vulgar words and everything against those people, you are just like them. You become them. Fight them with kindness or give them a kiss". Because it's no use fighting back swearing like that on social media, because everybody's looking at it and they all think that we're all the same. Just avoid those pages. Let them deal with it. When I fight back, I fight back with what's more important and I fight back with true stories of experience that we have. And we have to make sure that when we fight, we do not just fight to be heard, but we fight to be respected. We need to gain respect for what we are and who we are. Not because of the way we dress or anything like that.

It's hard. As part of our trainings that we do is train well-being on the girls, because some of our members come from broken families. And it's so hard to try and calm them down or change their mindset or even change their attitude because of the experiences that they go through, that they have gone through in their lives. I mean, I came through a hard life too, but I sacrificed a lot of things to be the person I am today. It takes a lot of guts. It takes a lot of forgiveness. I don't know how I survived all this time, because when I look back at it, I should be in a home of nuts, a mental house to fight back all those negativities all my life and what happened to me when I was young . . . I know I cannot forget, but forgiving works in mysterious ways. And I've seen it myself in a lot of the work that I do and a lot of the good that comes out of it. Sometimes, most times, it's hard to turn away, and I just fight back with a smile (laughter). And when they don't listen me, I start singing!

Being accepted within the churches, community and also having the opportunity to be ourselves in public and being accepted within churches and cultures is the main key. In most cases, some of us are strong believers in religion, you know? Some are discriminated at church. Some churches, they do not allow you to wear female clothes. And sometimes, social justice allows us to feel that sense of belonging again, also accepting LGBT people, which is the most important thing. [Based on] some of the research we did on discrimination within Tonga and the Pacific, homosexuality was only decriminalised in Nauru. However, here it's still under the threat of jail because of our sexuality. Tonga is one of the seven countries in the Pacific that haven't decriminalised homosexuality law.

So far, we have tried to fight on law reform and all those things, we've tried to do consultations, we've tried to do trainings within the rural areas. But there is always a backlash on these. It could take many forms such as increased public homophobic rhetoric, religious condemnation or even violent backlash, as was faced by few other leitis in our communities in the rural areas. However, some of the laws that we have here are not acted upon. Like the impersonation laws, that homosexuality law, because pretty much in Tonga everyone is related to someone and it's been raised a few times in parliament and someone would just push it aside. We've got better things to do, we've got more important things to discuss.

So, even though it has been raised and we still have those colonial era laws, we're still comfortable of being who we are because of the work that we have done to cut down a lot of the stigmatisation and all that. It's very hard to have our voices be heard in parliament or anything like that, because there's so much corruption going on, in our government. Sometimes we try and lobby through our consultations. At the same time, we don't want to open a can of worms, because most of the time when we start talking of legal reform and all that, they all jump into same-sex marriage, as if that's all we want. It's quite hard talking to people whose mindsets are already fixed. At the same time, it will take time for a country that has adopted religion as their culture. So, I don't know, maybe the next two, three or five years, we will have something that's suitable or we're able to change things here in Tonga.

"Religion as culture"

INTERVIEWER: How does the "adoption of religion as its culture" affect the place of leitis in Tonga?

JJM: The culture that we had didn't differentiate anyone. We had our own culture before Christianity came into this country. Then when the Christianity came into this country, we adopted another culture. It became a second culture of our country. It sort of differentiated gender a lot. Then gender came into the picture, but that was never an issue [before]. Our culture was a more loving, more caring, more [about] sharing with our community. There was no label-ling and all that. We knew where we belong. There were three statuses here in Tonga: which is the king, the noble and the commoners. That's it. There's no such thing as I'm a preacher, you're trans, you're homosexual, you're a sinner . . . nothing like that. And so, Christianity came into the picture, then – I mean nothing wrong with Christianity, but when you define Christianity to mock or to discriminate others because of their sexuality or because of their gender, because of their likings and their behaviour, then that becomes some-thing different. Every now and then, a preacher will stand up and preach on the radio or even on TV about us. Of these little churches that always have something against us. And that person will continuously say something about us. But it doesn't bother us anymore. They sound like a broken record.

INTERVIEWER: Would you say that a lot of the discrimination or stigma that leitis face in Tonga is due to religion or people's understanding of religious norms?

JJM: I do believe it has a lot to do with the religious beliefs. I had friends, very, very good friends that I grew up with in the same church, same school and same town, and we were in the same class and everything since childhood. Until that person turned or was so-called "born again" and became evan-gelist, then the majority of the people that she was around with do not like homosexuality or even having me around wearing what I wear and she kind of adopted that kind of attitude from those people and it became very uncom-fortable. I still call her my friend and all that, but the bonding that we had since we were kids, since we all grew up and even when she's had kids . . . I was always there . . . but it sort of cut out our relationship.

Strategies of resistance and change

INTERVIEWER: What strategies do you and the Tonga Leitis' Association use to overcome those that oppose you?

JJM: One of the main strategies that we use now is the talanoa methodology, and that's by telling stories without concealment. When we use the talanoa meth-odology, we bring everyone in a consultation. We bring in all the lawmakers, the decision-makers, the church leaders, the community leaders, district offi-cers, parents. After our first national consultation, we decided to find more funding to do more consultations, to bring everybody so we can sit down [at] a round table and talk face to face. Telling them the issues that we've gone through, what we need and all of that. The respect we want to gain from them. At the same time, they need to listen to the stories, to our stories. Because they assume that we are just sinners, that we're out there to rape everyone and all those people. But little do they know, it's the people out there that are out trying to find us at night and all those things. I mean, we don't want to name names. But in order for us to keep the peace and to be able to work with our communities and that, it's important for them to listen to make time for us to sit down and talk. They're listening to our stories.

After the first national consultation, there was a need from the district offices to take [it] to four or five districts of Tonga, which [are] the three districts, main districts in Tongatapu and one in the central area, and also to the Vavaʻu Islands, which is one of the biggest island group here in Tonga. We took the consultations over there and the outcomes from there was a lot of people agreed that we need to amend the law that we have. And not only that, but they wanted to take the consultations to each village. So, we were all so into it. We wanted to do that. Unfortunately, we don't have any more funding and the funds that we reserved for all those other consultations [were] totally used up when Cyclone Gita came and our whole office was blown. We had to use some of those funds to revive the office and also the living quarters, the living space. We see a lot of goodness when you sit down and talk to them face to face, instead of assuming, because of negativities that you faced yourself. So now, we're trying [to] see if we're able to get funding. Then we'll continue the consultations into the villages or the suburban areas.

Support, partnerships and allies

INTERVIEWER: When you are looking for funding for these kinds of activities, where have you found the most support?

JJM: First of all is the Miss Galaxy Pageant. Then, we were able to secure funding from the Canadian Fund. A small amount came from the United Nations Development Program (UNDP) through the Fiji Office. I think that's about it.

INTERVIEWER: Have there been any challenges in running the Miss Galaxy Pageant?

JJM: 2018 was our 25th anniversary! But in 2016 we could not run it.

When they started doing the march on CEDAW (Convention on the Elimination of all Forms of Discrimination Against Women), they thought that we were part of it. But no, that's a convention for women. Until our government would allow us to change our IDs into women, trans-women and all that, then we will consider our movement to be part of CEDAW. But we were actually one of the number one supporter for CEDAW to be ratified. Just because we supported it, everybody was thinking: oh, okay, there they go again!

INTERVIEWER: How did you build the relationship with businesses?

JJM: When we were looking for sponsorships for the Miss Galaxy, we actually went from door to door, from every single business and sat down with them and talked. One of the strategies of the Miss Galaxy is to be able to secure funding for scholarships for our school dropouts to go back to school. Not only that, but to assist with the HIV awareness programmes and all that. They were supportive of our goals and what we wanted to achieve. Every single year we seemed to be able to get the funds and, not only that, but we have one of the best programmes. It is much more fun and much more known and much more popular than the local "real" girls' pageant. It attracts a lot. It attracted a lot of media from overseas too.

It's not an easy job, because funding a pageant like ours, you're talking about 30–40 grands to be able to pull up a show like that: electrician, sound system, staging and everything cost a lot of money. And yet, we've been able to achieve it. But because of that relationship, the businesses know where their money is going and most of them have employed some of the graduates from the scholarship holders that have graduated from those technical schools. So, they know their money's worth and the support that they have done for the TLA and the Miss Galaxy is worth every single penny, because the returns keep coming back to them. So it's a win-win situation for both of us and not only our members, but, at the same time, the businesses that support us.

INTERVIEWER: How does your work connect to larger international human rights as well as international and Pacific transgender or LGBTQ movements?

JJM: The Pacific Sexual and Gender Diversity Network (PSGDN), I was one of the cofounders for that in 2007. Me and Ken Moala from Samoa and Carlos Perera from Fiji. But that's because we were invited to an Asia-Pacific conference on HIV and AIDS and all that in Australia, during the Gay Games. When we went to the conference, there was no such person from the Pacific at all. Australia and New Zealand, but they had no one from the Pacific Countries. So, we decided: okay, I think it's about time that we try and find out if we're able to do something for the Pacific and to be able to represent the Pacific in any of these international arenas. So we talked about it – this was in 2002 – and then finally, we were able to establish the PSGDN. I was nominated by the Australian-New-Zealand ILGA Board (the International Lesbian, Gay, Bisexual, Trans and Intersex Association) to represent the Pacific, including Australia and New Zealand, to go to ILGA World Conference. From there, I got connected to some of the international activists on trans and other LGBT networks. When we first started the PSGDN in Apia, Samoa, there was a representative from the Asia-Pacific Coalition for Men's Health that were there at the Gay Games at that conference I was talking about earlier and they came to be able to find someone from the Pacific to represent the 14 undeveloped countries, including Australia and New Zealand of course.

So, after a few talks on the first meeting in Bangkok, I insisted in my community from the Pacific, PSGDN supported me, that we need to differentiate the undeveloped countries from Australia and New Zealand. So we were able to achieve that. And so, through all those connections I got to develop a lot of relationships with other networks, donor agencies [and] other activists from everywhere in the world. When we got that exposure, we started working with a lot of international networks on projects to do with trans movement, researches. We were able to connect to the Global Fund and Robert Carr Fund and other agencies to fund some of the projects that we have here in the Kingdom, especially when it comes to HIV and AIDS: condom campaigns, HIV testing and all that, because they are very experienced. We were able to secure funding from those funders to be able to carry those programmes now, here in Tonga, for the LGBT community.

INTERVIEWER: Part of the royal family has been supportive of the leitis' movement and of your work. Can you speak about how it has helped the work that
you do?

JJM: When we first started in 1992, we took the actual project and we thought:
we'll find someone that has got the highest status in our society to be our
patron. And the only person I thought of was Princess Pilolevu because she
has always been a good supporter of leitis and she had always had leitis
around her. I was one of those fortunate ones that worked for her. So when
we took it to her, she said yes and that's when she got one of her eldest daughters to be our patron. And having someone like that, to have that kind of high
standard in society, it breaks a lot of barriers. When you have them, they are
so visible in a lot of ways in a lot of things that we do, and very vocal at the
same time. It has eased a lot of situations. We find it easier to have them be
there at the forefront, because a lot of people won't be able to say anything,
because she's there.

I see the results on our first Pacific Human Rights Conference. We had one of
those churches that came and stood with a banner and started shouting blah blah
blah from the wall front area, they could not even come near the actual thing.
They couldn't come to the actual convention centre, because they knew that she
was inside the whole conference, the whole time. They just got tired of shouting
and we didn't even care about what they were doing, we did not even bother. We
just told all our members, all our international delegates, to just stay inside, don't
bother, and when they go outside, to go to the market or anything, don't bother
saying anything, just go and just avoid them. And, of course, it did happen. They
just got tired and nobody bothered to respond to their shouting and all that, and
then [they] finally went home, because they were tired of shouting at nothing.
Our conference was still going on and the more they shouted, the louder we are
from inside. Everyone laughed at the thing. But that's one of the examples that we
faced and having them over there, having someone like that cuts a lot of barriers
and eases things for us.

INTERVIEWER: What is it about the Tongan context that allows for the co-existence
of laws that criminalises LGBT identity and at the same time allows for the
royal family to publicly be a patron?

JJM: Even though those laws are there, let's get to the reality of things. We are
human beings and we are part of everyone's family. When it comes to functions, to events and church events and conferences and everything, we are the
ones who do the dirty work. We're the ones who are preparing the church,
cleaning, making the flowers, cooking, serving. And the other countries, you
have servants and all that, but here in Tonga, it's us who are up there doing all
that, while the preachers sit there with their suit. I mean, if they try and pulled
us away into isolation and all that, because of gender, then who's going to
do that? Who's going to do the dirty job for them? Even with or without the
royal family as our patron, I don't think that they will be able to discriminate

anyone because of their gender or whatever one believes in, because pretty much everyone is related here in Tonga. This country is so bloody small for anyone to just to get anyone to be isolated.

Future: leadership and hopes

INTERVIEWER: From the outside, the leadership seems to be based on you. Would you say there's a multi-generation leadership that's growing within the leiti movement in Tonga?

JJM: I think there needs to be more to get the young ones' voices and, not only that, to groom them to be good leaders. I know I'm not going to be there for the rest of my life and we have quite a good team, but the only reason why I'm more visible, is because most of the time I don't shut my mouth (laughter). When it comes to facing anything from specially the government, they push me. I'm the one that stays at the forefront, facing all the consequences and all that.

But it will take a lot of time and it will take a lot of guts, a lot of work, a lot of money, to be able to groom some of our young ones to become the future leaders of this movement. We have a very, very good team. Very active team. We need to make sure that the one that we groom is someone that can carry forward the work that we started. As much as I love the work that I do, I would like to retire and pursue my music. And have a little rest and have a little fun (laughter). And get at least 8-hour sleep (laughter). You can't be an activist and a single mother at the same time.

INTERVIEWER: What are your goals or hopes for the leitis in Tonga?

JJM: I would like to see the leitis to live comfortably and be respected for who they are. No matter what they are. I want to see a Tonga that is full of love. I want to see a Tonga that is full of care, support, instead of labelling people. Because that's our biggest problem here. Not only that we label just the leitis, but we label our own family who's a single mother. I want to see a Tonga that is understanding, love and use the real godly love that God gave us, to use it as a tool to fight against hate, fight against discrimination, stigmatisation. I want to see a Tonga that is loving instead of hating others or hating you for who you are.

Conclusion

This interview brings key insights in relation to sources of insecurities, support and strength, as well as to localised approaches to effect social change in Tonga for a more inclusive society. Leitis face multiple levels of insecurities caused by marginalisation, labelling, physical and verbal abuse and, more recently, through social media. Christianity comes out as a site of tension, but also of personal strength. Joey Joleen Mataele highlights the tensions between certain understandings of Christianity and traditional indigenous Tongan culture, at the same time pointing out that leitis play a key role in church functions and that being part of their churches and communities are important for them. Tongan culture and power structures are again a site of both tension and resilience. While the government appears to have been less willing to tackle these questions, the support of the royal family has helped facilitate the work of TLA. While largely unenforced, changing laws that criminalise homosexuality and cross-dressing remain an important part of TLA's work and mission, in addition to creating awareness and changing the attitudes of perceptions towards leitis through a national conversation. This open dialogue approach is based on the indigenous methodology of talanoa and invites all types of stakeholders and parties to participate in discussions and sharing of experiences to move towards reconciliation and social transformation, building on the profound human ties within Tongan communities. Finally, the strategic role of the private sector is underscored, as businesses play a key role in supporting TLA's mission and in creating spaces and opportunities for leitis to work and perform.

References

Besnier, N. (1997). Sluts and superwomen: The politics of gender liminality in urban Tonga. *Ethnos, 62*(1–2), 5–31.

Ministry of Internal Affairs, Women's Affairs Division. (2019). *Gender equality: Where do we stand? The Kingdom of Tonga.* Government of Tonga. Retrieved from http://purl. org/spc/digilib/doc/oemo2

Tonga Leitis Association. (2019). *What we do.* Retrieved from www.tongaleitis.org/index. php/whatwedo

Part 3

Organisational culture, security providers, partner institutions and security outcomes

12 Contextualising policing in Melanesia

History, adaptation and adoption problematised

Danielle Watson and Sinclair Dinnen

Introduction

The Pacific Islands region comprises hundreds of islands spread over approximately 15% of the globe (World Bank, 2018). The region is loosely sub-divided into three broad cultural and geographic groupings – Polynesia, Micronesia and Melanesia. Although there are similarities within these groupings, Pacific Island Countries (PICs) have diverse histories, traditions and cultures that makes it difficult to generalise or to formulate all-encompassing Pacific specific narratives. Differences also manifest in their economies, the continued presence or influence of colonial relations and alignment to more powerful first-world countries. Most PICs are microstates with small populations dispersed across numerous islands and atolls. Around 90% of the region's population of approximately 11 million people live in the four independent Melanesian states of Papua New Guinea (PNG), Fiji, Solomon Islands and Vanuatu, with over 8 million in PNG which dominates the region in terms of land mass and population size.

Regional security and stability have been enduring priorities for Australia and New Zealand, the South Pacific's two main metropolitan powers and traditional donors. Rapid globalisation and institutional fragility have increased external concerns about the vulnerability of PICs to transnational crime (Walton & Dinnen, 2016), as well as the potential spill-over from internal security and stability crises in particular countries. The heightened strategic security environment post-9/11, 2001, gave rise to a distinctly more interventionist approach by Australia in its relations with its Pacific Islands neighbours (Fry & Kabutaulaka, 2008). This was in response to the perceived threats posed to regional security by internal conflict and political instability in several Melanesian countries, including PNG, Solomon Islands and Fiji. Australian strategic analysts posited the existence of "an arc of instability" surrounding their northern and eastern shores (Ayson, 2007). Consistent with Western responses elsewhere in the Global South, external interventions in the region had a strong emphasis on statebuilding, including on strengthening law enforcement, judicial and other central state agencies. The exemplar was the 14-year long (2003–2017) Australian-led Regional Mission to Solomon Islands (RAMSI) (Allen & Dinnen, 2010). While the "state-building moment" has likely passed in the Pacific as elsewhere (Mazar, 2014), capacity building programmes with regional security bodies, including police organisations, continue to be supported by Australia and New Zealand, with some minor involvement by China, Japan and other non-traditional donors (Dobell, 2003; McLeod & Dinnen, 2007). These kinds of engagement with PICs' policing organisations raise questions about the effectiveness of external police assistance and the forms of institutional transfer entailed in the diverse local contexts of the contemporary Pacific, as well as about whose interests they ultimately serve (Larmour, 2007; Dinnen & McLeod, 2009).

While police organisations in many PICs rely on foreign aid to help build capacity and mitigate resource shortfalls, few policy discussions acknowledge both the potential and limitations of such assistance and its implications for developing sustainable local policing approaches. Here, we focus on the contribution of external countries drawing on examples from various Melanesian countries. We look specifically at contributions to policy reform, conditional aid not cognisant of context and the likely impact of adopted foreign policing positions on police-community relations.

We organise our discussion around three areas that we perceive as critical to policing in Melanesia – historical, cultural and contextual factors; the existence of plural policing in PICs; and the realities associated with the transposition of foreign policies and practices – and further elaborate on the need for external entities to be cognisant of Melanesia's contextual realities.

Understanding Melanesia – historical, cultural and contextual considerations

PICs assumed their current political form during a colonial period that lasted around 100 years in most places. While indigenous experiences of colonialism varied enormously, the most common institutional legacy was the establishment of states. Prior to European expansion across the region in the second half of the 19th century, Pacific island societies were organised along traditional lines under the leadership of chiefs or big-men, usually with limited degrees of influence over prescribed areas. Fiji consisted of a number of warring chiefly confederacies (MacNaught, 2016). Elsewhere, and most markedly in Melanesia, authority was diffused widely across multiple indigenous polities whose small size – often around 200–300 people – provides the basis for the exceptional socio-linguistic diversity that persists to this day (Sillitoe, 2000).

In the relatively egalitarian Melanesian settings, authority was typically personalised in traditional leaders with few formal rules. Dealing with disputation and wrongdoing was embedded in everyday life rather than being mandated to specialised personnel operating through a differentiated legal system (Scaglion, 2004). The intrinsic inter-dependence of small-scale societies ensured that the restoration of social relations – what is now termed "restorative justice" (Dinnen, 2003) – was an important aim of dispute resolution within social groups, often involving compensation and other forms of ceremonial exchange. Retributive practices, including "payback", raiding and warfare, were also common in many places, particularly where no morally binding relationship existed between disputing groups (Knauft, 1990).

Policing in the larger Melanesian territories was a critical instrument of colonial pacification and administration (Dinnen, 2019). Early police work included suppressing indigenous resistance, ending fighting and raiding among local groups, safeguarding European interests, adjudicating infringements of "native regulations", and collecting head tax. Colonial policing was more military than civilian, and initial encounters between outsiders and local people were often violent (Ballard & Douglas, 2017). In PNG, the largest and most topographically challenging Pacific territory, the leading role of the police in extending and consolidating colonial influence prompted one early observer to label Australia's administration as a "benevolent type of police rule" (Lord Hailey quoted in Mair, 1948, p. xvi). Patrols consisting of members of the armed constabulary led by European district officers, called *kiaps*, provided the most visible face of colonial government (Kituai, 1998), while police patrols were also an important form of colonial governance in Solomon Islands. Vanuatu, administered jointly by Britain and France, was a colonial oddity with separate British and French police divisions, each dealing with their own citizens under English or French law and both dealing with locals under a "native" code.

As political independence approached, police forces across the colonial world were modernised, becoming more independent of government and often acquiring centralised command systems, specialised units and growing in size (Anderson & Killingray, 1992, p. ix). Decolonisation in Melanesia occurred mainly in the 1970s. Given their diversity, it is hard to discern a typical Pacific islands police force or colonial legacies shared by all of them. One similarity is that all have had relatively short histories as professional organisations dedicated to impartial law enforcement. The coercive and paramilitary aspects of colonial policing have left a marked legacy, particularly in PNG, Solomon Islands and Vanuatu, as manifested in police violence and limited public trust in the police. In most of these countries, the uniformed police continue to operate alongside diverse forms of community-based dispute resolution and social regulation, administered by chiefs or other local leaders and often legitimated in terms of *kastom* or tradition. The existence of diverse security providers underlies the plural reality of contemporary policing (see below).

Most Melanesian police organisations experience severe constraints in terms of resources and other support from governments with limited fiscal capabilities. The most serious consequences of underfunding are found in PNG where the size of the police force has not grown significantly since independence in 1975 despite significant population growth and serious "law and order" problems (Dinnen, 2017).

Plural policing in the Melanesia – beyond the blue and white

The pluralisation of policing provision represents an ongoing global transformation in security governance. Once viewed as the exclusive responsibility of national police organisations, it is now recognised that multiple actors and agencies are involved in the delivery of policing and security services. The pluralisation of policing and security, particularly as it has played out in the Global North, has attracted considerable interest among scholars across disciplines. Various terms are found in the burgeoning literature addressing this phenomenon, including "plural policing" (Jones & Newburn, 2006), "hybrid security" (Bagayoko, Hutchful, & Luckham, 2016), "non-state policing" (Baker, 2010) and "networked security" (Wood & Shearing, 2007). State police are understood by scholars as operating within broader "security assemblages" (Abrahamsen & Williams, 2009) whose shifting configuration varies across time and space. Plural policing encompasses diverse actors and relationships between them, including private policing forms secured *through* government; to transnational police arrangements taking place *above* government; to markets in policing and security unfolding *beyond* government; and to policing activities engaged in by citizens *below* government (Loader, 2000, p. 324).

Growing recognition of pluralisation has encouraged a broader conceptualisation of policing as a network of power and regulation going beyond a discrete institutional form, function and ethos. This broadening unsettles longstanding assumptions about the primacy of states (and governments) in security governance. While policing has always been plural in practice, allegiance to idealised Weberian notions of statehood premised on the state's monopoly over violence remains tenacious. This is evident in the area of international policing assistance. Despite a discernible shift in the rhetoric of many donors and other development organisations acknowledging the need to engage with a broader spectrum of policing actors (OECD-DAC, 2007, p. 163), international interveners continue to engage almost exclusively with state-based police organisations. This tendency is reinforced by the predisposition of international police-builders, typically drawn from home police organisations, to build in their own image.

Without questioning the need for external assistance to what are often poorly resourced and thinly stretched national police organisations, this allegiance to a universal institutional form neglects the plural realities of policing in most countries. As Bruce Baker has noted in African contexts, security provision "beyond the tarmac road" looks very different to that in the donors' home setting (Baker, 2008). His observation applies equally in Melanesia, with multiple policing and security providers co-existing and interacting in diverse ways across the region. The development of police organisations initially established under colonialism has been shaped by a combination of local and global influences. In most Melanesian countries, state authority, as embodied in national legal systems and agencies like the police, intermingles with older forms of authority and social organisation as they have adapted to change. In these hybrid orders, "diverse and competing authority structures, sets of rules, logics of order and claims to power co-exist, overlap, interact and intertwine, combining elements of introduced Western models of governance and elements stemming from local indigenous traditions of governance and politics" (Boege, Brown, & Clements, 2009, p. 17).

Arguably the most commonly experienced sources of authority and regulation in contemporary Melanesia are the state, *kastom* (custom) and the churches.

Kastom has proven to be highly dynamic and adaptive, although under considerable stress in the face of rapid socio-economic change in many places. Extended kinship networks and social relations continue to provide an important basis for individual allegiances and identities, and remain a critical framework for engaging in daily life across the region. Reflecting a long history pre-dating formal colonisation in many places, Christianity constitutes another. These various sources of authority are overlapping and interact in diverse and complex ways. As such, they are significant aspects of local policing contexts in different countries, playing an active role in dealing with local disputes.

Constraints on the resources and reach of the state contributes to continued reliance on extended families, traditional leaders, churches and other non-state actors for everyday security (Allen, Dinnen, Evans, & Monson, 2013). While some forms of decentralised or community-based policing practice are formally authorised or given tacit approval at state level, others are wholly unofficial. Recent processes of globalisation have introduced additional layers to the already multi-layered character of policing and security provision. This includes the marketisation of security and rapid expansion of private security (see Dinnen this volume), as well as the increasing role of regional, international and transnational regulatory regimes and actors, as exemplified in the RAMSI intervention and growing networked policing arrangements responding to transnational threats (Walton & Dinnen, 2016).

Permission from the community to police the community

The idea of acquiring social permission from civilian stakeholders to engage in acts of law enforcement is neither new nor specific to Melanesia (Edward, 2005; Shusta, Levine, Harris, & Wong, 2002). Police organisations in much of the Western world have shifted away from prioritised law enforcement through imposition to policing by consent (Edwards, 2005). Greater emphasis has been placed on police partnering with the population to promote ideas of self-regulation and to dissuade engagement in unacceptable social behaviours. This is primarily evident in the popularity of Community Policing and Crime-Prevention Policing Models amongst policing organisations globally. Much of the scholarly literature on policing by consent coming out of more developed countries highlights the need for forged police-community partnerships and also emphasise the need for strategies cognisant of societal diversity in a more globalised world (Jackson, Bradford, Hough, & Murray, 2012; Jefferson, 1990; Shusta et al., 2002). The idea of policing by consent is an interesting yet theoretically complex area for Melanesia, as "communities" vary enormously and longstanding traditional and cultural systems of policing necessitate the negotiation and navigation of power differentials between plural policing entities. Legacies of coercive colonial policing practice provide another complicating factor.

Communities in much of Melanesia (typically comprising rural villages and rapidly growing urban settlements) still draw on quasi-traditional forms of governance, with an important role for chiefs and other local leaders in addition to the administrative systems of modern statehood (Aina, 2002; White & Lindstrom,

1997). In indigenous Fijian villages, for example, there exists Village Chiefs and chiefly families who hold structural authority over the maintenance of law and order in their respective villages (Nabobo-Baba, 2006). Policing in rural Fijian communities is primarily done at the community level by local chiefs and councils of village elders. The elders of each family serve the primary policing role as they mediate all matters within the families. The power to punish or pardon community inhabitants for perceived crimes is also held by the chief and decisions made at the community level are in most instances respected and representative of "law enforcement". Hybrid approaches to policing and justice, drawing on diverse actors and different forms of authority (e.g. state, *kastom* and Christianity), also prevail throughout much of PNG, Solomon Islands and Vanuatu (Craig & Porter, 2018; Allen et al., 2013; Forsyth, 2007).

In outlining some of the varied forms and contexts of plural policing in the Pacific Islands, it is important to be aware of the limitations and risks associated with them. Traditional authority is highly contested in many areas, including over who is and who is not a chief, and is under sustained pressure from broader forces of social and normative change. In acknowledging the continuing role of older systems of regulation in these settings, there is the well-known risk of romanticising customary forms and other local practices (Richmond, 2011). Some of these can be oppressive and discriminatory towards particular groups and individuals, just as others can be respectful and empowering. *Kastom* is by definition conservative in orientation and can obscure significant imbalances in power and divisions along lines of gender, ethnicity, age or religion. The problematic treatment of women in particular is a widely recognised problem with traditional or *kastom*-based approaches to justice and policing in the Pacific (Bull, George, & Curth-Bibb, 2019). Likewise, customary practices can become corrupted when detached from their traditional social moorings. Informal policing initiatives that are inadequately regulated or supervised can be captured by partisan interests and become instruments of oppression. Likewise, church-led approaches that place a singular emphasis on forgiveness and reconciliation, can promote immunity for offenders and injustice for victims. Plural policing, with its implied options and choices, can also confuse those seeking clear pathways for the processing and resolution of their cases.

At the same time, it is important not to allow such challenges to obscure the potential and opportunities presented by plural policing and legal pluralism. Many of the same concerns raised in respect of non-state policing providers are also aired regularly in relation to government police organisations: for example, corruption, lack of accountability, brutality, discrimination against vulnerable groups (see, for example, HRW, 2005). If it is both desirable and possible to engage with and reform the latter, then why not with some of the former?

Adoption without adaptation problematised – borrowed policing policies and practices

Global concerns about potential security threats, including crime, continue to influence measures taken by policy makers and security service providers internationally, regionally and locally. Strategies anticipated to increase security and promote law and order are usually informed by context or the geographic remit within which they are created (Friman, 2009; Watson, Boateng, Pino, & Morgan, 2018). Where global solutions to identified or perceived threats are formulated and put forward as international declarations, it then becomes the responsibility of the country to interpret how such pronouncements are translated or localised to fit context. In many instances, ideas about social and political instability, and the high likelihood of groups or communities at risk in smaller less developed countries lead to assistance or initiatives being undertaken by larger developed countries to assist (Watson & Kerrigan, 2018). This usually translates to large-scale adaptation or adoption of foreign solutions to local problems, or local traditional and cultural practices being problematised for non-conformity to international standards of appropriateness. Here, we focus on three issues specific to outsider theorising in PICs policing – perpetuated ideologies of modernisation, international indicators of suitability and borrowed solutions – and provide context-specific examples to highlight the dangers of such non-contextualization for the Pacific.

Perpetuated ideologies of modernisation

Modernisation can be loosely explained as an attempt to reshape in the image of another. As a theory, it is loaded with assumptions about appropriateness and accepted standards to which others must aspire (Ekbladh, 2011). It ascribes to the ideologies of the powerful policy elites, represents their assumptions about what ideological positions should be prioritised, adopted, idealised or made a casualty of the modernising political agenda, and it projects the image of modernity to which others are expected to ascribe. In this sense, the modernisation agenda initially focussed on economic development mirrored after developed Western societies (Hunter, 1991). The developed "West" presented an ideal model of modernisation in turn projecting a path towards a universal ideal (Latham, 2000). Such positions on modernisation promote convergence around accepted standards of progress towards a more forward or "modern" approach and often oversimplifies development targets. All Melanesian countries are categorised as underdeveloped by international standards. For many of these countries, reliance on external funding sources, slow economic growth and low per capita income make them primary beneficiaries/targets for "development aid" to assist with modernisation or more specifically, alignment with the political agendas of their funders. We emphasise the impact of modernisation on policing approaches and organisational responses to technological advancements.

Policing approaches in much of the "developed" world have moved away from reactionary methods to more proactive community oriented approaches, which favour partnerships with stakeholders (Oliver, 2001; Watson et al., 2018). Such approaches are premised on police legitimacy and are primarily reliant on positive police-community relations (Sargeant, Wickes, & Mazerolle, 2013). In many Melanesian countries, there are strong community ties, cultural practices and established traditional systems for maintaining order at the community levels (Newton, 1998). The push for modernisation by donors sometimes translates to the introduction of approaches which may not be best suited to local contexts or in some instances, the premature introduction of approaches without consideration of contexts. What is also a likely occurrence is the reality of organisations being enticed by foreign approaches and trying to adapt them despite their inapplicability or financial non-viability. We make reference to New Zealand's Crime Prevention approach, which has had positive results since its implementation (Crawford, 2013; Unit, 1994). In 2017, a workshop was held by the New Zealand Police to share information about the successful approach to policing and to assist PICs in adopting the approach in their specific contexts. The documented success of the approach was likely to enhance its attractiveness, especially in contexts where there was an identified need to address crime, unmatched by available resources. What was not highlighted was the cost of such a modernisation undertaking or the acknowledgement that there were already informal crime prevention strategies operational in much of Melanesia. The cost of proper implementation beyond the establishment of a policy document would be too high. The availability of funding for training, developing effective cooperative approaches, establishing systems for monitoring and evaluation and contextualising likely exceeded most countries' operational budgets. Though crime prevention strategies and community policing tenants are visible in many PICs, the lure of modernisation moves countries to adopt practices reflective of international indicators of suitability perceived as "modern" or peddled as "policing best practice", without consideration of context appropriate best practices that may already exist.

Police organisations in much of the developed world have committed to modernisation to ensure efficiency and effectiveness of service delivery in societies marred by diversity, fragmentation and eclecticism (Waters, 2007). In Melanesia, modernisation efforts appear primarily concerned with the introduction and updating of technological products intended to improve police service delivery, efficiency and effectiveness. They also appear focussed on capacity building to reduce reliance on other countries and to facilitate service availability and delivery locally. Successful modernisation efforts are visible across Melanesia with notable examples in Solomon Islands through the Australia funded Police Development Program's capability building for fraud control, Fiji's Intelligence System and through the Pacific Islands Chief of Police (PICP) Secretariat coordinated Forensic Working Group and Transnational Crime Network. In contexts where intentions are unmatched by funding availability, solutions with little to no relevance are offered to smaller countries. What is also not uncommon in Melanesia is the introduction of relevant technologies without trained personal for operation or technology that cannot be maintained locally with no contingency plan in place for maintenance after funding is withdrawn or diminishes. In most contexts, the full cost of modernisation is not truly considered as what is proposed is usually a condensed or arbitrarily put together solution to a problem. For police organisations in Australia and New Zealand, the time and resources invested into the training of officers to use any newly introduced technology simply cannot be matched in contexts with strained human resources, limited financial capacity and the lack of trainers to conduct the required training (or update skillsets).

Borrowed solutions

Policing policies and practices across the globe continue to undergo modifications to meet the changing demands placed on policing organisations. The globalisation agenda perpetuated primarily by developed countries present crime as a global problem to be addressed through strategic alignment favouring policies and practices from the global North (Watson, 2014; Watson & Kerrigan, 2018). What this means for less powerful countries is a bombardment with policies and declarations with minimal contextual relevance being presented for adoption or localisation (Watson, 2016). This is in part due to privileging the security/policing priorities of the metropolitan countries/donors over those of the recipient countries where they are assumed to be the same. A menu option of policing policies usually becomes the marker reflective of adherence to international standards put forward by the UN, UNODC, World Bank and donor countries. The distinctiveness of Melanesia becomes secondary to alignment agendas, unconcerned or unfamiliar with historical, traditional, cultural political and economic contextual realities.

For countries such as PNG, Solomon Islands and Vanuatu, policing has been a relatively low priority of successive governments. This lack of prioritisation by political leadership has meant that police assistance/reform has been largely left up to donors like Australia and New Zealand. In most of these countries, including Fiji, the idea of modified policing has not been as successfully executed on the ground. This is not surprising as the theory behind the policing strategies used (Community Policing together with Broken-Windows Policing) 1) directly contradict each other and 2) have not been successfully implemented beyond the point of policy adoption. In such contexts underscored by problematic police-community relations and non-feasibility with established indigenous local policing practices or informal settlements comprised of multiple ethnic groups, it is unlikely that the external model allows for ease of implementation or adoption. If we consider the realities in other PICs context well known for scepticism of law enforcement (Solomon Islands, Vanuatu, Papua New Guinea) or limited police capacity (all PICs), it is likely that foreign theorising is not necessarily best suited to address local problems.

The borrowing of fleeting or poorly conceptualised policies also presents a challenge for Melanesian countries. We draw attention to the Broken Window and No-Drop policies from the US and New Zealand, respectively. The highly controversial Broken Window Theory is premised on the idea that visible signs of crime and criminality encourage further crime and criminality (Maskaly & Boggess, 2014; Wilson & Kelling, 1982). The theory makes assumptions about visible crime and criminality premised on poor infrastructure, prescribed standards of behaviour and northern notions of order and lawfulness. In so doing, it prescribes reactions to what might be regarded as acceptable or "normalized" behaviours in Melanesian contexts. In a country such as Fiji for example, where police policy makers have been known to reference this theory and align policing practices with the same, one of two assumptions can be made – either the theory has not been accurately understood or it is bound to become another casualty of non-contextualized borrowing. The No-Drop policy which was developed in New Zealand as a strategy to combat domestic violence was shelved after less than a decade (Pais, 2016). Despite New Zealand's acknowledgement of the inapplicability of the policy (due to the sensitive and complex nature of domestic violence), Fiji and Solomon Islands continue to struggle with the implementation of this borrowed solution to a major problem. What is interesting is the reality that New Zealand discontinued the policy despite available resources to support victims, training for officers to enact the policy and alignment from identification of an issue to prosecution. Such a high resource requirement and reliance of an effective prosecution system is likely to pose a challenge for most Melanesian countries, which would also increase the likelihood of the policy not being properly actioned.

Conclusion

Discussions about policing in Melanesia require initial acknowledgement of the diversity of the countries and the historical, traditional, social, political and economic distinctiveness of island states. While we acknowledge the existence of similarities among Melanesian countries, we caution against assumptions about sameness and transferability of policing interventions, practices and policies to all countries. Greater consideration needs to be given to country-specific problems and solutions should be contextualised within country-specific operational agendas. Watson and Kerrigan (2018) advise "ideas generated independently of the anticipated operational context are likely to present low-impact strategies or force-to-fit solutions" and this significantly affects the prospects of accomplishing projected outcomes (626). Our goal here is not to dismiss or trivialise the positive impact of external intervention and assistive strategies to policing in the Melanesian context. Instead, we highlight the need for contextualisation.

References

Abrahamsen, R., & Williams, M. (2009). Security beyond the state: Global security assemblages in international politics. *International Political Sociology*, *3*, 1–17.
Aina, S. (2002). Fa'a Samoa. *Amerasia Journal*, *28*(3), 135–147.
Allen, M., & Dinnen, S. (2010). The north down under: Antinomies of conflict and intervention in Solomon Islands. *Conflict, Security & Development*, *10*(3), 299–327.
Allen, M., Dinnen, S., Evans, D., & Monson, R. (2013). *Justice delivered locally: Systems, challenges and innovations in Solomon islands*. Washington, DC: World Bank.
Anderson, D., & Killingray, D. (Eds.). (1992). *Policing and decolonisation: Politics, nationalism and the police*. Manchester: Manchester University Press.
Ayson, R. (2007). The "arc of instability" and Australia's strategic policy. *Australian Journal of International Affairs*, *61*(2), 215–231.
Bagayoko, N., Hutchful, E., & Luckham, R. (2016). Hybrid security governance in Africa: Rethinking the foundations of security, justice and legitimate public authority. *Conflict, Security & Development*, *16*(1), 1–32.

Baker, B. (2008). Beyond the tarmac road: Local forms of policing in Sierra Leone and Rwanda. *Review of African Political Economy, 35*(118), 555–570.

Baker, B. (2010). *Security in post-conflict Africa: The role of nonstate policing.* Baton Rouge, LA, London, and New York: CRC Press.

Ballard, C., & Douglas, B. (2017). "Rough justice": Punitive expeditions in Oceania. *Journal of Colonialism and Colonial History, 18*(1). https://doi.org/10.1353/cch2017.0018

Boege, V., Brown, M. A., & Clements, K. P. (2009). Hybrid political orders, not fragile states. *Peace Review, 21*(1), 13–21.

Boege, V., Brown, M. A., Clements, K., & Nolan, A. (2008). *On hybrid political orders and emerging states: State formation in the context of 'fragility'.* Berlin: Berghof Research Center for Constructive Conflict Management.

Bull, N., George, N., & Curth-Bibb, J. (2019). The virtues of strangers? Policing gender violence in Pacific Island countries. *Policing and Society, 29*(2), 155–170. https://doi.org/10.1080/10439463.2017.1311894

Craig, D., & Porter, D. (2018, June). *Safety and security at the edges of the state: Local regulation in Papua New Guinea's urban settlements.* Washington, DC: World Bank Justice for the Poor, Research Report. Retrieved from https://elibrary.worldbank.org/doi/abs/10.1596/30260

Crawford, A. (Ed.). (2013). *Crime prevention policies in comparative perspective.* Devon: Willan Publishing.

Dinnen, S. (2003). Restorative justice in the Pacific islands: An introduction. In S. Dinnen with A. Jowitt, & T. Newton Cain (Eds.), *A kind of mending: Restorative justice in the Pacific islands* (pp. 1–34). Canberra: Pandanus Books.

Dinnen, S. (2017). Internal security in Papua New Guinea: Trends and prospects. In J. Pryke (Ed.), *Papua New Guinea: Seven snapshots of a nation.* Sydney: Lowy Institute.

Dinnen, S. (2019, April 1). Security governance in Melanesia: Police, prisons and crime. In E. Hirsch & W. Rollason (Eds.), *The Melanesian world.* London: Routledge, forthcoming.

Dinnen, S., & McLeod, A. (2009). Policing Melanesia: International expectations and local realities. *Policing & Society, 19*(4), 333–353.

Dobell, G. (2003). The reluctant Pacific nation: Policy taboos, popular amnesia and political failure. *Quadrant, 47*(5), 16.

Edwards, C. J. (2005). *Changing policing theories for twenty-first century societies.* Alexandria, Australia: Federation Press.

Ekbladh, D. (2011). *The Great American mission: Modernization and the construction of an American world order* (Vol. 6). Princeton, NJ: Princeton University Press.

Forsyth, M. (2007). *A bird that flies with two wings: The Kastom and state justice systems in Vanuatu.* Canberra: ANU Press.

Friman, H. R. (2009). Drug markets and the selective use of violence. *Crime, Law and Social Change, 52*(3), 285–295.

Fry, G., & Kabutaulaka, T. (Eds.). (2008). *Intervention and state-building in the Pacific: The legitimacy of 'cooperative intervention'.* Manchester: Manchester University Press.

Human Rights Watch (HRW). (2005, August 30). *Making their own rules: Police beatings, rape and torture of children in Papua New Guinea.* New York: Human Rights Watch.

Hunter, J. D. (1991). *Culture wars: The struggle to define America.* New York: Basic.

Jackson, J., Bradford, B., Hough, M., & Murray, K. H. (2012). Compliance with the law and policing by consent. *Legitimacy and Compliance in Criminal Justice,* 29–49.

Jefferson, T. (1990). *The case against paramilitary policing* (p. 16). Milton Keynes: Open University Press.

Jones, T., & Newburn, T. (Eds.). (2006). *Plural policing: A comparative perspective.* Milton Park: Routledge.

Kituai, A. (1998). *My gun, my brother: The world of Papua New Guinea colonial police 1920–1960.* Honolulu, HI: University of Hawai'i Press.

Knauft, B. M. (1990). Melanesian warfare: A theoretical history. *Oceania, 60*(4), 250–311.

Larmour, P. (2007). International action against corruption in the Pacific Islands: Policy transfer, coercion and effectiveness. *Asian Journal of Political Science, 15*(1), 1–16.

Latham, M. E. (2000). *Modernization as ideology: American social science and "nation building" in the Kennedy era* (Vol. 4). Chapel Hill, NC: University of North Carolina Press.

Loader, I. (2000). Plural policing and democratic governance. *Social & Legal Studies, 9*(3), 323–345.

MacNaught, T. J. (2016). *The Fijian colonial experience: A study of the neotraditional order under British colonial rule prior to World War II.* Canberra: ANU Press.

Mair, L. P. (1948). *Australia in New Zealand.* London: Christopher's.

Maskaly, J., & Boggess, L. N. (2014). Broken windows theory. *The Encyclopedia of Theoretical Criminology*, 1–4.

Mazarr, M. J. (2014). The rise and fall of the failed-state paradigm: Requiem for a decade of distraction. *Foreign Affairs*, January–February, 113–121.

McLeod, A., & Dinnen, S. (2007). Police building in the Southwest Pacific: New directions in Australian regional policing. In A. Goldsmith & J. Sheptycki (Eds.), *Crafting transnational policing: Police capacity-building and global policing reform* (pp. 295–328). Oxford: Hart.

Nabobo-Baba, U. (2006) *Knowing and Learning: An Indigenous Fijian Approach.* Suva, Fiji: Institute of Pacific Studies, The University of the South Pacific.

Newton, T. (1998). Policing in the South Pacific islands. *The Police Journal, 71*(4), 349–352.

OECD DAC. (2007). *Handbook on security sector system reform: Supporting security and justice.* Paris: OECD.

Oliver, W. M. (2001). *Community-oriented policing: A systemic approach to policing.* Upper Saddle River, NJ: Prentice Hall.

Pais, P. (2016). *Challenging the efficacy of no-drop prosecution policies in domestic violence cases: A comparative legal analysis.* PhD Dissertation, The University of Queensland.

Richmond, O. (2011). De-romanticising the local, de-mystifying the international: Hybridity in Timor Leste and the Solomon Islands. *The Pacific Review, 24*(1), 115–136.

Sargeant, E., Wickes, R., & Mazerolle, L. (2013). Social control in community context: Exploring the formal-informal nexus. *Australia & New Zealand Journal of Criminology, 46*(1), 70–87.

Scaglion, R. (2004). Legal pluralism in Pacific island societies. In V. S. Lockwood (Ed.), *Globalization and culture change in the pacific islands* (pp. 86–101). Upper Saddle River, NJ: Pearson Prentice Hall.

Shusta, R. M., Levine, D. R., Harris, P. R., & Wong, H. Z. (2002). *Multicultural law enforcement: Strategies for peacekeeping in a diverse society.* Upper Saddle River, NJ: Prentice Hall.

Sillitoe, P. (2000). *Social change in Melanesia: Development and history.* Cambridge: Cambridge University Press.

Unit, C. P. (1994). *The New Zealand crime prevention strategy.* Wellington: Crime Prevention Unit.

Walton, G., & Dinnen, S. (2016, October). *The dark side of economic globalisation: Politics, organised crime and corruption in the Pacific* (pp. 1–32). Development Policy Centre Discussion Paper 48. Australian National University.

Waters, I., Hardy, N., Delgado, D., & Dahlmann, S. (2007). Ethnic minorities and the challenge of police recruitment. *The Police Journal, 80*(3), 191–216.

Watson, D. (2014). Defining power margins: A classification of power within the discourses of police and civilian in a crime "hotspot community" in Northern Trinidad. *Journal of Multicultural Discourses, 9*(3), 227–250.

Watson, D. (2016). The power of community branding: An examination of the impact of imposed categories on policing a "crime hotspot community". *Journal of Multicultural Discourses, 11*(1), 51–68.

Watson, D., & Kerrigan, D. (2018). Crime, criminality, and north-to-south criminological complexities: Theoretical implications for policing "hotspot" communities in "underdeveloped" countries. In *The Palgrave handbook of criminology and the global south* (pp. 611–632). Cham, Switzerland: Palgrave Macmillan.

Watson, D., Boateng, F. D., Pino, N., & Morgan, P. (2018). The interface between exercise of state power and personal powerlessness: A study of police perceptions of factors impacting professional practices. *Police Practice and Research*, 1–14.

White, G. M., & Lindstrom, L. (Eds.). (1997). *Chiefs today: Traditional Pacific leadership and the postcolonial state*. Stanford, CA: Stanford University Press.

Wilson, J. Q., & Kelling, G. L. (1982). Broken windows. *Atlantic Monthly, 249*(3), 29–38.

Wood, J., & Shearing, C. (2007). *Imagining security*. Abingdon: Willan Publishing.

World Bank. (2018). *The World Bank in Pacific islands*. Retrieved from www.worldbank.org/en/country/pacificislands/overview

13 Policing sorcery accusation related violence in Papua New Guinea

Miranda Forsyth

Introduction

This chapter describes how the police in Papua New Guinea (PNG) respond to sorcery accusations and related violence (SARV). In so doing, it opens a portal through which the relationship between the police, the state and the public can be viewed and analysed. SARV offers a unique angle from which to view these relationships because it often involves a clear conflict between differing conceptions of what actions are in the public interest and what constitutes a source of insecurity. At its most extreme, SARV pits an entire community convinced of the need to torture and kill the sorcerer (or witch), whom they believe has killed and may kill again, against a state whose laws proscribe the death penalty for those who take such actions. The police, as one interviewee neatly put it, are the "meat in the sandwich".

This chapter first investigates the successive challenges the police in PNG face when seeking to police SARV. Like much of the literature in this area, it highlights the vast array of difficulties faced by the police – including their lack of sufficient personnel, training, resourcing and oversight. It also describes the *particular* problems SARV presents on top of this familiar litany of problems – the moral dilemmas faced by police officers when they themselves are convinced of the reality of the sorcery claims, and the risks to their own lives from the mob violence that often accompanies SARV incidents. In such a context, there are competing conceptions of security at play – the security of the community in terms of needing to be protected from potential supernatural harm, and the security of individuals needing to be protected from stigmatisation and attacks following accusations of sorcery. Not only does this pit individual security against public security, it also pits a magical world-view against a secular/scientific one.

The chapter then steps away from a "deficit lens" approach to policing and turns to describing a number of strategies used by those police who do respond effectively to SARV. Many of these strategies revolve around the non-policing relationships and resources that the police officers possess as members of clans and tribes, as members and leaders of different Christian congregations, as supporters of particular political factions and as participants and leaders in a wide range of community leadership roles.

The importance of non-state policing resources is a familiar theme in the literature of policing in the global South (and in the global North, within the frame of community policing and private security). However, the chapter does not identify the importance of this web of relationships in order to make the now familiar argument about the need to recognise and appreciate the broad range of non-state policing resources. Whilst it agrees with this standpoint, it goes further to ask what the empirical evidence about the policing of SARV tells us about the relationship between the police and the state, a relationship that has not been interrogated often, not even in the literature focussed on plural policing.

The chapter makes the argument that there are at least two models of relationship between state, police and community in PNG. One is the classic Weberian state, existing in some bureaucratic structures, institutional arrangements and most importantly, as an ideology. In this model the police, who have a legitimate monopoly on the use of force, carry out the wishes of the state *on* the community. The other model is a far older relational state, where the drivers of action are the relational properties that exist between individuals and institutions. In this model, the police and community are connected in multiple different ways and act on *each other*. The relational model views the police force and other institutions of government as just one of multiple sets of relationships within which individuals are situated. Both of these models of state exist in different configurations of dynamic interaction and domination throughout PNG and are implicated in policing practices, such as in policing SARV.

The chapter finally sets out some of the theoretical and policy implications arising from this insight. It suggests the ability of police to effectively provide security for the weak and the vulnerable in PNG society may be enhanced by embracing their relational resources, and providing them with the moral and ethical skills needed to navigate effectively between conflicting cultural and state norms around the acceptability of violence.

The various threats SARV poses to security in PNG

Throughout Melanesia, sorcery and witchcraft provide an explanatory framework that makes sense of events in the world, especially illness, death and misfortune. In 2009, the PNG Constitutional Law Reform Commission reported on its extensive consultation and research into sorcery beliefs in PNG. It found the majority of Papua New Guineans strongly assert that sorcery is real, regardless of levels of education, gender, religiosity, or whether they reside in urban (including overseas) or rural areas. One effect of believing in witchcraft is an assumption that others desire to do them harm. Ashforth (2005, p. 69) uses the notion of "spiritual insecurity" to explain the impact produced by belief in witchcraft, noting: "life in a world of witches must be lived in the light of a presumption of malice: one must assume that anyone with the motive to harm has access to the means and that people will cause harm because they can".

In PNG today, belief in sorcery frequently leads to accusations against individuals suspected of practising sorcery, particularly in the context of unexplained or unexpected sickness and death. Such accusations can lead to stigmatisation (and social isolation), violence and even death. Activists within PNG have coined the term "Sorcery Accusation Related Violence" (SARV) to refer to this bundle of harms, signifying that it is violence emanating from the accusation, rather than the supposed power of sorcery that underlies the harms. Increasingly, it is globally recognised that SARV (sometimes referred to as "witch-hunting") is a form of extreme human rights violation and that it is occurring in many countries (Forsyth, 2016; WHRIN, 2017).

The scope of the harms related to SARV have not yet been properly quantified. However, halfway through a multi-year research project documenting as many cases as possible in three provinces, the chapter's research team has recorded 357 incidents of sorcery accusations since 2016.[1] The data about each of these incidents is recorded on a standardised form by a network of local field recorders in each province, referred to below as "incident data".[2] So far the data shows 117 of these 357 incidents led to violence against 185 victims and 240 did not lead to violence. In almost a quarter of the SARV incidents, the victim's family had to temporarily relocate and 16 % did so permanently. Our analysis of cases reported in the national media and by the national courts over a 20-year period found that in the reported cases, almost half the accused were killed (42%), a third were wounded (34%) and a third (34%) were not physically harmed. (On average, there were more than 30 deaths and 72 victims per year (Forsyth, Putt, Bouhours, & Bouhours, 2017b).

The formal state legislative response to SARV in the past decade has involved the repeal of the Sorcery Act 1971[3] and the introduction of a new provision into the Criminal Code that creates a specific offence of "wilful murder of a person on account of accusation of sorcery" (s299A). Whilst each year there are between seven to eight convictions for murder involving accusations of sorcery,[4] the vast majority of cases of murder, grievous bodily harm, assault, arson and destruction of property associated with accusations of sorcery do not proceed very far, if at all, through the criminal justice system. This fact has been repeatedly commented upon by local activists and external commentators, including various United Nations (UN) human rights representatives.[5]

The challenges of policing SARV

As in many parts of the global South, security in PNG is provided by a broad network of actors and institutions, often acting together in assemblages (Lattas & Rio, 2011) or in nodal relationships (Shearing, 2005). SARV is therefore policed by a variety of different actors, particularly local leaders and faith-based organisations, but this chapter focusses principally on the police response.

The official police force in PNG is the Royal Papua New Guinea Constabulary (RPNGC), estimated in 2013 at around 5,724 uniformed police (Connery & Claxton, 2014), which is less than half the UNs' recommended minimum.[6] Given the uneven geographical distribution of police, with most clustered in urban areas, there are many areas of PNG effectively left unpoliced by the RPNGC. Training of uniformed police takes just six months. Uniformed police are supplemented by community auxiliary police (CAPs) and reserve police officers, both drawn from the wider community.[7] CAPs receive 2–6 weeks training and notionally get paid a small salary, which frequently fails to materialise.

The various challenges facing the RPNGC and the CAPs/ reserves have been detailed over the years without great variation, except perhaps with an increasingly negative and desperate tone (see Dinnen & McLeod, 2009). Peake and Dinnen (2014, p. 34) note that "[i]t is striking that the language used to diagnose the RPNGC's frailties in 2014 is practically identical to that used at the beginning of the first programme [25 years ago]". These challenges include the manifestly inadequate size of the force; lack of essential resources, such as vehicles and fuel; lack of regular training, such as investigatory techniques; substandard police leadership; factionalism; political interference in police operations; lack of responsiveness to community complaints and high levels of police brutality (Putt, Dinnen, Keen, & Batley, 2017). Extracurricular means of raising funds, through political patronage and "fuel" money from individuals seeking help or reporting a crime have also been reported (Dinnen, 2017). The last major review, in 2004 ("the 2004 review"), found "weaknesses in every area and aspect of the constabulary".[8] That review also noted that the most widespread philosophy amongst the Constabulary still carried a colonialist notion of "enforcing the rules on a suspicious population", despite prior recommendations in various reports to evolve to a community policing philosophy.[9]

These generalised capacity challenges impact the RPNGC's ability to prevent and intervene in incidents, and to bring perpetrators of SARV to justice. For instance, in one Highlands province, a CID officer explained they had no assigned vehicle since 2015 and could only access a station vehicle occasionally. Specialist squads, such as the homicide squad, no longer existed, and he described his policing approach as "investigating cases as they come in", rather than having capacity to go out to remote places to conduct interviews and investigate. He mentioned a case where a woman was accused and tortured, including by her brother, who is "still at large and won't surrender". In another case, a young girl was accused and tortured. Although the police have evidence to identify the suspects, the remoteness of the location, across two rivers with no bridge, makes it hard to arrest them. The police officer in charge explained how he went three times to try to arrest the suspects, but people refused to talk about it. He said that if he used force, then they would probably remove some of the bridges to trap him and try to shoot him. Instead, he had to resort to other more dialogue-based and relational tactics.

The policing response to SARV is further complicated by various factors that are more particular to the issue. These stem largely from the disjuncture between the official state response to SARV *as a crime* and broad community *support for* violence against those believed to have used sorcery, particularly where the accused sorcerer is considered to have killed someone through their sorcery and remains a threat. The impacts of this disjuncture are:

- Police are frequently not notified about SARV incidents. Based on our incident data collected in three locations, the police were called in just over a quarter of the incidents that resulted in violence.

- Police are hampered in intervening to protect those being attacked by the community (outnumbered and outgunned). In 23% of cases we have collected to date across the three provinces, over 50 perpetrators are involved, frequently blocking police access and threatening violence against police attempts to intervene.
- Police cannot persuade witnesses to testify in court. For instance, in one Highlands province, a CID officer said: "We need statements, most witnesses won't do it. Whole tribe against an individual. Nobody supports the victim. . . . The community decides what they want to say to the police".

Some police are complicit in SARV and act as passive bystanders or even perpetrators, sharing the same views as the community about the suspected sorcerer. In one recent case, the Northern Provincial police commander was even the instigator of SARV; he became convinced that his sore leg was caused by two individuals in his home village using sorcery against him, and sent two of his officers to assault them, leading to the death of one of the accused and serious bodily harm the other.[10]

As a result of all these (and other) challenges, the proportion of incidents that result in arrests is low, at 9% according to our incident data and at 20% according to the 20 years of reported cases in national newspapers and courts we have analysed. The percentage of incidents resulting in convictions is even lower.

A related issue for the police trying to police SARV is how they should respond if approached by community members concerned that a particular individual or individuals are practising sorcery. The strict legal position is that sorcery is not a crime under the criminal law, although the Village Courts have a number of sorcery-related offences that criminalise the *pretence* of sorcery. We have documented a wide range of responses to such concerns, including: police detaining the accused and launching full investigations;[11] explaining that "there is no evidence" to prove sorcery under the law and sending people back to their villages or communities to deal with the matter there; mediation (discussed in the next section); advising community members to seek compensation from the suspected sorcerer; imprisoning the suspect, sometimes with and sometimes against his or her will[12] and as mentioned earlier, becoming active participants in violence against those accused.

Police strategies to address SARV

There are multiple instances where police intervention does occur through prevention, intervention and prosecution, as well as provision of safety to those accused, despite significant obstacles lying in the way of police assisting the victims of SARV. Four main policing strategies in relation to the SARV cases emerge from the examples of cases we have documented.

The first strategy involves forming coalitions with local powerbrokers and local community members, in order to both engage in prevention and to intervene to stop violence or to remove those being accused. One senior police officer in the Highlands reflected that while he had believed "in arrest and the rule of law" when he first worked in the province more than 15 years ago, he has subsequently taken a more "flexible view". Despite being well connected politically and high in the police hierarchy, he has to rely on provincial or more local patronage to obtain resources, such as fuel for the police vehicles, in order to even get to sites where intervention is required. Once at a rescue site, negotiation and strategic collaboration with local leaders is essential, given the imbalance of manpower between police and community. In Bougainville, we documented a number of cases where unarmed police teamed up with armed ex-combatants and community government leaders in order to rescue accused sorcerers who were being detained and beaten by community members.

Second, police informally mediate cases at the police station or in villages, seeking to enable communities to deal with their anxieties around sorcery in ways that do not involve violence. This type of mediation often involves encouraging people to voice their concerns and provide evidence to support their accusations, and in turn, giving the accused an opportunity to publicly respond with explanations about the alleged suspicious behaviour. For instance, a person seen in an odd place at an odd time may be suspected of sorcery, but they may have a simple explanation for their presence at that time that dispels suspicion. Through such mediation, the police perform the role of bridging the strict demands of the state's legal position (sorcery is irrational nonsense) and the genuine concerns of communities. Sometimes the police conduct the questioning themselves, other times they provide security for the meeting, and exercise their convening power to bring together community leaders, pastors or Village Court magistrates to do the actual mediating.

Third, the police frequently offer the accused refuge inside the police station and in its cells. Whilst on occasion there is a lack of clarity around whether or not the intention is to offer safety, or in fact to lock away a dangerous public menace, we have documented a substantial number of cases (in Bougainville, Lae, Port Moresby and in the Highlands) where the motivation is clearly to protect the accused individual. One example occurred in Port Moresby in late 2018, when a female police officer offered refuge to a woman accused by her in-laws of using sorcery to make her husband sick. Despite the disapproval of her superior officers, she kept the accused woman in the police station for a week, paying for her food and her baby's supplies, and even slept in the station with her. She helped the accused woman to find family members willing to take her in and support her. When asked what had motivated her to do this, the police officer replied: "I had no choice. I could see she needed help". She observed she was not concerned the woman was a sorcerer, because she had carefully assessed the evidence and concluded that the woman truly loved her husband and so trying to make him sick made no sense. She reflected that she was trying to make a difference through assisting one person at a time, and hoped that her gesture would spread. She believed that maybe if one day the woman she had helped saw someone else in a similar situation, she would advise them "go and see [name] the police officer, she will help you".

Fourth, there are multiple cases where police have offered personal support and their own resources to care for victims of SARV and their families, taking them into their own houses at times, and exposing themselves to considerable risk to their own lives. In one case of SARV, one family's son was murdered, the fingers were chopped off another son and the father had had his whole hand chopped off. The police officer involved in the case stated: "my family agreed to assist these two on humanitarian grounds and so we allocated them some ground and some coffee plantation. They have been with us for four years now, we have not asked them for anything in return". When asked whether he was afraid of his own life for sheltering these men, he stated: "I am a paramount leader of my tribe. If anyone says anything bad against me they will be attacked by my tribesmen". This is an example of a police officer calling upon his tribal networks to allow him to exercise care and protection for victims, duties that are related to, but go well beyond, his role as a police officer.

Other police officers have set up initiatives within their own communities to avoid the type of extreme violence they have observed occurring in relation to SARV cases. For instance, one police officer in the Highlands described the way in which he had set up an association in his community to address social disorder: in cases of sorcery accusation, the association calls together members of different Christian denominations from within the community to weigh up the evidence, and find there is no real evidence. He further personally explains to the accusers that there could be other reasons behind the incident they have accused the "sorcerer" of causing, such as a biological explanation for sickness or death. This police officer observed that people listened to him because he has standing in the community and he has their respect, in part due to his role as police officer.

Insights for the relationship between the police and the state

It is helpful to situate this discussion in the context of a rich vein of scholarship on policing that has emerged over the past decade,[13] which has, in different ways, critiqued the dominant model of policing, termed here the "police legitimacy model", (borrowed from Mendez-Beck & Jaffe, 2019). This model involves "a relation where the police enforce a social and legal order posited by the state" (Mendez-Beck & Jaffe, 2019, p. 4). It is based on a Weberian understanding of the state, whereby the police have a monopoly on the use of force, and the goal of policing is as much about providing the state legitimacy as it is about providing security and justice for people (Bayley & Perito, 2010, p. 82). In this model, to use the helpful language of Braithwaite (2000), the state does "all the rowing and all the steering". Braithwaite (2000) argued that this model of the state reached its zenith in practice under a Keynesian ideology, later increasingly undermined by the turn to the market as regulator. In the context of policing, it means the police, as agents of the state, have the role of enforcing the law *on* the community.

Two interlinked policy-relevant consequences of these insights into the problems with the police legitimacy model of policing arise. One is the need for more active embrace by governments of "multi-choice policing" or "plural policing" to use policing resources outside of, or more loosely connected with, the state. The second is the turn to "community policing" as a way of recognising the need to involve communities more actively in both the steering and rowing of policing. The original, expansive vision of community policing was based on the logic that the police need to engage in lateral partnerships and collaborative efforts with other government organisations, structures of civil society and the private sector (Marks, Shearing, & Wood, 2009, p. 146). Both of these approaches have been strongly advocated also in the context of PNG (for example, Peake & Dinnen, 2014).

However, there has been strong resistance from governments in both the global North and the global South to any real engagement with both multi-choice policing and community policing as originally proposed (Marks et al., 2009). Both proposals have foundered at the point of the state being prepared to relinquish the ideological monopoly over policing within its particular territory. In regard to community policing, the notion has been "writ small" to become "[s]omething to make state police more effective by getting the community to help them" (Braithwaite, 2000, p. 230). In other words, the state enrols the community to do part of the rowing, but does not relinquish much real control over the steering, keeping intact its objectives to strengthen the legitimacy and effectiveness of the police (and hence the state).

The plural policing scholarship argues that it is important to recognise the existence of a diversity of policing actors in any given social field. A further, hitherto largely unexplored consequence of the insights emanating from this scholarship is that it is also necessary to rethink the model of the relationship between the police and the state. This, in turn, has implications for how the police interact with, influence and are influenced by, the other policing actors in the broader assemblages and networks within which they work.

In much of the literature discussed above, even that used to argue for community policing and plural policing, the police are seen as closed nodes tied very strongly to the state, reflecting the model strongly associated with the Weberian state. The emphasis is on control of police through rigid hierarchy and bureaucratic rationality. While the nodal governance literature encourages police to enrol others in their policing project, it still envisages them as a bounded entity – "the police" – and as total agents of the state (for example, [Shearing 2005]). Marks et al. (2009) envisage each node in the security governance, including the police, as "strong and distinguishable from the other" (p. 152). Any move of individual police officers outside this relationship of control is seen in purely negative terms, usually as corruption or co-option by non-police actors (be they criminal gangs, businesses, political parties or in a Melanesian context, *wantoks* [literally "one talk", meaning people from the same language group or family/clan/tribe]).

Yet, this model of relationship between the police and the state is very much at odds with the empirical reality, particularly in a country like PNG, but to some degree in many other countries as well. The reality is much more often the case that the police and other agents of the state exist within multiple relational networks wherein they exercise their powers to both steer and row governance at different scales.

Following these insights, this chapter suggests that the Weberian state is not the only form of state in existence in PNG (or indeed in many other countries). There is also a *second* form of state, the relational state. In this model, both the rowing and the steering rely upon the relational properties that exist between individuals and institutions as they are variously grouped and networked. The relational state acknowledges that relationships are the glue that holds the state together at a variety of different scales and the engine that drives much of the action – in many contexts they are the only things allowing it to operate at all. In the relational state, the police and community are connected in multiple different ways and act on *each other* and it is through these interactions that policing and the provision of security (as well as governance) largely occurs.

The relational state exists in dynamic interaction with the Weberian state in PNG, with each modifying and, in particular contexts, dominating each other. It is not correct, however, to conceptualise an evolutionary trend in which the Weberian state model slowly but surely dominates the relational state model (see, for example, the World Development Bank Report (2017) where this assumption is stark). Both the relational state and the Weberian state are better conceived as fully formed and fully modern, operating together to produce the governance arrangements of today. The consequence of this reframing means that it is a mistake to consider the relational state only in terms of the extent to which it can improve the Weberian state's scope, power and legitimacy. Instead, it should be asked how both might improve (and threaten) security and access to justice.

Evidence for the existence of the relational state largely comes from observations about how the police actually provide security to the victims of SARV. The strategies most frequently successful in this context can best be understood as belonging to the relational state, namely forming coalitions with other powerbrokers, use of informal strategies such as mediation, using state resources (such as police posts and prison cells) in ways unintended officially and personal donations of support and security. The relational state framing allows us to view what is happening not as the police failing to fulfil their functions (as in the classic diagnosis of "weak" or "failed" states), but as fulfilment of their functions through the modalities of the relational state, rather than the Weberian state.

The example of SARV shows that in order for the opportunities for less dominating visions of justice to emerge and be enforced, they must come from the interaction of both models with each other. A purely Weberian state approach achieves almost nothing in relation to SARV, because the state lacks the necessary manpower to apply an interpretation of security vastly at odds with community perceptions of security. A purely relational approach risks allowing mob violence to prevail, favouring tribal connections that are the strongest. However, the interactions between the two state models can provide the necessary range of resources, normative contestations and moral balancing that enable police officers to conceive and implement the various successful strategies outlined above. Whilst more research is needed to delve deeper into the various motivations of the police officers engaged in these approaches, the chapter has found a range of motivations. These include: perceptions of their obligations as police officers to provide security for those who seek their support; religious convictions; desire to maintain peace in their own communities and their compassion for the victims, which arises from a shared sense of humanity.

Following Braithwaite's injunction to seek to integrate the explanatory with the normative (2000, p. 235), it is necessary to consider the policy implications of the discussion above. One new policy orientation emerging from the nodal policing literature (Marks et al., 2009) is "minimalist policing". This approach advocates seeking to clearly delimit the police role to catching and charging perpetrators of crime, removing them from the more preventative work. However, this approach is unlikely to work in a country like PNG, as the approach is premised on a state that is strong and well-resourced enough to be able to effectively enforce a core role for the police. This chapter advocates a different approach: an embrace of the relational resources that police can and do draw upon to perform their role of provision of security writ large. Focussing only on the negatives associated with these relational resources (*wantokism*, corruption, etc.) ignores the reality that it is the relational leverage of police officers that allows them to perform any real role of security provision in PNG today. This means that conceptualising police as out-siders and neutral enforcers of the law may cut them off from the very resources they rely upon to do their job.

Conclusion

In conclusion, there is a need to understand that police officers and other state offi-cials always operate both within webs of relationships *and* within the institutional structures and ideology of the Weberian state. Thus, there is a need to equip them to make the best use of this dual reality in carrying out their policing and other gov-ernance roles. Challenging the normative legitimacy of violence is now a priority, as well as actively seeking to discover where the interactions of the two models of state best generate policing that achieves the visions of justice sought by commu-nity members, protection of the weak and promotes compassion for the suffering of others. It is also essential to identify where the Weberian state and the relational state can support each other in effectively discouraging abuses of power by police officers. For instance, it may be useful to draw explicit attention to the role of police in navigating between different normative systems as part of police training, as well as discussing the values behind state, religious and customary systems that support the provision of security, particularly in protecting the weak and vulnerable, who are often the most impacted by SARV. If any type of restriction in the role of the police needs to be considered, it should perhaps be a re-prioritising of their role in protecting the vulnerable and de-prioritising the legitimation of a dominating state.

Notes

1 Official records in PNG, such as court, police and hospital records, are fragmented or inconsistent (Lakhani & Willman, 2014). They often do not record whether or not a crime or injury resulted from sorcery accusations and lack the vast amount of SARV

never reported to state authorities. The research team behind this study therefore created a database in late 2016 to be updated until 2020, to detail incidents of sorcery accusations recorded by a network of local researchers in target provinces, using specially devised incident forms to capture violence and non-violence incidents related to cases of sorcery accusations in relevant communities.

2 Further details about the methodology of the project are available at Forsyth, Putt, Bouhours, and Bouhours (2017a).

3 The Sorcery Act 1971 created three main ways to address issues around anxieties about sorcery: offences that indirectly criminalised the practice of pretending to do, or holding oneself out, as practising sorcery; a partial defence for sorcery-accusation related murder; and the offence of falsely accusing someone of performing sorcery or being a sorcerer. When in force, charges were rarely laid under the Act that resulted in convictions in the National court, and records of District court decisions are so fragmented, it is impossible to say how widely it was used at that level, but it may have been used more widely as a strategy for mediation of issues by the police. The defence was almost never used, and indeed the courts since 2010 have been giving heavy penalties more frequently: see further Forsyth (2015, pp. 218–219).

4 See Forsyth, M. et. al. (2019). Ten preliminary findings concerning sorcery accusation-related violence in Papua New Guinea.

5 See https://un.org.au/files/2013/06/Statement-on-Sorcery-related-Killings-and-Impunity-in-Papua-New-Guinea.pdf.

6 The UN recommends a ratio of 1:450.

7 The last recorded figures found were of 1,703 Reserve Police and 3,538 Auxiliary Police in the 2004 review Report, retrieved from: www.inapng.com/pdf_files/Police_Review_Report_final.pdf.

8 www.inapng.com/pdf_files/Police_Review_Report_final.pdf.

9 www.inapng.com/pdf_files/Police_Review_Report_final.pdf, p. 50.

10 Top cop sidelined over sorcery claim, The National, 29 March 2018.

11 Alleged detained sorcerers released, Post Courier, 8 November, 2017.

12 In one particularly egregious case, the victim had been severely burnt and assaulted; the police detained her in the cells for a day before sending her to the hospital, a delay that was alleged to have led to her death: Woman dies from torture injuries, Post Courier, 1 November 2017.

13 The authors comprising this scholarship include: Shearing, Wood, Braithwaite, Dupont, Grabosky, Wulff, Kyed, Albrecht, Baker, Dinnen, Jean and John Comaroff, Beck and Jaffe, amongst others.

References

Ashforth, A. (2005). *Witchcraft, violence, and democracy in South Africa*. Chicago, IL: The University of Chicago Press.

Bayley, D. H., & Perito, R. M. (2010). *The police in war: Fighting insurgency, terrorism, and violent crime*. Boulder, CO: Lynne Rienner Publishers.

Braithwaite, J. (2000). The new regulatory state and the transformation of criminology. *British Journal of Criminology, 40*, 222–238.

Connery, D., & Claxton, K. (2014). *Shared interests, enduring cooperation: The future of Australia-PNG police engagement*. Retrieved from https://s3-ap-southeast-2.amazonaws.com/ad-aspi/import/SR72_AFP_PNG_engagement.pdf?8Qt36WDQ4iChLvNyEydnHZf2FApOBcjJ.

Dinnen, S. (2017). *Internal security in Papua New Guinea: Trends and prospects*. Retrieved from https://interactives.lowyinstitute.org/archive/png-in-2017/png-in-2017-internal-security-png-trends-prospects.html.

Dinnen, S., & McLeod, A. (2009). *Policing Melanesia – International expectations and local realities*. Retrieved from www.researchgate.net/publication/232861742_Policing_Melanesia_-_international_expectations_and_local_realities.

Forsyth, M. (2015). A pluralist response to regulation of sorcery and witchcraft in Melanesia. In M. Forsyth & R. Eves (Eds.), *Talking it through: Responses to sorcery and witchcraft beliefs and practices in Melanesia* (pp. 213–239). Canberra: ANU Press.

Forsyth, M. (2016). The regulation of witchcraft and sorcery practices and beliefs. *Annual Review of Law and Social Science, 12*(46), 331–315.

Forsyth, M., Putt, J., Bouhours, T., & Bouhours, T. (2017a). *In brief 2017/28 sorcery accusation related violence in Papua New Guinea, Part 1: Questions and methodology*. Retrieved from http://ssgm.bellschool.anu.edu.au/experts-publications/publications/5782/ib201728-sorcery-accusation-related-violence-papua-new-guinea

Forsyth, M., Putt, J., Bouhours, T., & Bouhours, T. (2017b). *In brief 2017/29 sorcery accusation related violence in Papua New Guinea, Part 2: Key characteristics of incidents, victims and perpetrators*. Retrieved from http://ssgm.bellschool.anu.edu.au/experts-publications/publications/5784/ib201729-sorcery-accusation-related-violence-papua-new-guinea

Forsyth, M., Gibbs, P., Hukula, F., Putt, J., Munau, L., & Losoncz, I. (2019). *Ten preliminary findings concerning sorcery accusation-related violence in Papua New Guinea*. Development Policy Centre Discussion Paper No. 80. Retrieved from SSRN: https://papers.ssrn.com/sol3/papers.cfm?abstract_id=3360817.

Lakhani, S., & Willman, A. M. (2014). *Trends in crime and violence in Papua New Guinea* (English). Research and Dialogue Series No. 1. Washington, DC: World Bank Group. Retrieved from http://documents.worldbank.org/curated/en/992741468287127441/Trends-in-crime-and-violence-in-Papua-New-Guinea

Lattas, A., & Rio, K. M. (2011). Securing modernity: Towards an ethnography of power in contemporary Melanesia. *Oceania, 81*(1), 1–21. https://doi.org/10.1002/j.1834-4461.2011.tb00090.x

Marks, M., Shearing, C., & Wood, J. (2009). Who should the police be? Finding a new narrative for community policing in South Africa. *Police Practice and Research: An International Journal, 10*, 145–155.

Mendez-Beck, M., & Jaffe, R. (2019). Community policing goes south: Policy mobilities and new geographies of criminological theory. *The British Journal of Criminology, 59*(4), 823–841. https://doi.org/10.1093/bjc/azy046

Peake, G., & Dinnen, S. (2014). Police development in Papua New Guinea: The need for innovation. *Security Challenges, 10*(2), 33–51.

Putt, J., Dinnen, S., Keen, M., & Batley, J. (2017). *The RAMSI legacy for Pacific policing*. In Brief 2017/20. Retrieved from https://openresearch-repository.anu.edu.au/bitstream/1885/141341/1/IB2017.20%20Putt%20et%20al.pdf

Shearing, C. (2005). Nodal security. *Police Quarterly, 8*, 57–63.

The Witchcraft and Human Rights Information Network (WHRIN). (2017). Retrieved from www.whrin.org/

World Development Bank. (2017). *World Development Report 2017: Governance and the law*. Retrieved from www.worldbank.org/en/publication/wdr2017

14 Insecurity, policing and marketisation

Papua New Guinea's changing security landscape

Sinclair Dinnen

Introduction

The growth of the private security industry is a global phenomenon, with the fastest expansion in recent years occurring in the Global South. Worth an estimated $180 billion in 2017, the global market for private security (including private guards, surveillance and armed transport) is forecast to grow to $240 billion by 2020 (Provost, 2017). Many countries, including China, the US, Canada, Australia and the UK, now have more private security guards than public police officers. Although there is limited data available, the Pacific islands appear to be broadly conforming to this international pattern. Private security vehicles, uniformed personnel, guard dogs and company logos have become ubiquitous throughout the region, particularly in its rapidly growing urban landscapes. The industry has become a significant source of employment and a favoured form of business investment in many of these countries.

While extensive research has been done on private security in the Global North by scholars in various disciplines, including criminology (Jones & Newburn, 2006) and international relations (Abrahamsen & Williams, 2011), its growth in the Global South has attracted less attention (Diphoorn, 2015). This chapter examines the rise of private security in Papua New Guinea (PNG), the region's largest and most populous country. With an abundance of natural resources and situated at the crossroads between Asia and the Pacific, PNG has been undergoing rapid economic globalisation over the past two decades. Since its independence in 1975, it has acquired notoriety for its problems of crime, violence and disorder. PNG was also the location of the so-called Sandline Affair in 1997, when the government engaged a private military contractor (PMC) to deploy South African "mercenaries" to defeat a secessionist rebellion on the island of Bougainville (Dinnen, May, & Regan, 1997; Dorney, 1998). This was the first appearance of a PMC in an independent Pacific island country and attracted regional and international attention, as well as precipitating a major political crisis in PNG, including a military revolt, urban riots and the eventual standing down of the prime minister.

While there has been no further resort to PMCs operating in an offensive capacity, PNG is now home to a bewildering array of private companies offering a range of (non-military) security services. The dramatic growth of the industry in recent decades raises questions about the drivers and character of this expansion, how it impacts and interacts with other forms of security provision in PNG's plural policing environment, issues of accountability and regulation, and questions about who benefits and who stands to lose from these developments in the country's security governance.

The chapter examines the growth of private security in PNG in the context of broader changes underway in this, the largest and most socially diverse, independent Melanesian nation. The first two sections examine the background to the expansion of private security in recent decades, and, in particular, the pervasive insecurity found in PNG's fast growing urban centres and in parts of the Highlands region, as well as the shortcomings of the Royal Papua New Guinea Constabulary (RPNGC). The chapter then turns to the character and development of the industry itself. Relations between private and public security are then examined before a concluding section that touches on the political economy of this sector and its potential implications for security governance in PNG in the years ahead.

The growth of private security in PNG

The growth of PNG's private security sector reflects a number of intersecting currents. The first is the high level of insecurity that has prevailed over many years, particularly in the towns and cities. Secondly, is low and declining confidence in the capabilities and integrity of the national police force, the RPNGC. Thirdly, is the growing investment in private security as a commercial enterprise that occurred during the decade-long mining and petroleum boom from 2003 that saw robust growth in the national economy (Fox & Schröder, 2017). Fourthly, the sector's fortunes have also been enhanced by the hosting of Australia's controversial offshore detention facilities on PNG's Manus island, which has provided commercial opportunities for a succession of private security companies in recent years. Finally, the country's recent hosting of APEC in 2018 provided another other significant, albeit temporary, boost for the industry in the national capital, Port Moresby.

"Law & order" and insecurity

PNG's first national security policy, launched in 2013, identified "law and order" as a "level one threat" that poses a "grave and immediate danger to national life" (GoPNG, 2013, p. 43). The term "law and order" is used in PNG to refer to problems of crime and disorder, and official responses such as policing and other suppressive measures. For example, in his foreward to the policy, Prime Minister Peter O'Neill emphasised additional support to the RPNGC and justice system as his government's main response.

Concerns with "law and order" have a long history in PNG. They acquired their initial prominence during decolonisation as the old colonial administrative system was gradually dismantled and replaced with the institutional framework of independent statehood, including a centralised police force and modern justice system. During this period, the "fundamental opposition between indigenous people and colonial powers was displaced by a far messier array of local divisions" (Otto & Thomas, 1997, p. 4). These became evident in the outbreak of localised conflicts such as that on the island of Bougainville associated with the construction of Panguna gold mine. Some of the emergent problems of order related to the accentuation of longstanding antagonisms between local groups, while others arose from stresses of more recent origin. The most serious included the appearance of micronationalist movements in some of the more developed regions, notably Bougainville and the gazelle Peninsula in East New Britain Province, the revival of inter-group conflict or tribal fighting in parts of the highlands and a growing moral panic around urban crime in Port Moresby.

The revival of tribal conflict in the Highlands, which had been successfully suppressed for much of the colonial period, was viewed by some as indicative of an effective withdrawal of state from rural regions following the dismantling of the old devolved system of colonial administration. Under that system district officials, known as *kiaps*, and their armed police, played a leading role in bringing a loose form of government to the territory's widely dispersed rural population (Oram, 1973). That system was credited with contributing to the successful suppression of inter-group conflict for much of the colonial period (Dinnen & Braithwaite, 2009). Re-emergent problems of tribal conflict were also associated with what many Papua New Guineans saw as the weakness of the modern justice system, including its formalistic character compared with the more pragmatic and flexible system of colonial regulation that it replaced (Strathern, 1972). The authority of formerly powerful colonial police was also viewed as seriously diminished with the advent of legal formalism, including being subject to regular and humiliating "defeats" in court, often on obscure technical grounds. Older forms of violent self-help reappeared in the Highlands against in this broader context of political and institutional change, becoming more lethal and difficult to resolve with the introduction of modern firearms (Haley & Muggah, 2006).

Concerns around a growing urban crime problem increased as Port Moresby's population increased during the 1960s and 1970s. With the lifting of colonial restrictions on the movement of Papua New Guineans, young migrants flocked to town. Levels of recorded crime increased and contributed to a growing chorus, particularly among expatriate residents, about deteriorating "law and order" (Clifford, 1976). PNG's towns have since acquired unsavoury reputations, with the national capital regularly depicted as one of the world's most unsafe cities. Although PNG has the lowest urbanisation rate (at 13%) among Pacific island countries, its substantially larger scale means that it has the biggest urban population in the region (ADB, 2016, p. 13). High levels of insecurity manifest themselves in the fortifications, razor-wire and private security presence across the urban landscape. During the 1970s, 1980s and for much of the 1990s, *raskol* gangs provided the "folk devils" in the larger moral panic around urban insecurity (Harris, 1988; Goddard, 1995). Port Moresby experienced cyclical patterns of crime waves followed by special crime control measures, sometimes involving curfews and other emergency measures and invariably entailing heavy-handed and militarised policing of the informal settlements viewed as the incubators of *raskolism* (Dinnen, 2001).

While "law and order" concerns remain focussed on urban areas, many rural areas are also seen as increasingly "lawless" with the spread of violent crime and threat of conflict in the Highlands. Tribal conflict, still predominantly a Highlands phenomenon, has changed considerably over the years. The use of high-powered weapons, along with the introduction of local mercenaries or "hire-men" and guerrilla tactics, has dramatically altered the ground rules of tribal fighting and fueled escalating cycles of conflict that are difficult to resolve through either policing interventions or traditional peacemaking. Tribal conflict has also been aggravated by heightened contestation around elections, as well as over the distribution of the economic and other benefits to local stakeholders from the large natural resource projects located in a number of Highlands provinces (Dinnen, Porter, & Sage, 2010).

Violence against women and girls, including rape and other forms of sexual abuse, remains an enormous challenge. Deeply embedded attitudes towards gender relations are slow to change, while the effects of contemporary patterns of economic globalisation, including deepening inequalities, disproportionately affect women and girls. Human Rights Watch has claimed that family violence in PNG has reached "emergency" levels, with more than two-thirds of women experiencing some form of it, and, in some areas, 80% of men admitting to committing sexual violence against their partners (HRW, 2015). An Australian police officer attached to the RPNGC described levels of domestic violence as "pandemic, equaling something in a war zone" (Cochrane, 2015). An ongoing epidemic of sorcery-related violence, often directed against women, has become another major concern and has precipitated a concerted campaign of law reform, awareness and other interventions by government, churches and donors (Forsyth & Eves, 2015).

Despite their centrality in shaping, particularly external, perceptions of postcolonial PNG, there is little reliable data to accurately gauge the scale of PNG's "law and order" problems. Relatively few incidents are reported or recorded, rendering available police statistics patchy and unreliable. While media reports, surveys and anecdotal evidence suggest that victimisation rates are extremely high by global standards, other data indicate some stabilisation in the first decade of the new millennium (Lakhani & Willman, 2014a). Given PNG's diversity, significant variations are likely to exist within and between different parts of the country, as well as over time. While perceptions of insecurity are widespread, they vary according to factors such as gender, age, wealth and location.

The declining effectiveness of public policing

The ineffectiveness of the RPNGC has been viewed as a major contributor to the country's "law and order" problems, mainly through the lack of deterrence and high levels of impunity this gives rise to. At independence in 1975, police coverage was estimated to extend to only 10 % of the country's total land area and 40 % of the population (Dorney, 2000, p. 304). In the intervening decades, the size of the RPNGC has only increased by around 30% (Dorney, 2016) while the overall population has almost quadrupled. In 1975 the police-population ratio was 1:476, with approximately 4,100 uniformed police for a population of around 2 million. Figures from 2013 indicated the police-population ratio had decreased to 1:1,275, with 5,724 uniformed police for a population of around 7.3 million (Connery & Claxton, 2014, p. 26). More recent estimates put the size of the force at between 7,000–8,000 officers, while the population now exceeds 8 million. Limited recruitment has also contributed to an ageing workforce with around 15% of serving officers in 2014 having passed the mandatory retirement age, with another 29% expected to reach that age by 2018 (ibid). Recent government pledges to significantly increase the size of the force, such as that by PM O'ONeill, appear unlikely to be realised in the austere fiscal climate that has followed the end of PNG's latest mining boom.

Police authorities have sought to compensate for lack of numbers by relying on auxiliary and reserve police. Some municipal authorities have also established local security groups, as with Port Moresby's City Rangers who were tasked with assisting to enforce a ban on the sale and consumption of betel nut in the National Capital District (NCD). The latter, as with other kinds of untrained and poorly supervised auxiliary police, have been regularly accused of harassment and intimidation (The National, 2018). With most government resources concentrated in urban centres, rural-based citizens continue to rely on extended families and informal approaches to meet their everyday security needs. Where state police are absent, local responses in some rural communities include culturally inflected self-policing initiatives, such as the "community police" established in response to tribal conflict and sorcery-related violence in the Gor area of Kundiawa-Gembogl District, Simbu province (Bal, 2015). While accounts from Gor are generally positive, there are obvious risks attaching to these unofficial initiatives, notably in terms of potential abuses of power against vulnerable individuals and groups such as women.

Household victimisation surveys confirm that lack of trust in the police is a major contributor to insecurity in urban areas (Guthrie, 2013). Although they are more accessible in the towns, the RPNGC are widely viewed as unresponsive to requests for help. Lack of funds to buy fuel for police vehicles is a common reason (or excuse) provided for non-attendance and payment is often a pre-condition for rendering assistance. Flat-lined budgets cover salaries but leave little to fund operational expenses, and this has encouraged some elements of the police to pursue rent-seeking opportunities. These can include payment for "turning a blind eye" to alleged infringements and imposition of on-the-spot fines. It also renders the police susceptible to reliance on wealthy patrons, including political and business leaders, with the risks this poses to police integrity.

While unofficial forms of policing rightly arouse concerns about potential abuses, elements of the RPNGGC are regularly accused of brutality and excessive force. This has generated considerable fear of the police in many quarters. Officers have been implicated in unlawful killings, torture, routine beatings and rape (HRW, 2005). Mobile squads, in particular, have acquired notoriety for the rough justice they dispense. The last major government review of the police noted that outstanding legal claims against the state arising from unlawful police actions amounted to more than double the total police budget in 2004 (GoPNG, 2004, p. 48). Its findings included substandard leadership, inadequate resourcing, poor budgeting, a culture of indiscipline and unaccountability, political interference in police operations and an almost complete breakdown in public trust.

The integrity of the force has been further eroded by the penetration of extensive patronage networks in recent years. These have affected senior appointments and the conduct of some investigations and accentuated growing factionalisation within the organisation. The high turnover of police commissioners, as well as the suspension, sacking or marginalisation of officers investigating allegations of corruption against powerful individuals, are indicative of an alarming trend that has profoundly damaged the organisation (Walton & Dinnen, 2019a, p. 428).

As PNG's leading donor, Australia has provided substantial assistance to the RPNGC since the late 1980s, typically entailing training and other technical services provided by civilian advisers. A more robust approach was adopted in 2004 with the Enhanced Cooperation Program (ECP), which provided for around 230 Australian police to be seconded to the RPNGC with executive policing powers. The ECP provoked strong resistance among elements of the political elite and was successfully challenged in PNG's Supreme Court in 2005, leading to the withdrawal of the Australian police. Under the Papua New Guinea-Australia Policing Partnership that commenced in 2008, the Australian Federal Police provides advisory assistance to the RPNGC with deployed AFP officers serving in Port Moresby and Lae. Despite substantial external policing assistance over many years, it remains hard to identify many beneficial outcomes that have been sustained in terms of overall RPNGC performance (Peake & Dinnen, 2014).

Private security providers

Spokespersons tend to explain industry growth as a response to the security gap left by the inadequacies of the RPNGC. The corporate and business sector has been a major force behind the development of the sector, both as a consumer and supplier of private security services. PNG's crime problems have long been viewed as a major additional cost of doing business there. For example, a 2012 business survey found that 80 % of respondents reported that crime had affected their business and investment decisions, and there was little confidence in the police and judicial system (INA/ADB, 2012). As well as providing extra security for employees and property, businesses pay high insurance premiums and claim to have difficulty in attracting international staff. World Bank research indicates that concern with crime and violence among the PNG business community is more than four times the regional average in East Asia and the Pacific, and comparable with countries like El Salvador, Venezuela and the Democratic Republic of Congo

(Lakhani & Willman, 2014b). The same research indicates that business investment in security personnel and infrastructure, at around 84% of all companies surveyed, is significantly higher than the average for the East Asia and Pacific, Sub-Saharan Africa and Latin American regions.

According to PNG's Security Industries Authority (SIA), which issues licences to security companies, the number of licenced companies grew from 173 in 2006 to 464 in 2016, with a total workforce of around 27,709 security guards (Isari, 2017). These figures do not include what are believed to be a large number of unlicensed security companies and personnel, estimated by the SIA in 2016 to be around 219 unlicensed companies with 7649 guards. The number of licenced guards is still well over three times that of serving police officers and exceeds the combined strength of PNG's three "disciplined" services (RPNGC, PNGDF and the Correctional Service). According to some, private security is now the country's third largest employer. Companies vary in size, services offered, areas of operation, as well as national origins. They range from transnational security corporations with global reach, large locally-owned firms through to numerous smaller and often short-lived operators. SIA figures indicate that the three largest companies in 2016 were Guard Dog Security (around 3,622 guards), G4S Secure Solutions Ltd (around 3,390) and Black Swan International (around 780). Prior to its closure in 2017 following a PNG Supreme Court decision, security at the controversial Australian-funded offshore refugee processing facilities on Manus was provided by a number of different companies, including G4S and Wilsons Security. According to the SIA the Australian-owned Wilsons Security had around 622 employees on the island in 2013 and sub-contracted with a local landowner company that employed a further 280 guards.

Security companies tend to be concentrated in PNG's main urban centres, but also operate in the rural areas where major resource projects are located, including Southern Highlands, Western Highlands, Hela and Enga, as well providing security at the offshore facilities on Manus. Services offered by the private sector include static asset protection at extractive projects, agricultural plantations, government offices and other facilities, shopping centres, airports, hospitals, schools, banks, embassies and private residences. Other services include close personal protection, escorting mobile assets, security training, security assessments, emergency evacuations, rapid response capabilities, security fences and increasingly the supply, installation and monitoring of sophisticated electronic surveillance systems.

The SIA conservatively estimated the value of the industry in 2016 as between PNGK833 and PNGK1 billion. The larger mining companies also often have significant in-house security capabilities. For example, Barrick Gold, operator of the Porgera gold mine in Enga province, employed around 500 security personnel in its asset protection department in 2015.

Regulation

PNG is one of only two Pacific island countries (the other being Tonga) that have legislation covering the regulation of the private security industry. The Security

(Protection) Industry Act 2004 established the SIA and vests it with a number of functions, including the issuing (and revocation) of operating licences. The SIA is chaired by the RPNGC Commissioner and includes representatives from the security, insurance, mining, agriculture and manufacturing industries, as well representatives from the trade unions and churches. Its effectiveness is hampered by limited resources (around 12 staff all based in Moresby) and rapid industry growth. There are still no clear guidelines for the issuing (and cancelling) of licences. Other challenges include the large number of unlicensed operators, discipline problems, underpayment of security guards and the provision of unapproved training courses by some operators. With strong industry input, the SIA has drafted 88 recommendations to clarify ambiguities in the 2004 Act and improve its effectiveness. However, these have yet to be approved by the National Parliament.

At a regional level, the Pacific Islands Forum has recently resumed discussions around the growth and weakly regulated character of private security in the Pacific islands, raising the prospect of a regional regulatory framework (ABC News, 2016).

Relationship between private and public security providers

A close and increasingly interdependent relationship exists between private and public security sectors in PNG. This has been viewed as a potential opportunity for assisting the under-resourced police, but also as a potential risk to their integrity as providers of a public service. Both sets of security providers share the same challenging operating environment and, in the case of the larger companies, undertake many of the same activities. The SIA website states that security companies "play a important secondary role as a quasi law enforcing agency beside the Police force" (SIA). Strong informal networks exist, with many senior industry employees having previous police (or military) experience in PNG or overseas. These links are reinforced through having the RPNGC Commissioner chair the SIA, upon which private providers depend for their operating licences. Bigger operators, such as Guard Dog Security, regularly assist their under-resourced RPNGC colleagues by, for example, providing fuel and tires for vehicles, while informal networks facilitate intelligence sharing. Superior resources available to the high-end of the private market include communications, surveillance and tracking systems that are unavailable to the RPNGC. Some private security employees also serve as part-time reserve constables exercising the same powers as regular officers.

Collaboration between the police and business community has a long history in PNG. This includes special policing services provided to logging and mining projects operating in remote rural locations. Such arrangements are often covered by formal agreements or MOUs between the parties and might include the payment of allowances, transport costs and provision of meals and accommodation. There have also been frequent allegations of serving officers moonlighting as security for private clients, often while wearing uniforms and using police equipment. Such unofficial arrangements have been regularly condemned by senior police officials.

Although extensive interaction between police and private security occurs in practice, concerns are regularly raised about the potentially negative impacts of the burgeoning private sector on the performance and standing of the police. These include sensitivities about private providers encroaching on areas that police believe should remain their exclusive preserve, concerns that the growing prominence of private providers diverts attention away from the need to strengthen the police, as well as perceptions that public-private security collaborations might entail privileging powerful business interests over police responsibilities to ordinary citizens.

Some of these issues were highlighted in PNG's 2013 National Security Policy, which warned of a proliferation of foreign-owned companies engaging "in areas designed for PNG state agencies" (NSP, 2013, p. 37). According to the Policy, the involvement of these companies "undermines the state's ability and authority to deliver public safety and security" and "is compounded by the growing negative public sentiments against their presence which is viewed as undermining and denying local participation in the industry" (NSP, 2013, p. 37).

Political economy & future directions

While the growth in private security has, in many respects, followed the declining capabilities of the police, it also relates to broader changes in PNG's political economy. Economic growth has generated rising demands for security services among corporate and business clients, domestic and international organisations, as well as among wealthy individuals living in secure urban enclaves. As well as providing significant numbers of low-paid jobs to Papua New Guineans, the demand for private security presents an attractive opportunity for both foreign and local investors.

While reliable data is elusive, it is widely believed that there has been significant domestic investment in private security companies, ranging from landowner groups that have benefitted from resource rent windfalls through to wealthy members of PNG's political and business elite who have established or bought into companies. In this respect, the "proliferation" of private security companies highlighted in the National Security Policy is not just a result of foreign companies entering the market but also the growth of domestic investment and entrepreneurship. The NSP nevertheless identifies a likely growing source of contestation as influential domestic interests seek to dominate this lucrative and dynamic sector by restricting the role of international players. The recent activism of the SIA, as indicated by its proposed reforms to strengthen the regulatory provisions in the 2004 Act, also suggest attempts by the larger companies to consolidate their dominance by driving out smaller competitors.

PNG presents a challenging operating environment for all businesses, including security companies. Corruption has long been viewed as a major and growing problem, with much attention focussed on the perceived predatory behaviour of members of the political elite (Clarke & Walton, 2018). While such indices are crude instruments, PNG was ranked a lowly 138 out of 180 countries on

Transparency International's 2018 Corruption Perceptions Index. Fierce political rivalries, nepotism and patronage play a significant role in decision making around the allocation of government and other contracts for private security services. Tendering procedures and the awarding of lucrative contracts are often shrouded in secrecy, suspicion and allegations of corruption. The shady side of private security contracting in PNG was highlighted in February 2019 following dramatic media revelations about a $423 million contract awarded to a little known company, Paladin, to provide security and other services at the offshore facilities on Manus (Grigg, Shapiro, & Murray, 2019). Australian interest in the case was intense because the contract was awarded by the Australian Department of Home Affairs, and involved the award of a massive contract to an obscure company through a manifestly opaque and abbreviated tendering procedure. The case aroused heated debate in Australia and led to the Commonwealth Auditor-General announcing an investigation into the Department of Home Affair's management of security and welfare contracts for the offshore facilities in Manus and Nauru (Baker, 2019). While there has been no evidence of corruption in this case, numerous allegations were aired on PNG social media including that improper payments were being made to senior PNG political figures in order to ensure their continuing acquiescence in hosting the offshore facilities on Manus (Walton & Dinnen, 2019b).

In addition to concerns about vulnerability to corruption, growing levels of elite investment in private security in PNG also raises the issue of the disincentive for political decision makers to adequately support and strengthen struggling public security agencies such as the police. While investing in building effective law enforcement capabilities might be viewed cynically as not in the interests of members of the political elite involved in predatory activities, the growing investment in, and reliance upon, private security providers, might be another factor behind continuing government neglect of public security providers. That neglect, in turn, leaves the vast majority of Papua New Guineans who cannot afford private security, including already highly vulnerable groups such as women, most at risk.

For a major donor like Australia that has invested millions of dollars into capacity-building engagements with the PNG police over many years, the massive expansion of private security and its impact on public policing has attracted surprisingly little interest. While there are many potential risks involved, there are also opportunities presented in relation to addressing many of the problems of insecurity that PNG experiences. These would include opportunities for moving beyond viewing private security as essentially a gap-filling response to the inadequacies of public policing on the part of those who can afford private services. This would entail serious consideration of how more deliberate and transparent engagement between the two sectors might contribute to improving the quality and reach of security provision for all Papua New Guineans, including its most vulnerable groups.

PNG's national security landscape is self-evidently multi-layered and dynamic. It comprises diverse, though, often, overlapping, sets of providers – state, private and community-based actors – existing in different configurations in different parts of the country. Among the many gaps in our knowledge about security governance in PNG are the politics and power relations that are animating this changing landscape and that will shape the future of both security and insecurity in this Melanesian nation.

References

Abrahamsen, R., & Williams, M. C. (2011). *Security beyond the state: Private security in international politics*. Cambridge: Cambridge University Press.

Asian Development Bank (ADB). (2016). *The emergence of pacific urban villages: Urbanization trends in the pacific islands*. Mandaluyong City, Philippines: ADB.

Australian Broadcasting Corporation (ABC) News. (2016). *Calls to regulate the growing industry of private security in the Pacific?* Retrieved from www.abc.net.au/radio-australia/programs/pacificbeat/calls-to-regulate-the-growing-industry-of-private/7441832

Baker, R. (2019, April 1). Auditor-General launches proble into home affairs off shore contracts. *Sydney Morning Herald*. Retrieved from www.smh.com.au/politics/federal/auditor-general-launches-probe-into-home-affairs-offshore-contracts-20190401-p519mt.html

Bal, C. (2015). *Kumo Koimbo*: Accounts and responses to witchcraft in Gor, Simbu Province. In M. Forsyth & R. Eves (Eds.), *Talking it through: Responses to sorcery and witchcraft beliefs and practices in Melanesia* (pp. 299–307). Canberra: ANU Press.

Clarke, L., & Walton, G. (2018). Drivers of electoral and institutional money politics in Papua New Guinea. *The Australian Journal of Asian Law, 18*(2), 1–13.

Clifford, W. (1976). Urban crime in Papua New Guinea. In D. Biles (Ed.), *Crime in Papua New Guinea*. Canberra: Australian Institute of Criminology.

Cochrane, L. (2015, February 19). Papua New Guinea's rates of violence at 'pandemic' levels, Australian police officer says. *ABC News Online*. Retrieved from www.abc.net.au/news/2015-02-19/png-facing-a-domestic-violence-pandemic,-afp-officer-says/6150064

Connery, D., & Claxton, K. (2014). *Shared interests, enduring cooperation: The future of Australia-PNG police engagement*. Canberra: Australian Strategic Policy Institute.

Dinnen, S. (2001). *Law and order in a weak state: Crime and politics in Papua New Guinea*. Honolulu, HI: University of Hawai'i Press.

Dinnen, S., & Braithwaite, J. (2009). Reinventing policing through the prism of the colonial kiap. *Policing & Society, 19*(2), 161–173.

Dinnen, S., May, R., & Regan, A. J. (Eds.). (1997). *Challenging the state: The Sandline affair in Papua New Guinea*. Canberra: National Centre for Development Studies, the Australian National University.

Dinnen, S., Porter, D., & Sage, S. (2010). *Conflict in Melanesia: Themes and lessons*. World Bank, Development Report 2011, Background Paper, pp. 1–39.

Diphoorn, T. (2015). *Twilight policing: Private security and violence in urban South Africa*. Oakland, CA: University of California Press.

Dorney, S. (1998). *The Sandline affair: Politics and mercenaries and the Bougainville crisis*. Sydney: ABC Books.

Dorney, S. (2000). *Papua New Guinea: People, politics and history since 1975*. Sydney: Random House.

Dorney, S. (2016). *The embarrassed colonialist*. Sydney: Penguin Random House Australia.

Forsyth, M., & Eves, R. (Eds.). (2015). *Talking it through: Responses to sorcery and witchcraft beliefs and practices in Melanesia*. Canberra: ANU Press.

Fox, R., & Schröder, M. (2017). After Papua New Guinea's resource boom: Is the Kina overvalued? *Asia & The Pacific Policy Studies, 5*(1), 65–76.

Goddard, M. (1995). The rascal road: Crime, prestige, and development in Papua New Guinea. *The Contemporary Pacific, 7*(1), 55–80.

Government of Papua New Guinea (GoPNG). (2004). *Report of the administrative review of the Royal Papua New Guinea Constabulary.* Retrieved from http://www.inapng.com/pdf_files/Police_Review_Report_final.pdf

Government of Papua New Guinea. (2013). *National security policy.*

Grigg, A., Shapiro, K., & Murray, L. (2019, February 10). Cashing in on refugees, duo make $20 million a month at Manus Island. *Australian Financial Review.* Retrieved from www.afr.com/news/policy/foreign-affairs/cashing-in-on-refugees-duo-make-20-million-a-month-at-manus-island-20190210-h1b2e5

Guthrie, G. (2013). Social factors affecting violent crime victimisation in urban households. *Contemporary PNG Studies: DWU Research Journal, 18,* 35–54.

Haley, N., & Muggah, R. (2006). Jumping the gun: Armed violence in Papua New Guinea. In *Small arms survey 2006: Unfinished business* (pp. 165–187). Oxford: Oxford University Press.

Harris, B. (1988). *The rise of rascalism: Action and reaction in the evolution of rascal gangs.* Port Moresby: Institute of Applied Social and Economic Research, Discussion Paper 54, pp. 1–52.

Human Rights Watch (HRW). (2005). *Making their own rules: Police beatings, rape and torture of children in Papua New Guinea.* New York: Human Rights Watch.

Human Rights Watch. (2015). *Bashed up: Family violence in PNG.* New York: Human Rights Watch.

Institute of National Affairs (INA) and Asia Development Bank (ADB). (2012). *The challenges of doing business in Papua New Guinea.* Retrieved from https://www.adb.org/sites/default/files/publication/31209/challenges-doing-business-papua-new-guinea.pdf

Isari, P. K. (2017, April 20). *Information paper on the security industry in PNG' Security Industries Authority.*

Jones, T., & Newburn, T. (Eds.). (2006). *Plural policing: A comparative perspective.* Abingdon, UK: Routledge.

Lakhani, S., & Willman, A. M. (2014a). *Trends in crime and violence in Papua New Guinea.* Washington, DC: World Bank.

Lakhani, S., & Willman, A. M. (2014b). *Gates, hired guns and mistrust: Business as unusual.* Washington, DC: World Bank.

The National. (2018). *City rangers giving NCD a bad name.* Retrieved from www.thenational.com.pg/city-rangers-giving-ncd-a-bad-name/

Oram, N. (1973). Law and order: Maximum participation at all levels. *New Guinea, 7*(3), 4–22.

Otto, T., & Thomas, N. (Eds.). (1997). *Narratives of nation in the South Pacific.* Amsterdam: Harwood Academic Publishers.

Peake, G., & Dinnen, S. (2014). Police development in Papua New Guinea: The need for innovation. *Security Challenges, 10*(2), 33–51.

Provost, C. (2017, May 12). The industry of inequality: Why the world is obsessed with private security. *The Guardian online.* Retrieved March 14, 2019 from www.theguardian.com/inequality/2017/may/12/industry-of-inequality-why-world-is-obsessed-with-private-security

Security Industries Authority (SIA). Retrieved from www.sia.gov.pg/seccomps.html

Strathern, M. (1972). Official and unofficial courts: Legal assumptions and expectations in a highlands community. *New Guinea Research Unit, Bulletin, 47*, 1–166.

Walton, G., & Dinnen, S. (2019a). The Pacific islands – Politics, organised crime and corruption. In F. Allum & S. Gilmour (Eds.), *Handbook of organised crime and politics* (pp. 418–435). Cheltenham, UK and Northampton, MA: Edward Elgar Publishing.

Walton, G., & Dinnen, S. (2019b, March 15). *Gulag politics? Perceptions of PNG-Australia relations and the Paladin contract*. DEVPOLICYBLOG. Canberra: Development Policy Centre, Australian National University. Retrieved from www.devpolicy.org/gulag-politics-perceptions-png-australia-relations-paladin-contract-20190315/

15 Mapping military reform in Fiji

Timing it right

Natasha Khan

Introduction

The Royal Fiji Military Forces (RFMF) originated as the Armed Native Constabulary (ANC) established in 1871 by Ratu Cakobau, the highest chief at that time, but commanded by British Officers. It was tasked to suppress any resistance from the local tribes that were not aligned to Ratu Cakobau and his alliance with the British settlers (RFMF, 2010). By the Second World War (WWII), New Zealand was tasked to exercise control over Fiji's military responsibilities; hence it was renamed RFMF and its military capacities were increased, leading to deployment to the Solomon Islands during WWII (ibid.). From 1978, RFMF entered into another phase, which is still relevant today: their participation in UN peacekeeping operations. Between 1978 and 2018, approximately 34,000 RFMF soldiers have served in peacekeeping missions, bringing an income of about US $200 million to Fiji (ibid.). In recent years, participation in the Iraq war increased that income as approximately 1,000 Fiji Islanders have worked as escorts, guards and drivers for private companies in Iraq, remitting money back to Fiji (Firth & Fraenkel, 2009).

The contemporary RFMF has a relatively small manpower of 3,596 active soldiers and 4,425 reservists (FBC, 2019); however, most Pacific Island countries do not have any military capacity at all. RFMF is a highly structured and professional military. However, RFMF is composed almost entirely of indigenous Fijians and the military structure reflects the iTaukei[1] traditional chiefly system, as many high-ranking officers are from chiefly iTaukei families. For instance, both Epeli Nailatikau and Epeli Ganilau, Commanders of the Fiji Military Forces in the 1980s and 1990s, respectively, are high chiefs in their own right. Additionally, they are both sons-in-law of the late Ratu Sir Kamisese Mara, who was the Commander in Chief of the military in Fiji in his role of former President of Fiji, as well as being the highest-ranking chief prior to his death. As the military structure is intertwined with traditional iTaukei society, military personnel are accorded respect similar to that bestowed on the warrior class in the pre-modern era. The military is generally viewed as an iTaukei institution both physically and symbolically and largely viewed by iTaukei people as the ultimate guarantor of iTaukei power (Lal, Chand, & Naidu, 2008; Baledrokadroka, 2015).

The military in Fiji has been intertwined with coup d'états since 1987 and continues to play a significant role in the political arena, with the increasing presence of former military personnel at many levels of government and politics. After the 1987 and 2000 coups, the military was glorified by most iTaukeis for its role in the overthrow of democratic governments to retain iTaukei hegemony in politics (Ratuva, 2006b). However, when the military overthrew the government in 2006 on the basis of bad governance, the military was glorified by many of the Indo-Fijian community, but was held in lesser regard by significant numbers of the iTaukeis as they saw the military as going against "their own" (Chang, 2008).

Various reasons are postulated for the different coups and each coup has been linked with others, particularly through key players. The first coup, executed by military personnel, Brigadier Sitiveni Rabuka, was largely carried out to reclaim the iTaukei hegemony in the political arena and stifle non-racial discourse. The second coup, again by Commander Rabuka, saw the end of Fiji's ties with the Commonwealth that very same year, when the country was declared a republic and the theme of hegemony was reiterated. The third coup was a civilian one in 2000, but accomplished with the assistance of an elite military faction, the Counter Revolutionary Forces and was the bloodiest in Fiji's documented history (Firth, Fraenkel, & Lal, 2009). While it was initiated to give political power back to iTaukeis, this coup brought to the forefront previously hidden divisions among them. It also exacerbated factions within the Fiji military (Firth et al., 2009). The roots of the 2006 coup can be traced to the 2000 coup: the former was an overt manifestation of a praetorian military against a weak government unable to exercise civilian control over its military (Firth et al., 2009; Chang, 2008). The 2006 coup was also executed by a military Commander, Commodore Bainimarama.

With each coup, the military became more politicised and less accountable to the democratic government oversight. This was starkly demonstrated by the public display of frictions between the military and the Qarase government in late 2006. In addition to this, after each coup by the military, all coup perpetrators were granted full impunity. In the words of Chang (2008, p. 21): "The seeking and granting of amnesty has become a customary feature in the planning, execution, resolution and legitimation of coups, a strategy Bainimarama has gleefully adopted from Rabuka and Speight". However, Speight, who was a civilian, is the only coup leader who has been held accountable for his actions and is currently serving a prison sentence. This can be interpreted as an example of the influence of the military organisational culture in Fiji and highlights the need for military reform.

The military centrality theory argues that in many developing countries, post-independence, the military is more professionalised in comparison with other state institutions and thereby are more powerful (Jenkins & Kposowa, 1990). In addition, they may harbour political aspirations, thus increasing their likelihood to intervene in politics through coups d'état (Nordlinger, 1977; Finer, 1988; Jenkins & Kposowa, 1990). In most countries, colonial military institutions were largely formed to suppress internal uprising, therefore the military had been accustomed to political interference (Jenkins & Kposowa, 1990, p. 862). As the military powers increased in some post-colonial countries and the newly democratising countries lacked strong political institutions to maintain civilian control over the military, military intervention increased (ibid.). According to Collier and Hoeffler (2005), military intervention in the political arena can be minimised by increasing military budget, hence placating army grievances. However, this can lead to rebellion from other sectors of society, because governments can be deemed as repressive in their intent to potentially use the military against their populations (ibid.). Some elements of this theory are applicable for coups in Fiji as the military is more organised and professional in comparison with other state bodies and RFMF was created to suppress internal disturbances during the colonial period.

It has been argued that to maintain democracy, it is crucial for the military to be politically neutral and controlled by civilian authorities (Joinet, 1997; Orentlicher, 2005), while allowing the military some level of professional autonomy (Finer, 1988; Huntington, 1968; Janowitz, 1981). Lack of civilian control of the military would indicate failure of political institutions, creating space for the military elite to entrench themselves within the political system, which could lead to military coercion in domestic security (Luckham, 1971). The military should be apolitical and allied to the democratic government and not to ruling parties or politicians within preferred parties (Ashkenazi, 1994; Kemp & Hudlin, 1992). Alliances between political parties and the military could be used to allow the preferred political party to lead unfair electoral processes, suppress opposition and commit human rights abuses while providing leverage to the military. Conflict analysts have stated that military's disengagement from politics is linked to strengthened democracy and lowered threats of coups d'état (Welch, 1975).

In countries coming out of conflict and making attempts to deal with the past, sequencing of reform efforts is crucial to ensure that stability and peace are achieved (Murithi, 2010). Research undertaken in 2015 to investigate military reform in Fiji indicates that some respondents were sceptical about reform as Fiji military remains strong and enjoys its monopolistic position as the only armed institution in the country. Others also indicated that such reforms can be done by the former Military Commander and current Prime Minister, Voreqe Bainimarama, since he has a strong following within the military and because as the elected Prime Minister, he could legitimately start implementing reforms. Such reforms would need to be done gradually and need to be seen to be working with and not against the military. If reforms are too fast and the military are not engaged deliberately in the process, a praetorian military, such as Fiji's RFMF could derail the whole reform process. Additionally, Bainimarama also has a proven track record of reforming problematic structures and policies in Fiji. Some of these reforms of were almost inconceivable in the past, for instance, the dissolution of the Great Council of Chiefs, the electoral reforms and the use of the term "Fijian" for every citizen of Fiji, irrespective of ethnicity, among others. It could be argued that Bainimarama needs to utilise his current political and military clout to carry out reforms as history shows that by the time former Military Commander and former Prime Minister Sitiveni Rabuka realised the errors of his ways and wanted to de-politicise the military, he no longer had the patronage of the military.

Bainimarama still continues to enjoy military patronage (Baledrokadroka, 2015) and this gives him a unique opportunity to carry out military reform.

Any Security Sector Reform (SSR) design and implementation would need to consider factors such as the nature and type of democracy within a given country; the role of the military in the political arena and level of praetorianism[2]; the ethnic composition of the reformed military; sustainable attitudinal change amongst relevant stakeholders and the wider community's view towards the military. This paper argues that SSR programmes should align technical and social reforms to deconstruct ideologies to change attitudes on issues of security, safety, justice and human rights. It also argues that SSR programmes would be more effective in countries with structural conflicts, such as Fiji, than in countries coming out of violent conflicts.[3] SSR reforms are fraught with challenges such as impunity, fragmentation within the security sector, donor driven programmes and lack of local ownership, capacity problems and contextual and structural barriers.

The paper argues that while most security sector reforms are taking place in countries with a history of overt violence such as Afghanistan, Iraq, the Democratic Republic of Congo (DRC), East Timor, etc. SSR would be more effective in countries experiencing structural conflict without widespread violence, as is the case in Fiji. It argues that advocates of transitional justice need to reconceptualise their various mechanisms to target countries such as Fiji to prevent structural conflicts escalating into protracted conflicts in the future.

Methodology

In consideration of the various strengths and weaknesses of both quantitative and qualitative methods, a combination of methods was utilised. In total, three specific methods were used to obtain data for this research: focus groups, semi-structured questionnaires and key informants. Although triangulation has been criticised for assuming a single fixed reality (Seale, 1999), it is still a useful tool in qualitative research, as it allows the researcher to reflect on reasons for the differences in data obtained from different methods used and document them as part of the research process. However, the focus group interviews were discarded after the first focus group interview due to the lack of trustworthiness of data obtained in this session. For the rest of this paper, the term "respondents" will mean the respondents of the semi-structured interviews and the term "informants" will mean key informants.

In total, 59 individuals were interviewed using semi-structured questionnaires and 16 key informants were interviewed using an in-depth approach. While the number of respondents may seem low, the rationale for this research is not to have generalised findings, but rather to get rich data with many issues identified and discussed in depth. For the semi-structured interviews, purposive sampling was utilised to identify individuals who had some understanding of these issues, such as youths, military personnel, civil servants, tertiary students, civil society organisation staff and smaller number of unemployed persons. This was to acquire their views on military personnel and organisation in link with security.

Key informant interviews were also used. Generally key informant interviews are used to obtain data about a pressing and/or sensitive issue from a limited number of experts in the area of interest or those who have insider knowledge and usually entail in-depth interviews with each informant (Marshall, 1996). Accuracy can sometimes be doubtful because individuals usually have different perspectives on the same event, they are most likely to distance themselves from bad decisions they made in the past and they may not accurately recollect significant facts or details (Lilleker, 2003). To minimise this, any unusual and/or incorrect data will be verified against other sources for same or similar information. While key informants are advantageous given their insider and in-depth knowledge of a particular issue, their perspective can be elitist. Additionally, informants can also be subjective based on their positions and even misleading in an attempt portray their organisation in a positive light (Field-Springer, 2018).

To minimise the issue of elitism, some interviews were conducted with individuals who have insider information, but are not high-ranking public figures, such as an administrative officer and two university students. The administrative officer works in the judicial office and interacts daily with many key political and legal officers. This informant was particularly useful in substantiating information related to abuses of office, weak rule of law, corruption and so on. The student informants were both from prominent iTaukei political and military families, but had distanced themselves from their kinship links in coup related events and were able to provide an informative insider perspective on kinship ties, chiefly and military patronage politics and many related issues. Additionally, more than one informant was interviewed within some similar organisations or in relation to particular events to minimise the subjectivity of a singular point of view. For the purpose of this study, 21 potential key informants were identified. They represented past and present coup perpetrators, members of past and present governments who were removed from office by a coup, human rights activists, the legal fraternity, academics and chief officers of NGOs and other agencies. In total, 16 key informants were interviewed, yielding a 76% response rate. The interview time ranged from an hour to a maximum of two and half hours.

Security sector reform

The United Nations Security Council defines the security sector as "both State and non-State actors that have a stake in security and justice provisions" (UN Security Council, 9 February 2007, p. 2), but it limits the definition only to "traditional" security institutions (UN, 2008: §§ 14, 17). The OECD DAC and the Democratic Control of Armed Forces (DCAF) expand the definition of Security Sector Reform (SSR) to include the media, civil society organisations (CSOs), the judiciary, the executive and the legislature (OECD, 2007; DCAF, 2008). The UN and OECD have also emphasised that as well as effectively providing security, security sector institutions should be accountable to the population and adhere to rules of governance, democracy and the rule of law (UN General Assembly Security Council, 2008; OECD, 2007).

The military has strong links with violent conflicts in three ways: through structural causes of conflict, as a trigger factor and by perpetuating societal cleavages (Clingendael, 2002). For instance, the issue of iTaukei hegemony in the military is widely accepted, but the dominance of iTaukeis in the military is often perceived as a threat by Indo-Fijians during times of tension. In 1987, this was overtly felt when the military singled out Indo-Fijians for harassment and threats (Firth et al., 2009). However, in 2006, the military commander singled out Methodist Christians and the traditional chiefs for harassment through various restrictions (Firth et al., 2009).

Secondly, the military has triggered conflicts in Fiji in the most overt form by threats of executing coups d'état and use of harassment to suppress any resistance to its position (Trnka, 2008). In the past, the alignment of some, if not most of the military personnel with the nationalist factions triggered underlying disparities and in 2000 this led to street riots against Indo-Fijians (Trnka, 2008). Additionally, the two coups in 1987 and 2006 were carried out by the military. The 2000 coup was undertaken with the assistance of 30 Counter Revolutionary Warfare Unit (CRWU) members, an elite unit within the military (Trnka, 2008). This unit was formed after the 1987 coup d'état as an intelligence arm of the military, but was disbanded after a mutiny by some members against other sections of the military in late 2000 (Trnka, 2008).

Thirdly, the military can also perpetuate social cleavages by being part of factors that prolong conflicts. For instance, since the 2006 coup in Fiji, a number of statutory bodies, state enterprises and public service departments such as the police force, immigration, justice, prison, airport authority and the Commission against Corruption have been militarised by appointment of military personnel to senior positions across all these bodies (CCF, 2014). The military has explicitly stated that it has plans to be part of politics and to monitor government activities in future (Robertson, 2017). This oversight role that military has given itself has and may continue to perpetuate further conflicts unless the military is brought under civilian control.

Multi-ethnic military

Institution reform is a common concept in Security Sector Reform and this section will link the concept of military reform with the issue of inducing civic trust, through pluralism in the military. Armed forces which do not reflect the social composition of the broader society tend to be distrusted by the minority within the society in times of conflicts (Adekanye, 1996). This is particularly problematic in multi-ethnic states and could lead to diminishing trust towards the military by minority groups (DCAF, 2006), as it can be perceived as representing the interests of a single ethnic group (Mason, 2007). To minimise this, the military should have a common unifying "vision that transcends the different identities of its members in order for them to perform cohesively and effectively in the field" (DCAF, 2006, p. 2). A military which is more representative of the population "will also better understand the concerns of all population groups because its representatives will speak their languages, comprehend their cultures, appreciate their traditions" (Mayer-Rieckh & Duthie, 2009, p. 232) and could help to foster inter-ethnic tolerance. This was observed in post-apartheid South Africa, where power sharing arrangements at the political level were also reflected in the military hierarchy leading to a more stable situation during that period (Nathan, 1996). By contrast, in Fiji, the military personnel and politicians have manipulated each other by citing traditional iTaukei and chiefly allegiance.

During times of peace, the ethnic composition of the military might not be an issue. However, during and after conflict, the military's composition can lead to certain groups aligning with or against government, particularly if the military was involved in the conflict, as they may perceive this as "them" against "us". For instance, prior to the 1999 elections in Fiji, it was not uncommon to hear nation-alist groups utilise the fear of another coup to deter people from voting for the Labour Party, which had a larger number of Indo-Fijian supporters. Indo-Fijians considered this a real possibility as only 15 of the approximate 4000 military per-sonnel in Fiji were Indo-Fijians in 2010 (Firth & Fraenkel, 2007). As a result, it was perceived that iTaukeis had inside information regarding a coup.[4]

While the Fiji Military Forces do not explicitly exclude Indo-Fijians from their recruitment, their portrayal as an overtly Christian organisation may have deterred Hindus and Muslims. SSR programmes would need to emphasise active recruit-ment of different ethnic groups for the military to calm the fears that minority populations have towards the military in post-conflict situations.

Having different ethnic groups within the military may also lead to the mili-tary being less intrusive in the political arena. While recognising that military institutions in general tend to be organised in a very hierarchical manner and that questioning authority is often associated to insubordination, one could argue that cultural differences between the indigenous and Indo-Fijian communities related to authority could influence the military's relationship to politics. For instance, in Fiji, iTaukeis have a strong allegiance to the traditional chiefly system and the military is seen as an extension of this system. The military commanders have an almost unquestioned authority over junior officers in the particular iTaukei con-text. However, the history of the Indo-Fijian community has led it to have a less hierarchical community structure and a history of questioning political authority. As such, perhaps having significant Indo-Fijian military personnel may lead to this sub-group questioning the commander or senior military personnel actions, particularly with regard to interference in politics.

Democratic rules require that political parties accept defeat at the polls or through legislative process and until a country's political system matures to that level, a new democracy is always at risk (Mason, 2007). While democracy is under threat in many parts of the world, it is even more under threat in ethnically divided societies as political parties are often formed along ethnic lines (Horow-itz, 1985). Attempts to form multi-ethnic parties are challenged by nationalist groups (Mason, 2007) and when population groups are increasingly dissatis-fied with the government in power, either the state uses its military to suppress potential uprisings (Mason, 2007) or the military becomes praetorian: that is, it assumes control of civilian authority forcefully (Uzgel, 2003).

Praetorian military

The military becomes praetorian when it threatens to use or uses force to dominate the political arena (Nordlinger, 1977). It is argued that the following conditions allow praetorianism to develop: ineffective civilian government; lack of legitimacy of the civilian regime; failure of political and social institutions to provide legitimate space for channelling political participation and mediating social conflicts; polarisation of social groups; and the military gaining high levels of popular support, at least in the initial stages of its involvement in the political arena (Perlmutter, 1981).

Coups d'état by the military are the most overt form of praetorianism. For instance, the military has retained a strong link with the political process in Fiji since the 1987 coup and minimising its role abruptly may lead to an escalation of the conflict. SSR programmes need to take into account the strength of the military and their role in the political sphere (Malan & Weir, 2007). Interventions need to engage with the military to rebuild a stable civil-military relationship, but I argue that gradual changes would be more effective. A praetorian military could derail the whole reform process unless it is deliberately courted. Lessons learnt from DDR (demobilisation, demilitarisation and reintegration) programmes show that when the military is engaged and given incentives, it is willing to embrace that reform (Smyth, 2004). Similar approaches could be used in SSR reform, particularly if the military is to be downsized, as not involving them could be perceived as threatening their existence. For instance, when Andrew Hughes was appointed by the Qarase government in 2003 to reform and strengthen the Fiji Police Force, which involved setting up an armed police unit, the military became convinced that this unit would be used against them (Khan, 2015). As a result, the unit was summarily disbanded on the day of 2006 coup. Additionally, the military ensured that Hughes would not return to Fiji and appointed a senior military person in his place (Ramesh, 2006). The Qarase government and Hughes could have justified to the military why the armed police unit had been established in order to placate their fears rather than side-lining them on the basis that the military had no place in political decision making.[5]

In designing SSR some issues to consider are: the role of the military; appropriate civilian control and professionalising security personnel; oversight bodies; allocation of resources; institutional separation of duties as well as supporting reformers and minimising the impact of spoilers (Wulf, 2004; Ball, 2004). Many of these factors align with liberal democratic principles, with the understanding that the military needs to be under civilian control.

Where civilian control of the military is promoted in SSR, it also needs to be emphasised that the democratic government should follow democratic principles and good governance. In many newly democratic governments, including some elected governments in Fiji, have come to power through corruption, repression and nationalist tendencies, which do not give them much legitimacy among the professional military (Firth & Fraenkel, 2007). Reiterating the above notion, oversight bodies also need to promote good governance principles, rather than assuming a dogmatic approach. For instance, in Fiji, the National Security Council (NSC) exists as an oversight body for the security sector, but it consists only of members of the government and its work is shrouded in secrecy. The NSC should be expanded to include the police, military and civilian experts on national security, as well as representatives of relevant CSOs to allow inclusion of different viewpoints (Ratuva, 2006a). This would also establish a transparent and democratic process within the security governance framework and ultimately regain trust for different agencies (ibid.).

Perception of military in the community

The glorification of the military by different communities also gives the military added legitimacy for their actions. SSR and transitional justice would need to understand how to address such an abstract issue if civilian oversight of the military is to develop. For instance, the 1987 coup undermined the military's international image and was vilified by the Indo-Fijians, but the nationalists hero-worshipped the new leaders (Ratuva, 2006b). This view became so pervasive amongst the iTaukeis that anyone voicing their concerns against the military was taunted for siding with the vulagi (migrant) Indians (Ratuva, 2006b). However, when the military overthrew the government in 2006 on the basis of bad governance, the military was glorified by many Indo-Fijians for removing Qarase, who was increasingly perceived by them as racist (Ratuva, 2006b). At the same time, the military was vilified and demonised by the iTaukeis as they saw the military "going against their own" (Chang, 2008). SSR and transitional justice need to work with the wider community to identify how glorification of the military after upheavals can encourage the military to be praetorian. Communities' perception of the military also needs to undergo a paradigm shift through education and awareness of democratic principles. Such programmes should emphasise a demarcation between the government and the role of the military in statebuilding.

Timing of military reform in Fiji

The issue of Fiji's military reform has been discussed widely since the late 1990s, but to date no constructive reform has occurred. Both the 1997 Fiji Defence Review (Parliament of Fiji, 1997) and the 2005 Fiji Defence White Paper (Lowy, Firth, & Vitusagavulu, 2004) questioned the need for a military as there was no external threat to security in Fiji. In most countries, the military is usually retained for external security so it was suggested that the military in Fiji be downsized or even disbanded altogether. Unsurprisingly, these ideas were strongly resisted by the Fiji military (Radio NZ International, 2006).

Table 15.1 shows that only 14% of the respondents felt that the military should be disbanded and 25% considered downsizing as a reform measure. A significant 29% wanted the military to remain the same and 14% wanted to increase it.

Table 15.1 Do you think Fiji military should be?

Do you think military in Fiji should be:	Total
Disbanded	14%
Downsized	25%
Increased	14%
Remain the same	29%
Don't know	12%
NR	7%
Total	59

Table 15.2 gives the reasons for their suggestions. Similar to the Defence Review suggestions, 20% of the respondents stated that there was no need for a military in Fiji. Fifteen % of respondents were concerned about the military's interference in politics even though two-thirds of this group of respondents wanted the military to remain as it is, but 19% felt that the military was doing a great job and they considered either increasing the military's size or letting it remain the same.

Aquila Yabaki, Director of Fiji's Citizens' Constitutional Forum, believes that we may never be able to disband our military, as their UN peacekeeping missions are a major source of income for many families and relatives: "The reality is that in the last 20 years or so the peacekeepers brought in a lot of foreign exchange for their families and thereby for the country. Therefore, disbanding it would be almost impossible". The respondents did not feel so strongly about this view as only 3% considered the military as a source of income, but both respondents in this group wanted the military to retain its present size.

The Fiji White Paper (commonly known as the 2005 Defence White Paper) recommended that the military should be downsized from 3,330 to 1,700 personnel, as this number was optimal for partaking in peacekeeping operations (Lowy, Firth, & Vitusagavulu, 2004). Despite Brigadier Aziz's comment, Radio NZ International (2006) reported that the military felt threatened by the changes suggested by the 2005 Defence White Paper and highlighted the social and security implications of such changes if they were to be implemented.

Respondents who had suggested disbanding or downsizing the military were asked what should be done with the military personnel who would be affected by the reform process. Thirty-five percent of the respondents suggested that such personnel should be resettled in the villages to farm the land, 22% recommended secondment to a civil sector job and 17% indicated seeking employment in the international security sector. Figure 15.1 addresses the issue of allaying fears for any reforms relating to disbanding or downsizing the military. A considerable 50% of the respondents stated that any concerns of the military personnel could be addressed through creating awareness of such reforms. Eight percent suggested work assurance and 8% considered other effective measures such as secondments to other government departments and specialised trainings for the remaining personnel, while 21% stated that the military is too powerful at the moment to be disbanded or downsized.

Table 15.2 Reasons for suggested military reform (or not)

Reasons why military should or should not be disbanded, downsized, increased, remain the same.	Disbanded	Downsized	Increased	Remain the same	Don't know	NR	Total	Percent
No need for military in Fiji	6	5		1			12	20%
Military should not interfere in politics		3		6			9	15%
Invest in infrastructure		3		1			4	7%
Don't trust military anymore	2						2	3%
Hold military accountable		1			1		2	3%
Military is a source of income				2			2	3%
Military is doing great			6	5			11	19%
Mixed responses		2	1	1	2	1	7	12%
NR		1	1	1	4	3	10	17%
Total	8	15	8	17	7	4	59	100%

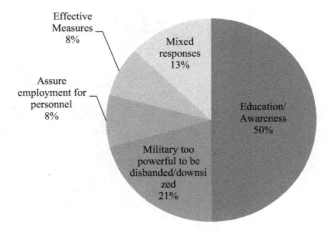

Figure 15.1 How to address fears of military personnel for any disband/downsize reforms?

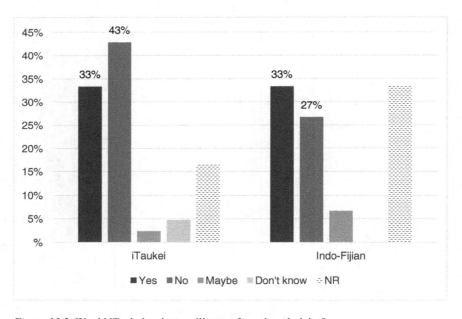

Figure 15.2 Would iTaukei resist to military reform, by ethnicity?

As the Fiji military is largely viewed as an indigenous body and also as a source of employment for many iTaukeis, it was important to consider the perception of any resistance from this group. Figure 15.2 illustrates that 33% of iTaukeis and a similar proportion of Indo-Fijians believe that iTaukeis would resist military reform, but interestingly, 43% of the iTaukeis do not think that there would be resistance from their group. This sentiment would need further investigation if and when any military reform is planned to ensure wider acceptance of reforms and reduction of any potential threats of violence.

The Republic of Fiji Military Forces (RFMF) are largely seen as an iTaukei organisation as the majority of the personnel are iTaukeis with only 4% Indo-Fijians. In pluralistic/multicultural societies like Fiji, it is usually best practice for the military to be more representative of the different ethnic populations (Khan, 2015). In Fiji, the military system seems to parallel the chiefly system for the iTaukeis as both are very closely aligned with most of the military elites coming from chiefly families. The argument is that, if representative numbers of Indo-Fijians are recruited into the military, with their lack of chiefly allegiance, there is a possibility that it could reduce tension amongst Fiji Islands military and may also induce trust towards the military amongst the Indo-Fijian community. Table 15.3 shows that the majority of the respondents from both communities are receptive to having more Indo-Fijians in the military with 53% agreeing to this.

Figure 15.3 illustrates the reasons respondents believed recruitment of Indo-Fijians in the military should or should not be carried out. A significant proportion of the respondents (25%) were agreeable to the idea and justified their preference on the basis that integration in the military might lead to peace with others, stating that all citizens should be given equal rights as Fiji Islanders. Twenty-two percent of the respondents stated that since Fiji is a multiracial society its military and other sections of the government should reflect this more closely.

Despite the support for Indo-Fijian recruitment to the military, respondents also noted in interviews the challenges to this process. For example:

> The recruitment of Indo-Fijians could be done through policies as you can use human rights law to promote affirmative action within government institutions because government institutions are funded by the tax payers' money. But they also need to make the institutions amenable to the Indo-Fijians. For instance, if they bring Indians in but don't provide their food, emphasise only Christian values with military then it would be difficult to recruit even with affirmative action policies. The culture of Indo-Fijians is not reflected in the way that they live in the barracks, so how will that encourage Indians to join?
>
> (Imrana Jalal – Human Rights Activist, Personal Communication, 23 March 2010)

Table 15.3 Should the military actively recruit more Indo-Fijians?

Yes	53%
No	8%
Maybe	2%
Don't know	3%
NR	34%
Total number	**59**

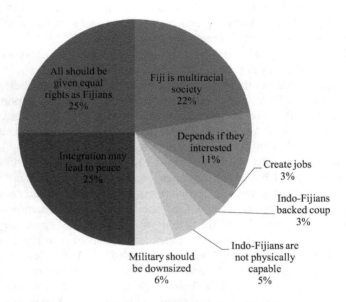

Figure 15.3 Why should Indo-Fijians be recruited in the military?

In addition, as discussed earlier, there is also an assumption that the military culture in Fiji is specifically aligned with the indigenous structure of authority and warrior identity:

> The Fijian military personnel, I believe see themselves very much on the concept of 'bati' [traditional warrior class in Fijian culture], so military and rugby both perpetuate that mentality. So military is very much an expression and extension of that culture in Fiji. Inherent in that is the protection of the chief at all costs so these are the cultural values that are perpetuated within the military as well. So if the Commander says to do something, they will do it due to their cultural thinking and their military discipline on top of that.
>
> (Andrew Hughes – Former Commissioner of Fiji Police,
> Personal Communication, 10 March 2011)

Discussion

Military reforms have been suggested for the Fiji military since the 1990s, but no government in the past has been able achieve this. Some people are sceptical about military reform in Fiji while it remains so strong and enjoys its monopolistic position as the only armed institution in the country. The research responses also indicated that while many would like to see the military reformed, they also accept that this is unlikely to happen soon.

I argue that military reform in Fiji is possible, but it needs to be done gradually and the military community's concerns and apprehensions should be taken into consideration. Some criticisms of military reforms mooted in the past were:

1   The suggested downsizing was too and much too soon: the 2005 recommendation was to downsize the military by almost 50%. A more gradual downsizing of 5% per year for the next 10 years would be less dramatic and the redundant military personnel could be better absorbed in other employment sectors.
2   The 2005 reforms were suggested by the Qarase government, which was already on antagonistic terms with the military at the time. The military considered the suggested reforms as a reprimand and retaliated with anger and resentment (Khan, 2015). Any military reform should be implemented by a government that works closely with the military and the reforms need to take into consideration the military's concerns.
3   Suggested reforms in the past were always recommended by a civilian aligned government and as the military in Fiji is praetorian, it would take such recommendations as offensive and react in a militaristic way. As such, one could argue that Bainimarama may be well placed to recommend military reforms as he is a career navy and military officer and his views are likely to have wider acceptance within the military.

Additionally, Bainimarama also has a proven track record of reforming problematic structures and policies in Fiji, reforms which were almost inconceivable in the past. But the window of opportunity may not be open for long. It is argued that Bainimarama needs to take this unique opportunity to carry out military reform as he continues to enjoy the patronage of the military, and that otherwise, it would be a missed opportunity, as Sitiveni Rabuka wanted to de-politicise the military, but it was too late, as by that time he no longer had the patronage of the military.

While vetting of military personnel by incoming government was considered in the questionnaire as a means of reforming the military, the research responses indicated that vetting could be difficult to implement for the military only and although the link to vetting is weak the Fiji Independent Commission against Corruption (FICAC) has started some work to combat corruption.

Notes

1 In this paper, the term "iTaukei" is used to refer to indigenous descendants of Fiji and the term "Indo-Fijian" is used to refer to descendants of indentured labourers and free settlers who arrived from India in the late 19th and early 20th centuries. Within Fiji, the two groups are usually referred to as "Fijian" and "Indian", respectively. The term "Fiji Islander" is a collective reference to all peoples of Fiji.
2 The military is considered praetorian when it uses explicit or implicit force to control governance of the country.
3 Structural violence is linked to Galtung's work on negative peace and is defined as the implicit form of violence that is embodied by the social, political and economic structures of the society (Galtung, 1969: 167–191).

4 Data obtained from a Fiji Military Forces presentation which was accessed on 26 December 2009 from www.forumsec.org.fj/_resources/article/files/Etueni%20Caucau-Military%20Presentation-RFMF.pdf
5 Particularly as at that time, the military and the Qarase government were on confrontational terms, the armed Police Unit setup was viewed suspiciously by the military.

References

Adekanye, B. J. (1996). Rwanda/Burundi: Uni-ethnic dominance and the cycle of armed ethnic formations. *Social Identities*, 2(1), 37–68.

Ashkenazi, D. (Ed.). (1994). *The military in the service of society and democracy*. Westport, CT: Greenwood Press.

Baledrokadroka, J. (2015). The super confederacy: The military in Fiji's politics. *The Round Table*, *104*(2), 127–135. https://doi.org/10.1080/00358533.2015.1017251

Ball, N. (2004). Dilemmas of security sector reform: Response to SSR in developing and transitional countries. In C. McCartney, M. Fischer, & O. Wils (Eds.), *Security sector reform: Potentials and challenges for conflict transformation*. Berlin: Berghof Research Center for Constructive Conflict Management.

CCF. (2014). *Fiji in transition: Towards a sustainable constitutional democracy*. Retrieved August 20, 2019 from http://news.ccf.org.fj/wp-content/uploads/2014/12/Fiji-in-Transition1.pdf

Chang, K. (2008). After the storm of 2000. Fiji's troubled path toward justice and reconciliation. In W. Salim & K. Sagoo (Eds.), *Sustaining a resilient Asia-Pacific community*. Honolulu, HI: East-West Center & Cambridge Scholars Publishing.

Clingendael, International Alert & Saferworld. (2002, August). *Towards a better practice framework in security sector reform; Broadening the debate*. Occasional SSR Paper No. 1. The Hague and London: Clingendael-International Alert-Saferworld.

Collier, P., & Hoeffler, A. (2005, August). *Coup traps: Why does Africa have so many Coups d'Etat?* Centre for the Study of African Economies, University of Oxford, Preliminary Draft. Retrieved December 12, 2010 from http://users.ox.ac.uk/~econpco/research/pdfs/Coup-traps.pdf

DCAF. (2006). *Multiethnic armed forces: Backgrounder*. Geneva: Geneva Centre for the Democratic Control of Armed Forces.

DCAF. (2008). *Democratic control of armed forces: Backgrounder*. Geneva: Geneva Centre for the Democratic Control of Armed Forces.

FBC. (2019, 14 June). *RFMF to increase women recruits*. Retrieved August 20, 2019 from www.fbcnews.com.fj/news/rfmf-to-increase-women-recruits/

Field-Springer, K. (2018). Informants. In M. Allen (Ed.), *The Sage encyclopedia of communication research methods*. Thousand Oaks, CA: SAGE Publications, Inc. Retrieved August 21, 2019 from https://methods.sagepub.com/base/download/ReferenceEntry/the-sage-encyclopedia-of-communication-research-methods/i6548.xml

Finer, S. (1988). *The man on the horseback: The role of military in politics* (2nd ed.). London: Pinter.

Firth, S., & Fraenkel, J. (2007). *From election to coup in Fiji: The 2006 campaign and its aftermath*. Canberra: ANU Press. Retrieved August 21, 2019 from https://press.anu.edu.au/publications/election-coup-fiji

Firth, S., & Fraenkel, J. (2009). The Fiji military and ethno-nationalism: Analyzing the paradox. In S. Firth, J. Fraenkel, & B. V. Lal (Eds.), *The 2006 military takeover in Fiji:*

A coup to end all coups? Canberra: ANU E Press. Retrieved November 15, 2010 from http://press.anu.edu.au/publications/2006-military-takeover-fiji

Firth, S., Fraenkel, J., & Lal, B. V. (Eds.). (2009). *The 2006 military takeover in Fiji: A coup to end all coups?* Canberra: ANU E Press. Retrieved November 15, 2010 from http://press.anu.edu.au/publications/2006-military-takeover-fiji

Galtung, J. (1969). Violence, peace, and peace research. *Journal of Peace Research, 6*(3), 167–191.

Horowitz, D. L. (1985). *Ethnic groups in conflict.* Berkeley, CA: University of California Press.

Huntington, S. P. (1968). *Political order in changing societies.* New Haven, CT: Yale University Press.

Janowitz, M. (1981). *Political roles and military rulers.* London: Frank Cass.

Jenkins, C., & Kposowa, A. J. (1990). Explaining military coups D'Etat: Black Africa, 1957–1984. *American Sociological Review, 55*(6), 861–875.

Joinet, L. (1997). *Revised final report. Question of the impunity of perpetrators of human rights violations (civil and political).* ECOSOC, UN. E/CN.4/Sub.2/1997/20/Rev.1. Retrieved October 20, 2008 from http://ap.ohchr.org/documents/alldocs.aspx?doc_id=6960

Kemp, K., & Hudlin, C. (1992). Civil supremacy over the military: It's nature and limits. *Armed Forces Society, 19*(1), 7–26.

Khan, N. (2015). *Do transitional justice strategies address small island developing states niche conflict needs? Preventing the recurrence of Coup d'états: Study of Fiji.* Thesis. Retrieved August 20, 2019 from http://etheses.whiterose.ac.uk/17877/

Lal, B. V., Chand, G., & Naidu, V. (Eds.). (2008). *1987: Fiji twenty years on.* Lautoka: Fiji Institute of Applied Studies, USP.

Lilleker, D. G. (2003). Interviewing the political elite: Navigating a potential minefield. *Politics, 23*(3), 207–214. https://doi.org/10.1111/1467-9256.00198

Lowy, R., Firth, S., & Vitusagavulu, J. (2004). *National security and defence review: Safeguarding peace and prosperity.* Ministry of Home Affairs, Government of Fiji.

Luckham, A. R. (1971). A comparative typology of civil-military relations. *Government and Opposition, 6*(Fall), 5–35.

Malan, M., & Weir, E. (2007, December 13). *Democratic Republic of Congo: Transition without Military Transformation.* Bulletin, Refugees International.

Marshall, M. N. (1996). The key informant techniques. *Family Practice, 13,* 92–97.

Mason, T. D. (2007). *Sustaining the peace after civil war.* Carlisle: Strategic Studies Institute. Retrieved April 20, 2009 from www.StrategicStudiesInstitute.army.mil/

Mayer-Rieckh, A., & Duthie, R. (2009). Enhancing justice and development through justice-sensitive security sector reform. In P. de Greiff & R. Duthie (Eds.), *Transitional justice and development, making connections.* New York: Social Science Research Council.

Murithi, T. (2010). The role of security sector reform in dealing with the past. *Politorbis: Swiss Review of Foreign Affairs,* Special Edition on Dealing with the Past, No. 50(3/2010), 65–70. Bern: Swiss Ministry of Foreign Affairs.

Nathan, L. (1996). *The new partnership. Stabilising civil-military relations in Africa.* Paper Presented at Conference on Military and Civil Society, organised by Africa Leadership Forum, 23–25 September 1996. Retrieved July 6, 2009 from http://ccrweb.ccr.uct.ac.za/archive/staff_papers/laurie_pship.html

Nordlinger, E. (1977). *Soldiers in politics: Military coups and governments.* Englewood-Cliffs, NJ: Prentice-Hall.

Organisation for Economic Cooperation and Development (OECD). (2007). *OECD DAC Handbook on Security System Reform: Supporting Security and Justice*. Paris: OECD. Retrieved from www.oecd.org/dataoecd/43/25/38406485.pdf

Orentlicher, D. (2005). *Updated set of principles for the protection and promotion of human rights through action to combat impunity*. ECOSOC, UN. E/CN.4/2005/102/Add.1

Parliament of Fiji. (1997). *Defending Fiji: Defence White Paper*. Parliamentary Paper No. 3.

Perlmutter, A. (1981). *Political roles and military rulers*. London: Frank Cass.

Radio NZ International. (2006). *Fiji military ups tone about Defence White Paper*. Retrieved October 26, 2013 from www.radionz.co.nz/international/pacific-news/162601/fiji-military-ups-tone-about-defence-white-paper

Ramesh, S. (2006, December 11). Fiji's slow march toward a military takeover. *WordPress*. Retrieved August 21, 2019 from www.worldpress.org/Asia/2599.cfm

Ratuva, S. (2006a, November 3). Our security dilemma. *The Fiji Times*. Retrieved from www.fijitimes.com/story.aspx?id=50989%20

Ratuva, S. (2006b). The pre-election "Cold War": The role of the Fiji military during the 2006 election. In J. Fraenkel & S. Firth (Eds.), *From election to coup in Fiji: The 2006 campaign and its Aftermath*. Canberra: ANU E Press and Asia Pacific Press.

RFMF (Royal Fiji Military Forces). (2010). *History*. Retrieved January 2, 2011 from www.rfmf.mil.fj/news/history.html

Robertson, R. (2017). *The general's goose: Fiji's tale of contemporary misadventure*. Canberra: ANU Press. Retrieved August 21, 2019 from http://dx.doi.org/10.22459/GG.08.2017

Seale, C. (1999). *The quality of qualitative research*. London: Sage.

Smyth, M. (2004, Autumn). The process of demilitarization and the reversibility of the peace process in Northern Ireland. *Terrorism and Political Violence, 16*(3), 544–566. Retrieved December 24, 2016 from https://doi.org/10.1080/09546550490509865

Trnka, S. (2008). Tourism or terrorism. In B. Lal, G. Chand, & V. Naidu (Eds.), *1987: Fiji twenty years on*. Lautoka: Fiji Institute of Applied Studies.

United Nations General Assembly Security Council. (2008, January 23). *Securing peace and development: The role of the United Nations in supporting security sector reform*. Report of the Secretary-General. UN Doc. A/62/659–S/2008/39.

United Nations Security Council. (2007, February 9). *Letter dated 8 February 2007 from the permanent representative of Slovakia to the United Nations addressed to the Secretary-General*. UN Doc. S/2007/72.

Uzgel, I. (2003). Between praetorianism and democracy: The role of military in Turkish Foreign Policy. *The Turkish Yearbook, XXXIV*, 177–211. Retrieved from http://acikarsiv.ankara.edu.tr/browse/3993/3203.pdf?show

Welch, C. E. (1975). Continuity and discontinuity in African military organisation. *Journal of Modern African Studies, 13*(2), 229–248.

Wulf, H. (2004). Security sector reform in developing and transitional countries. In C. McCartney, M. Fischer, & O. Wils (Eds.), *Security sector reform: Potentials and challenges for conflict transformation*. Berlin: Berghof Research Center for Constructive Conflict Management.

16 Organisation repositioning for improved security provision

Lessons from Guam on implementing community policing

Danielle Watson and James Johnson

In May of 2015, Joseph Cruz (JC) was appointed by Guam's Governor and con-firmed by the 33rd Guam Legislature as Guam's 12th Chief of Police. His 32-year professional career includes service in the United States Military and the Guam Police Department. His military career includes eight years as an enlisted US Marine and 14 years as a commissioned officer in the US Army. His law enforce-ment career includes ten years as a police officer in the Guam Police Department. His policing career was, in part, motivated by the desire to emulate his older brother who returned to law enforcement after retirement from the military. Chief Cruz states that his military background and academic training as a criminolo-gist made his return to law enforcement a "natural choice". Importantly, he has received multiple awards for a myriad array of service activities. Finally, he is an enthusiastic member of the Pacific Islands Chief of Police body. We had the plea-sure of interviewing Chief Cruz at the Pacific Police Training Advisory Group Meeting in Brisbane, Australia on 26 May 2017.

THE INTERVIEW

Policing then versus policing now

Moving away from traditional policing

INTERVIEWER: Tell me about Traditional Policing in Guam

JC: Traditional policing, in theory and concept, is very reactive. There is the Police Department and the community with no interaction between the two. Crime exists, they [the police] respond to crime. There are no initiatives; there is no engagement to collaborate with the community. So crime preven-tion is minimal. With Community Oriented Policing, the approach taken is very proactive. The Police Department reaches out to the community, almost embeds itself within the community to understand what their [the commu-nity's] needs are and to be able to implement policies, implement initiatives and best practices that focusses on crime prevention. It is more about getting the community involved and having them be a part of the solution and not so much a part of the problem. What I have seen over the years is an acceptance of Community Oriented Policing verses traditional policing.

INTERVIEWER: How have policing priorities changed over the years?

JC: Most of the changes you see surround gender, cyber related crimes and the sharing of intelligence. There is a huge need for gender equality and greater inclusion of women in the profession of policing because they play a huge part in the issue of crime prevention and law enforcement. When you think about policing in the 21st century, cybercrime is an issue in Guam. We recently had an issue related to cyber offences and that is something my officers and especially the older ones are struggling with because they are still embracing the older methods of law enforcement. So the acceptance of modern technology and that crimes are being committed in cyberspace to them it is a hard concept to wrap their minds around. Intelligence sharing or the lack thereof is another policy issue that the Guam Police Department is dealing with. Because of the tyranny of distance here in Guam and because of the vastness of the Pacific region, the ability to share intelligence is in my honest opinion huge. Unlike in the US, we do not have the ease of access to share intelligence with neighbours nearby. On Guam we face challenges because we have limited resources so the sharing of intelligence and using modern technology to share that intelligence has become a challenge.

INTERVIEWER: Have these policing priority changes been met with modified officer training?

JC: Absolutely! I tell my new recruits now; "it is a thinking man's game". It is less brawn and more brain. The application of what you know verses what you physically can do makes you a better police officer. In the classes that are being taught at our training academy, we've kept the foundational courses, those courses that in theory and in concept are important, like Police Theory, Criminal Law, Procedural Law and other areas critical to officers understanding of policies and procedures. We have also revised our curriculum to focus more on addressing the needs of the community as mandated by legislation enacted on Guam.

INTERVIEWER: Are there economic factors that have affected the policing organisation in Guam?

JC: It is very interesting that you mentioned that because right now the way our legislature works and how the government of Guam works with regard to the annual budget process, we are getting ready to go into a new budget season. Because we operate on fiscal years from October of one year to September of the next year, we are looking at getting ready for our fiscal year 2018 budget. We have experienced budget cuts over the years. Over the last two years that I've been the Chief, we've always missed the mark in terms of the amount requested to sustain the Guam Police Department over the fiscal year, so budget adjustments are always necessary. Without the right fiscal resources it affects personnel, logistics, administration and other areas which all have a resounding effect on police operations. This basically affects everything we do and the extent of our efforts. For example, how we are able to coordinate Community Oriented Policing is significantly affected by budget cuts.

We are working with a budget that has historically been reduced anywhere between $ 2M to $ 4M per fiscal year so for us, we are challenged in that regard. I make a point to promote *fiscal responsibility* throughout the entire Guam Police Department. Being frugal and judicious with the monies that we have is where we have to exercise and demonstrate flexibility and wisdom. We are basically required to do more with less, if you will, and focus on making things happen.

Policing philosophy

INTERVIEWER: What do you think should be the role and function of the police?

JC: My personal opinion is that the whole concept of Community Oriented Policing is the strategy that we need to move forward with. So much so that we have taken the US Department of Justice's Community Policing Model and we've adopted it in the Guam Police Department (Cruz, 2016). We have even coined it the Mandana Order Policing Strategy. In my language Mandana means *together*. The entire concept of togetherness means coming together as an entire community across the full spectrum, whether it is the residents themselves in the villages, the government agencies, the non-governmental agencies, non-profit organisations, the military, private businesses and working together to make our community a safer place. That concept in and of itself is something that I take very personally and everybody knows this. When you talk about the Mandana Community Ordered Policing Strategy in Guam, they say that strategy is Chief J.I.'s strategy. He's the guy that kicked it off; he's the one that brought it in. I've pushed the Guam Police Department so that we have embraced this type of policing completely. There are three fundamentals that allow this strategy to really work in its entirety. It includes collaboration across the board in GPD and throughout the entire community, there must be *collaboration*. To be able to continue to make this work there must be *organisational transformation*. If you do not position your organisation in such a way as to facilitate transformation, then Community Oriented Policing cannot be embraced fully. You have to focus your resources, all your energy and all your attention into that Community Oriented Policing strategy and those initiatives that allow you to collaborate with the community. The third part is the *problem solving*. After you're working with the community, after you've set the conditions for success in your agency or in your organisation then the problem solving begins. Those are the three pillars or fundamentals of Community Oriented Policing and in the Guam Police Department. We have totally revamped the way we do things to totally embrace that concept of the Mandana Community Ordered Policing Strategy.

INTERVIEWER: Do you believe officers in Guam are required to extend themselves beyond the call of duty?

JC: In our collaborating with the community and through no fault of the community, we deal with many areas outside of our purview. This is because members of the community do not know who else to contact. Many issues that involve social services are referred to the Guam Police Department. We are called upon to deal with alcoholism, homelessness and other similar problems which in my opinion are issues related to education, awareness and socio-economic issues. In my opinion these are not functions of law enforcement. I emphasise to our leaders that these issues are outside of my league and they should not be the responsibility of the Guam Police Department or any law enforcement entity. We are not suitably equipped to take on socio-economic issues or to take care of purely social issues and education awareness. These are issues that persons in their respective areas need to address in order to truly aid the community.

Factors impacting policing

INTERVIEWER: What factors, if any, hinder police-community relations?

JC: A major hindrance is *resistance to change*. I have had a few of my staff officers wanting to hold on to the old way of doing things. There is that resistance to change that I like to call complacency. Some officers have gotten so used to doing things a certain way that they initially reject change. This is the biggest issue that I have run into; that resistance to change and then the lack of communication and cross talking. There is a lack of communication in collaboration with partner organisations that we need to liaise with regularly. The problem exists communicating information in a timely manner between police and the Department of Public Health and Social Services, in talking to the Guam Behaviour Health and Wellness Centre, in talking to the Judiciary which is our third branch of government. This lack of communication sometimes results in the creation of *sticking points* in being able to effectuate change for our community because we are not cross talking enough.

INTERVIEWER: Are there any other obstacles that get in the way of effective policing?

JC: Forensics. I am not saying it stands in the way of policing but it is not where it should be. It could be better. We have faced constraints as a result of budget cuts. It is one of those areas we are developing but the reality is we are just not moving fast enough. This for me is a work in progress.

INTERVIEWER: In terms of all those problems identified, which would you say is the greatest problem facing Guam Police?

JC: The biggest issue we face at this point is probably the issue of the intelligence gathering. The gathering of information and even more so, is the sharing of that information. We have what is called a Mariana's Regional Fusion Centre (MRFC). The MRFC is supposed to be able to analyse information/intelligence, both open and closed source. I've supported the MFRC by having an officer assigned to this Fusion Centre to serve as a liaison officer between GPD and the MRFC. However, trying to get tangible products to take out to my police officers in the field and say here is what we are seeing, or here is what the community is experiencing based on information they are gathering is still a challenge. Intelligence sharing has direct links to being able to deal with the cybercrimes being committed.

INTERVIEWER: Why are there problems in terms of gathering of the information?

INTERVIEWEE: Again, I think again it goes back to agencies just being very territorial. For one reason or another silos of information are being built and there seems to be no connection of those silos of information. I am struggling with the fact that we have all these mechanisms in place yet trying to make the connection or the link almost requires having to change an entire mindset. So the gathering and sharing of information continues to be a real problem.

INTERVIEWER: Is there a case where the gathering and sharing is only a problem at organisational levels or is it also happening at community level?

JC: I think it is more so at the organisational level, yes.

INTERVIEWER: So the communities welcome the police?

JC: The way the community sees it is they see what we're doing as a breath of fresh air. For them it's like finally the police are doing something. You hear them say "finally I see a police officer". We have town hall meetings where the Lieutenant Governor of our island and myself meet with the residents so that we can hear what their concerns are. I don't see a problem at the community level. And I will tell you our Mandana initiative is so aggressive that we have village mayors calling asking for our presence in their villages. We also have residents requesting our presence because we have this programme called the Neighbourhood Watch Programme and it's through those programmes that we listen to what they have to say and make adjustments accordingly in the Guam Police Department to be able to meet the needs of the community. So its very community oriented, its very community based. If the community says this is a problem, we adjust ourselves to meet the needs of the community. Because like I tell my staff, if it were not for the community we would be out of the job. We are here to serve them, to protect them, to keep them safe. The problem is not at the community level, it's at the organisational level and I'm trying to have people who have been in these organisations for over 20 years to change that mindset. Change is like a paradigm shift, almost insurmountable.

Policing priorities

INTERVIEWER: What do you think should be priorities for your Police service?

JC: In addition to Community Oriented Policing, the whole issue of dealing with cybercrime is a priority. We seem to be more frequently required to deal with issues pertaining to accessing intelligence and forensics. I prioritise forensics because of the fact that the tyranny of distance between Guam and our closest US counterpart is Honolulu, Hawaii, and that is a seven-hour plane ride with another five hours to get to the US mainland. Forensics is one of those areas that can completely compromise the success of investigations. It has the potential to facilitate a criminal's continued existence in a community or suspects continued community victimising. We are working towards getting our forensics initiatives to a point where we are accredited and self-sustaining to counter the challenges distance creates for us.

The significance of policing theories and practices on policing in Guam

INTERVIEWER: How have what you've learnt over the years impacted on your practice now?

INTERVIEWEE: I try to impart what I have learnt over the years on primarily my staff officers because I figure if I can start with them and a part of my senior management team, then it helps to sow positive seeds. Just by embracing a new concept of policing or having to explain to them in theory and practice what Community Oriented Policing was and then get them to embrace it and break it down to a more practical or operational level showed the effect of my own training on my professional behaviours as a leader. This imparting onto them police theories and police concepts is significant. Guam Police Department, as an organisation, has more college graduates than any other law enforcement entity on the [Pacific] islands because our laws are written if you want to make it to the rank of Captain or go higher, you must have a degree.

INTERVIEWER: Can you run me through how the ranking works?

JC: Sure. So we start out with a police officer trainee and then we go to police officer 1, 2, 3 and then we have Sergeant 1, 2, then you have Lieutenant, Captain, Major and then Colonel and then above Colonel is the Chief. Very military, very military structure.

INTERVIEWER: Are officers exposed to policing theories as part of their training?

JC: I would say they are. Officers are exposed to several models during training. Even my Police Officer Trainees, when they first graduate from the academy, are able to understand Community Oriented Policing. They are able to understand and appreciate different models and theories but yet they see value in the acceptance of our community-oriented approach. In police theory, we introduce them to the other concepts that are out there, the other theories about police management and organisation, but yet they embrace what we are doing. They are well able to execute what they learn when they go out into the communities. So there is practical application, but it starts with an understanding of theories and the understanding and acceptance of the concept of Community Oriented Policing. I believe I've introduced a new model, a different theory, and it has been accepted at all levels within the organisation.

Successes as chief

INTERVIEWER: There has been acceptance of your community-oriented approach at all levels within the organisation?

JC: It took more time but officers with many years of service have come on board. One of the main reasons is because over the years, the Guam Police Department saw some very dark times unfortunately and I say that not to discredit my predecessors but it just simply happened that there was not enough going on. Crime was happening in the community and little to nothing was done about it. Approaches were very reactive, wait for crime to happen and then respond, take a report, investigate, but nothing was done to effectuate that. We have seen so much positive reaction from the community and significant improvements in areas inclusive of personnel, logistics and administration. With the new paradigm shift to accept Community Oriented Policing, even the more senior officers, although a few of them were very resistant, understood the new approach and they said this is what we need to do. This is that shot in the arm, that inoculation that we have been needing for the longest time. While a few officers were somewhat hesitant to embrace change, they went with it and because the results are so positive, they love it.

INTERVIEWER: Why do you think that was not the case before Joe Cruz?

JC: The last two Chiefs spanned over 12 years [and] almost 15 years [respectively]. They came up through the ranks and they took with them the traditional way of doing things. When I first came in, the complacency, it was killing me . . . the frustration! If I could get a dime for every time somebody said "Chief this is not the way we do it". Even though sometimes it would make no sense or simply be the wrong way, it continued because this was what they knew. I had to say we are not doing it that way anymore unless we can justify why that way is the best way. There was a need for significant changes in mindset. I think the problem was complacency and leaders at the very tail end of their Police careers preserving what they knew. They simply wanted to exist in the here and now. It was more about doing their time and getting their pay check and being able to walk away having made it to the top rank. But nothing was done for the department; nothing was done for the community.

INTERVIEWER: So basically you upset the balance?

JC: We saw the attrition rate for our senior officers go up because they couldn't handle the change, they couldn't embrace it and the change was so aggressive. I use the analogy when I showed up, the ship was sunk in the mud at the bottom of the ocean. We managed to resurrect that ship and now we are sailing in the right direction and not only are we sailing but we are sailing very fast and we are moving and those officers that can't keep up, end up retiring. But the good thing about that is the pot is stirred you know the analogy I use is when you cook a pot of soup all the bits that rests at the bottom, you stir that pot, you get everything going again.

The impact of external organisations

INTERVIEWER: How has the impact of external factors affected what takes place in Guam?

JC: This is significant because we are a US territory. Everything we do, from the way our laws are written, the laws that we have to be in compliance with at the federal level and at the local level is influenced by our mother country, the United States. The US plays a huge part in our style of policing. There are also communities of people that come to Guam because of a treaty called the Contract of Free Association between The United States of America and the Federated States of Micronesia, The Royal Marshall Islands and the Republic of Palau. This allows free movement back and forth between those island nations and the island of Guam or any other US territory for that matter, to include any of the 50 states. Guam is therefore influenced very heavily by a very diverse migrant population. We have to deal with a large migrant population from a certain migrant state within the Federated States of Micronesia and this has influence on the laws that we write, the policies and procedures that we have in the Guam Police Department. From an organisational standpoint, organisations like the Federal Bureau of Investigations (FBI), Drug Enforcement Administration (DEA) and all our federal partners influence the Guam Police Department. Also being a part of the Pacific Islands Chiefs of Police is starting to affect what we do in the Guam Police Department. The Guam Police Department never in its history of roughly 65 years had a strategic plan. Two years ago, I implemented a strategic plan and do you know where I got the model from? The Pacific Island Chiefs of Police. I simply looked at the concept that they are using, I looked at how they put their strategic plan together and how they go forward and I simply adopted their model for a strategic plan and I started with this two years ago and just last year in November we were able to develop and put together a viable, working, living, breathing strategic plan that the Guam Police Department has never seen before. To me, that strategic plan is enormous because it defines how we go from where we are at now to where we are going in three years.

INTERVIEWER: What do you think you bring to the table in terms of positive influence to the rest of the Pacific Islands Chief of Police group?

JC: I would like to think and it is very interesting that you mentioned it because Guam is looked to be a leader in Micronesia with regards to policing and law enforcement. What the Pacific Islands Chiefs of Police do is we meet as Chiefs. I am also a part of the executive leadership team. We look at strategies to assist each other in terms of policing challenges and we discuss ways of improving organisational practices. Guam offers assistance to our brothers and sisters in Micronesia with implementation of plans and training of officers or whatever areas we are called on to assist.

Democratic policing

INTERVIEWER: What do you see as the key element of democratic policing?

JC: In my understanding, there are three key areas that democratic policing looks at. Number one is the rule of law and that any police agency or organisation, regardless of where you are, must understand that they are not above the law and that they are also part of the rule of law and they are subject to the law.

The second thing is that although we as officers of the law can intervene depending on the powers that are given to us, the authority given is based on legislation that is to say it is limited or is carefully controlled based on certain circumstances. So when you look at the US model of policing and how we do things in America, obviously our foundation doctrine is our constitution, the constitution of the United States. So you have all that is afforded to a citizen to include all the different amendments. Those amendments forbid law enforcement and police officers to do things like illegal searches and seizures, protection against self-incrimination. Although we have authority, those are limited and they are controlled and they all have to be in accordance and compliance with the law. So when you think about democratic policing, you need to keep those things in mind and that public accountability is significant, primarily because of the fact that police organisations exist for the community and if it was not for the community, the police organisation would not need to be there. The whole idea of democratic policing in my mind and as I understand it is to take away from being that long arm of the law or that arm of a governing body that imposes its will on the people and that is not what the police should be used for. The police should not be used to tread on anyone's civil rights or civil liberties. They are there to protect the community, to serve the community, not to serve any one person in power, not to serve any one body in power, it's not an extension of authority per se. It is for the purpose of maintaining law and order in the community.

INTERVIEWER: Can the Guam Police resist demands from the government?

JC: We cannot entertain any request that violates citizens' rights. The government cannot force the police to prevent protests so long as protests are peaceful. Even where actions are against the government, police do not intervene. What is not excused is the breaking of the law.

INTERVIEWER: Is corruption an issue the Guam Police has to deal with on a regular basis?

JC: Because of the dynamics in our community, because we are a very small community, I'd say corruption does not exist in the Guam Police Department. We are a small island, only 39 miles long by 19 miles wide at its widest point and everybody knows each other. In the Guam Police Department we all know each other; the probability of somebody doing something that is corrupt per se is very unlikely. It is extremely frowned upon and when you talk about public accountability, we all hold each other accountable, I as the Chief all the way down to the lowest ranking police officer. So the issue of corruption is not something that exists in the Guam Police Department. I will tell you though, there have been police officers who have broken the law and they have been arrested and some of them have been imprisoned and that is something separate and apart from corruption per se. We do not go out and we do not extort; we do not go out and take bribes; we do not do things of that nature. At least I am comfortable as the Chief to say corruption is not an issue that we have to deal with.

The way forward

INTERVIEWER: In terms of looking ahead, what do you see as the most likely developments happening in policing in Guam?

JC: What I see happening in policing is the full implementation of our Community Oriented Policing strategy. I say that because it really is everything that we do, everything that we think. I see a full implementation in theory and concept that drives all that we do. I see a full implementation on the horizon and our practices extending to other territories. The Governor from one of the other islands came to see me and he asked if I could send my officers to that island state to teach them Community Oriented Policing. So to answer your question, I see this spreading throughout all of Micronesia because our Governor hosted what is called the Micronesian Island Forum a few weeks ago, where I had to deliver a briefing on public safety in the region and I will tell you it was the most engaged 30 minutes of the entire forum. Based on what I was hearing from each one of those Presidents or Governors was that they had heard about our strategy of policing, they like the positives, the change that we have and they are all asking what we can do to better collaborate so that we can spread this throughout the region. There was a time when it was merely a thought, it was a theory, it was a concept and now that it is a reality, there is practical application. For me this is beyond awesome. Because we did it and we are working towards a full implementation throughout the whole of the community, I am even more besides myself. Our Community Policing Initiative has gone to a whole new level that I did not imagine. When those presidents and those governors said we need to spread this throughout the entire region and it all started with one person coming in there and getting the agency, the organisation to understand it and because we were able to effectuate it into our community, into Guam, the region now sees the good, the positives that are being brought because of this model of policing. I almost want to say my work is done here.

INTERVIEWER: Thank you for your time.

Conclusion

Chief Cruz's responses to our questions provide valuable insight relevant to policing PICs. Not only does he highlight the need for police reform, he also highlights how important it is for policing policies to be contextualised for maximum effectiveness. He suggests that it is important for police officers to take ownership of new initiatives if they are to be truly effective. It is also important to note that while he acknowledged the necessity of change within policing organisations, he reveals that what is necessary is not easy and the process of buy-in is not without challenges. His accounts provide a guide to policing policy adaptation and adoption, which directly aligns with international policing best practices. Security is presented as a community project requiring input from all stakeholders. In essence, he confirms that repositioning is critical to improved security provision.

Reference

Cruz, J. (2016). *Guam Police Department's citizen centric report*. Guam Police Department. Dipåttamenton Polisian Guåhan ipåttam.

Conclusion

17 Security, resilience and resistance in the PICs

Aligning priorities and relocating responsibility

Sara N. Amin, Christian Girard and Danielle Watson

Aims and outcomes

Security is a complex concept, which raises challenging questions about how insecurities are produced and how security can be enhanced. The multidimensionality of security, the inter-relatedness of the different aspects of security (and the causes of insecurity), the embeddedness of (in)security in multiple institutions and the costs of insecurity (whether to individuals, communities and/or states) make policymaking and activism related to security practically difficult, ethically sensitive and politically contested, both locally and internationally. Chapters in the volume brought into focus and contextualised complexities of security in the Pacific, examined how a range of (in)securities are produced and resisted in the region and explored the implications for theorisation and policymaking on security.

Part 1 Reframing Security in the Pacific centred Pacific experiences and perspectives on economic security (Dornan, Chapter 3); environmental security (Dvorak, Chapter 4; Chand and Taupo, Chapter 5); precarity, vulnerabilities and identities (Carnegie and King, Chapter 2) and the place of women, the arts and faith in reducing security in the Pacific (Dvorak, Chapter 4). In contrast to much of the policy discourse on security in the Pacific that locates insecurity in smallness, remoteness, lack of resources and "traditions", the chapters in this section locate the sources of insecurity in the Pacific to (neo-)colonialism, neoliberalism, Northern militarism and economic globalisation. Taken together, these chapters move away from the tendency to mainly frame security in the Pacific through the geopolitical and geostrategic interests of the Global North, while highlighting the agency of Pacific Island communities and states in (re)defining and enhancing their own security.

In *Part 2 Sources of Gender Insecurity in the Pacific*, the authors help to map out the complex causes of gender insecurity in the Pacific, bringing into focus the tensions between religio-cultural institutions and international-liberal agendas related to gender equality. Schoeffel (Chapter 6) and George (Chapter 8) highlight how gender inequality can be reinforced when interventions are externally designed and implemented, without appropriate contextualisation of programmes and building of relationships with targeted communities (Schoeffel, Chapter 6;

George, Chapter 8). Kopf, Fink and Weber (Chapter 9) critique the tendencies of humanitarian and disaster relief action to both ignore gender inequalities in particular aspects of recovery and governance, and reproduce women as passive victims of disaster, ignoring the knowledge and relations they bring to reducing insecurity during disaster and post-disaster situations. While Amin, Trussler and Johnson (Chapter 7) map attitudes that rationalise and normalise violence against women and sexual minorities and point to the centrality of religious ideologies in reproducing such attitudes, Davis (Chapter 10) develops an important argument on the possibility and necessity of articulating a Pacific theology against domestic violence. The final chapter (Amin and Girard, Chapter 11) in Part 2 showcases how these tensions between local and international norms and institutions, cultural, religious and human rights discourses and indigenous practices can be productively mobilised to reduce insecurity.

The chapters in the final section of the book (*Part 3: Organisational Culture, Security Providers, Partner Institutions and Security Outcomes*) map the costs and benefits of moving away from state-centred conceptions of security provision in the Pacific. Dinnen (Chapter 14) brings into focus the growing influence of private security providers in the Pacific, arguing that while the private security sector is filling an important security gap in PNG and thus facilitating economic development and entrepreneurship, the private security sector is politicised in similar ways as the public sector, leaving the most vulnerable groups, including women, without much security provision. Khan (Chapter 15) argues for the importance of considering the place of iTaukei culture and social structure in efforts at reform of the Republic of Fiji Military Forces. A key argument in this final section is that policing action that builds on police officers' individual cultural relations with the community and other authorities can and do have positive outcomes for security in many Pacific contexts (Watson and Dinnen, Chapter 12; Forsyth, Chapter 13; Watson and Johnson, Chapter 16). This has important implications on how security sector reform (SSR) is designed and implemented, pointing to the need for external agencies and donors involved in SSR in the Pacific and for Pacific institutions to recognise the value of alternative paradigms of security provision.

Complexity and inter-relatedness of security: aligning local and global priorities in security

In security studies, there has been a tendency to both separate domestic and external security threats and prioritise the latter. This can be argued about the way that Australia, New Zealand, the US, China and Japan have influenced and set the security agenda of the PICs, focussing on militarisation in the region and maritime border control. However, for many Asia-Pacific states, Masys and Lin (2018) argue that "domestic security challenges are becoming blurred with regional and global external security considerations" (p. vii) and that the former are at least as important as the latter. This is particularly the case of the PICs where the domestic and external security issues are often linked in both direct and complex ways to global issues, dynamics and systems, especially when it comes to the transnational issue of climate change, often perceived as the most important security threat currently faced by the region. For example, water security, usually considered a domestic issue, is a national issue in the Pacific given the limited access to fresh water supplies and the challenge of waste disposal (Manton, 2014). However, climate change is exacerbating water and food security issues in the Pacific (Heath et al., 2014) and the causes of climate change are largely located outside of the PICs, brought about by external actions and levels of industrialisation and carbon emissions to which the PICs have only marginally contributed to. In addition, as argued by Chand and Taupo (Chapter 5), the nature and scope of climate change as a security threat in the PICs include the potential loss of sovereignty and nationhood, making the common distinction between domestic and external security inadequate.

Furthermore, the PICs continue to find themselves in a situation where the actions of their geopolitical allies often directly conflict with the security needs of the PICs. An example of this is what happened during the most recent Pacific Islands Forum meeting in August 2019 when Tuvalu and the other PICs articulated the urgency of climate change for their security. In response, Australia pledged AUD 500 million to fight climate change in the PICs, while at the same time it rejected the framing of climate change as a crisis, refused to examine its use of coal, sea-bed mining and extractive industries as major contributing factors in the environmental security threat faced by the PICs, and focussed on its own concerns related to the growing influence of China (Clarke, 2019; Lyons, 2019). This type of conflicting dynamic is common as highlighted by what Glover (2012) defines as "Australia's Policy Paradox" in relation to fossil fuels and carbon emissions, what Barrett, Kurian, and Wright (2015) refer to as the "Contradictory Politics of New Zealand's Climate Change Policies in the Pacific", and what Dvorak (Chapter 4) describes in relation to the United States' nuclear agenda in the region. These actions and policies do not only contradict the very own discourse of many allies supporting the PICs, but also often comes into conflict and represents a direct security threat for the PICs.

A key issue here is the tendency to de-link the different types of securities. For example, Elliott (2015) points out that environmental security tends to be "divorced" from human security:

> The concept of environmental security, on the other hand, has become increasingly divorced from its potentially heterodox and critical roots in human security. Rather it has been captured by an orthodoxy that focusses primarily on non-traditional threats to traditional referents (i.e. the state) and that increasingly perceives 'environmental security' as a synonym for the threat multiplier dimensions of climate change. Rather than empowering a people-centred approach that places emancipation at the centre of human/ environmental security, the author argues (following Mason and Zeitoun) that this has foreclosed rather than protected human freedom and dignity.
> (p. 11)

This is particularly important, relevant and problematic for the PICs as the international agenda and environmental movement sometimes neglect certain questions and aspects of human security, the impact on livelihoods and the socio-economic challenges and needs of vulnerable populations (see for example Forsyth, Leach and Scoones (1998) on the tension between exclusionary measures and livelihoods or Gray and Moseley (2005, p. 16) on how some conservation efforts have led to "livelihood systems [being] outlawed and criminalised", as well as Bolnick et al. (2006) and McGranahan and Satterthwaite (2002) for the specific tensions in development and urban planning between the environmentalist "green" agenda and the human and public health "brown" agenda focussing on water, sanitation and housing), even though it is acknowledged that environmental security and sustainable development are also key to poverty reduction (Ohlsson, 2000) and that both are linked in complex ways (Nadkarni, 2000; Angelsen, 1997). In the words of Dalby (2015):

> The crucial point is that climate change is about much more than traditional environmental concerns with parks, pollution, preservation and population. According to those who specify climate change in terms of national or human security, it is a much more important issue, potentially leading to major social disruptions and possibly wars, and hence a much higher policy priority.
>
> (p. 83)

The reality of geopolitical power at the international level has often meant that the PICs have been forced into an agenda dominated by external powers that does not necessarily correspond to their main priorities and concerns, that continues to ignore the connections between environmental security, human security and freedom from violence and war, and that a major source of their continued insecurity remains in the actions of powers and centres outside their direct control and authority. The perverse outcomes of an externally defined security agenda can be seen in a different security issue. As Schoeffel (Chapter 6) and George (Chapter 8) show, external powers utilise aid and development mechanisms to influence PICs' governments and institutions to prioritise gender equality in political and economic institutions as the primary means by which gendered insecurity is reduced. Here the issue is less that this is not a priority of Pacific Island communities and states, but rather lies in the processes by which the agenda is set, as well as in how it is implemented. Importantly, context-specific needs of women and sexual minorities in the region are often not taken into account in both agenda setting and implementation processes and, as a result, interventions can reinforce gender inequalities, delegitimize policies and laws designed to support women and sexual minorities and even produce additional violence and insecurity against these groups.

The links between global and interconnected/interrelated risks and human and environmental security are shared by Africa, Asia and the Pacific Islands (Behnassi, Gupta, & Pollman, 2019) and some levers for successful management of and response to these issues are beyond regional and local powers and lie more at the global level. On the one hand, this means that concerns, efforts and solutions can be shared with actors outside the Pacific region to mobilise action and support to tackle these issues, but on the other hand, it also limits the impact that PICs can have on their own. As such, if priorities are not aligned, the global impact and the activities of major global players, especially in relation to climate change, can counter the efforts done by PICs themselves, highlighting once more the importance of cooperation.

This does not minimise the impact and influence PICs can have within their own borders and to influence the international and global agenda. The success of regional power and mobilisation against nuclear testing in the 1980s testify to the leadership and capacities of the PICs in this regard. In fact, as the chapters by Dornan (Chapter 3), Dvorak (Chapter 4) and Chand and Taupo (Chapter 5) highlight, the scale and urgency of the security threat posed by climate change for the Pacific has created an important movement in the Pacific, especially through PICs' regional bodies, that underscores the need to challenge the status quo and rethink our model of economic development and economic security, our frameworks of responsibility and accountability, as well as to reconfigure power relations. In the next section, we specifically outline sources of Pacific agency and resilience in reconstructing the meaning, practice and provision of security.

Agency, relationships and resilience: relocating responsibility of security provision and reconfiguring power relationships

From the focus on security and vulnerability has risen the interest in resilience, basically the flip side of vulnerability. While Chambers (2006/1989) associates risks, shocks and stress to the external dimension of vulnerability, he associates the "the lack of means to cope without damaging loss" (p. 33) to its internal dimension. Resilience can be linked to the latter dimension and can be understood as the capacity and means to cope with risks, shocks and stress (Ombati & Ombati, 2016; Sirven, 2007) or to "bounce back" aftershocks or crises (Boas & Rothe, 2016; Davies, 1993). It could be argued that the traction behind this term in policy and development circles lies in its forward-looking perspective to tackle current and incoming challenges that shifts the focus towards action, implementation and empowerment (Boas & Rothe, 2016):

> Resilience discourse stresses rationales and practices such as adaptation to risk, shared responsibility, and self-capacity to achieve human security. In line with such a discourse, empowerment of vulnerable communities by funding adaptation projects in the global South became reconsidered as a part of a broader security strategy.
>
> (p. 2)

This type of resilience discourse tends to produce a devolution of responsibilities of providing security from states to communities, individuals, the private sector and the civil society (Boas & Rothe, 2016; Chmutina, Lizarralde, Dainty, &

Bosher, 2016; Joseph, 2013; Oels, 2015). This leads to a privatisation and individualisation of issues, risks and responsibilities. This "privatisation of responsibility, disguised as freedom" is also associated to the discourse of empowerment (Dawson, 2012, p. 313). It is also often linked to utilising market logics to find adaptive solutions, which can continue to maintain existing power relations: the green economy to deal with climate and environmental insecurities (Goodman & Salleh, 2013; Bakker, 2010), women's (and more recently men's) education and women's entrepreneurship to deal with gender insecurities (Batliwala, 2007; Bexell, 2012; Kabeer, 1999; Stromquist, 2015), privatisation and marketisation of security services to reduce insecurities produced through violent crime (Huggins, 2000; Goldstein, 2005). As Dinnen (Chapter 14) argues, while privatisation of security can produce and support innovation, entrepreneurship and economic opportunity, it can also simultaneously increase insecurities by entrenching existing power inequalities.

There is however a different and parallel resilience and empowerment discourse that is oriented towards the transformation of the logics and orders that have produce the insecurities in the first place (Parpart, Rai, & Staudt, 2003; Kabeer, 2005; Tschakert, 2009). For example, Oels (2015, pp. 189–190) argues that the discourse that presents climate change as inevitable and that focusses on resilience and migration as a result, "depoliticises the issue of climate change in a radical way" and contributes to "legitimizing the displacement of millions of people", taking away the responsibility of industrialised countries to reduce emissions. Refusal to disconnect the causes of climate change to the solutions proposed is an important act of discursive resistance that aligns with the position and reactions of PIC leaders as highlighted by Chand and Taupo (Chapter 5). In this discourse, notions of responsibility and accountability are centred on those who have been the perpetrators of producing the insecurities faced by the populations of the Pacific. Dvorak (Chapter 4) argues this in relation to the Marshall Islands' continued efforts, especially by women, for justice beyond simple monetary compensation in relation to the ravaging effects of nuclear testing.

Efforts to reorder and relocate responsibility can be seen in different types of activity from the Pacific. For example, in 2014, the Pacific Climate Warriors Campaign, involving 30 Pacific Islanders and hundreds of Australians used kayaks and traditionally built canoes to occupy the harbour and succeeded in turning away ten of the 11 coal ships set to collect their cargo from Newcastle, Australia (Fair, 2015). This very material and symbolic action was explicitly designed to make visible the "connections between the actions of the Australian fossil fuel industry and the impacts that anthropogenic climate change is having on many Pacific Islands" (Fair, 2015, p. 58). Another recent example is the Pacific Island Students Fighting Climate Change (PISFCC), who are currently pressing Pacific leaders to bring up the issue of climate change with the International Court of Justice (ICJ) and ask for "advisory opinion on the obligations of states under international law to protect the rights of present and future generations against the adverse effects of climate change" (Vanuatu Climate Action Network, Media Release 7 August 2019). Linked to larger movements of climate justice in which environmental degradation and effects of climate change are understood as ethical and political issues (instead of simply environmental), this type of work is attempting to redefine crime, justice and international frameworks around responsibility to protect beyond their current focus on war and physical violence to issues of environmental crime broadly (White, 2013) as (some) researchers acknowledge the relevance of and links to security, violence and crime, from water issues (Brisman, McClanahan, South, & Walters, 2018) to natural disasters and climate change (Kaldor & Rangelov, 2014).

In these resistances, reframings and recentrings, resilience and empowerment are located in radically different worldviews that peoples can bring to deal with the global climate change and environmental security problem. Indigenous ways of being that emphasise connectivity, inter-relatedness and responsibility in relation to both people/communities and the environment are central to what PICs and Pacific communities are asserting. These require going beyond extractive practices and technological solutions in reducing environmental insecurity and instead imply reconsidering the dominant logic of capitalist economic development. Pacific communities argue that sustainability of "security" and resilience to deal with change and insecurity will require re-ordering the current global political and economic regime (Mar, 2016; Parker & Grossman, 2012; Hanlon, 2009; Hau'ofa, 1994).

A similar argument of locating "traditional" systems as potential sites of resilience can be found in relation to discussions about food security. Campbell (2015) points to the need for revitalising traditional food security systems in the PICs. While there are many policy efforts at INGO, governmental and media/civil society levels focussing on awareness of traditional food systems and practices, such efforts tend to fall back on individualising responsibility for the provision of food security. However, for traditional food security systems to be viable and sustainable, one cannot ignore the current causes of food insecurity in the PICs, brought about by colonisation, neoliberal globalisation and environmental degradation linked to climate change (Campbell, 2015). Again, resilience and empowerment located in tradition or community participation can only be sustainable and meaningful in the context of reconfiguration of power relations.

This is not limited to issues of environmental and food insecurity produced through the climate change crisis or extractive, neoliberal, globalising capitalism. The modernisation discourse, in part globalised and imposed through moments of colonialism and then the development project, centres the citizen-state relationship as the primary relationship to order behaviour (Castells, 2011; Tilly, 1995, 2003). All other relationships (religious, cultural, gender, etc.) are meant to be secondary and subordinated to the relationship to the state, to ensure the security of both the state and its subjects (Castells, 2011; Tilly, 1995). However, this approach has produced many types of insecurities, including directly through violence used by states against specific populations to subordinate alternative identity and community groups (Castells, 2011). In addition, neoliberal globalisation has not only led the state to be unable (or unwilling) to provide for the economic and health security of its population, but also weakened the ties that could facilitate security outside of the state (see Carnegie and King, Chapter 2). As Ratuva (2014) argues in relation to understanding social protection in the Pacific, the modernisation discourse has also created a deficit in thinking about security provision. By locating relationships beyond the state as both subordinate and often problematic, socio-cultural relationships and communities are ignored as a potential source of security enhancement. Yet, as George (Chapter 8), Amin and Girard (Chapter 11), Watson and Dinnen (Chapter 12), Forsyth (Chapter 13) and Watson and Johnson (Chapter 16) show, these non-state relationships located in faith, wantokism, *kastom* and other cultural communities have been central in the PICs to ensure (public) security provision.

These chapters highlight the power of relationships and cultural communities working with "modern" states to enhance security. Such a perspective, central to many key tenets of Pacific ideas of governance, is able to take the individual not as an abstract citizen stripped of their identities and relationships, but instead embedded in relationships which, if recognised by the state and others, allows a governance embedded in care. In such a perspective, resilience is not located in the individual or vulnerable community coming up with their own solutions and adaptations. Resilience instead comes from resources and knowledge that can be mobilised because of the relationships and interconnectedness between individuals, (local, regional and global) communities and the state.

An argument to centre relationships and relationalities in security provision needs to address the reality that many aspects of culture and religion have been utilised to produce and reinforce insecurities against certain groups, especially against women, sexual minorities and cultural/ethnic minorities. Schoeffel (Chapter 6), Amin, Trussler and Johnson (Chapter 7), George (Chapter 8), Kopf, Fink and Eberhard (Chapter 9), Davis (Chapter 10) and Amin and Girard (Chapter 11) all document the different ways in which patriarchal heteronormative structures have normalised and rationalised direct and indirect violence, exclusion and marginalisation of women and sexual minorities in the PICs. Khan (Chapter 15) also points to the way that relationships located in iTaukei culture impact on not only who is included in the military and military culture, but also produce insecurities at a national level for excluded groups.

However, these chapters do not argue for a decentring of relationships and communities. What they suggest is that instead of marginalising or excluding non-state relationships and authorities, communities and identities in efforts to reduce gender (or other) insecurity(ies), it is necessary to take them into account both in recognising their role in producing insecurities and in their potential to enhance the security of women, sexual minorities and cultural minorities. The key here is to draw on context-specific resources (leadership, relationships, ideas, discourses) that simultaneously 1) challenge the reification of culture, tradition and identity as monolithically patriarchal and/or exclusive of certain ideas; and 2) resist standardisation of the gender equality agenda. Meo-Sewabu's (2016) work on cultural agency among indigenous Fijian women, Kapur's work on feminism and religion in India (2014), Mahmood's work on Muslim women in Egypt (2011), Hernández Castillo's work on indigenous Latin American women's movement (2010) and the work by leitis in Tonga documented by Amin and Girard (Chapter 11) are just some examples of both scholarship and activism that embody how the goal of enhancing gender security can be reconciled with culture, tradition and religion in ways that are potentially mutually transformative and more sustainable.

Future directions for research and action

Locating this volume on mapping security in the Pacific in the larger *Routledge Studies in Crime and Justice in Asia and the Global South* and the aim of bringing into focus Southern research on crime and justice issues have allowed us to do the following: 1) reframe security from within the Pacific in terms of both explaining insecurity and understanding security provision; 2) identify the ways that Pacific states and communities are acting to enhance their own security and 3) explore some implications of this reframing and these actions for thinking about and policymaking on security.

There are gaps in this volume in all these efforts, including an absence of focussed analyses of and documentations on actions related to food security, energy security, space security, cybersecurity, as well as an absence of scholarship utilising Pacific epistemologies in researching and writing (in)securities. The question of migration and its implications for both security and insecurity has also not been addressed in a focussed manner, even though it has been discussed in different ways in Dornan (Chapter 3), Dvorak (Chapter 4) and Chand and Taupo (Chapter 5). This is a topic with major implications for individuals, communities and nations, in relation to socio-economic dimensions (e.g. work, education and remittances) and to physical dimensions, food security and spatial survival. In this regard, some countries have bought or have been offered land for relocation and agriculture in other PICs and Australia as a consequence of climate change and rising sea levels. When it comes to temporary migrants in the Asia-Pacific region, Tazreiter, Weber, Pickering, Segrave, and McKernan (2016) have developed the concept of "fluid security" to look at the specific characteristics and skillsets that people carry "across spatial, temporal and imagined borders" (p. 17) to better understand the sources of both insecurity and resilience for these workers.

Moreover, while this volume contributes to contextualised analyses of security-insecurity in the Pacific, comparative analysis would yield deeper and richer theoretical gains. Despite Pacific specificities, given that the securities and insecurities are embedded in a global-regional-local nexus and that some structures and dynamics in the Pacific are shared by communities in different contexts, comparative analyses (both within and beyond the Pacific) is also important for developing context-specific solutions. Future collections and research should address these gaps.

Despite these gaps, we believe it is important to consider each of the chapters individually, as well as collectively, for the argument in this concluding chapter: If security and resilience are to be sustainable and ongoing, there is an urgent need to align security priorities locally and globally, as well as reconfigure the political economy of relationships, identities and "traditions" and their place in the "modern" state as potential sources of resilience in security provision. We understand that in translating both of these into action, one will run into the real-politik of power relations in which the West, military and capitalistic logics, economic "super" powers, and the modernist project dominate. However, current possibilities offered by the scope of contemporary security crises, a revitalisation of indigenous worldviews and knowledge (Smith, 2013), a push for Southern theorisation (Connell, 2014) including in crime and justice studies (Carrington, Hogg, & Suzzo, 2016) and technologies that facilitate collective action and the creation of solidarity (see Titifanue, Kant, Finau, and Tarai [2017] in the context of the PICs and Castells [2015] more broadly) have created an emergent opportunity to produce new ways of reconfiguring power relationships between different states, as well as – and perhaps more importantly – between communities and states within and beyond national borders.

References

Angelsen, A. (1997). The poverty–environment thesis: Was Brundtland wrong? *Forum for Development Studies*, *24*(1), 135–154.

Bakker, K. (2010). The limits of "neoliberal natures": Debating green neoliberalism. *Progress in Human Geography*, *34*(6), 715–735.

Barrett, P., Kurian, P., & Wright, J. (2015). Environmental security and the contradictory politics of New Zealand's climate change policies in the Pacific. In I. Watson & C. Pandey (Eds.), *Environmental security in the Asia-Pacific* (pp. 157–178). New York: Palgrave Macmillan.

Batliwala, S. (2007). Taking the power out of empowerment: An experiential account. *Development in Practice*, 17(4–5), 557–565.

Behnassi, M., Gupta, H., & Pollmann, O. (2019). *Human and environmental security in the era of global risks: Perspectives from Africa, Asia and the Pacific Islands*. Cham: Springer.

Bexell, M. (2012). Global governance, gains and gender: UN–business partnerships for women's empowerment. *International Feminist Journal of Politics*, *14*(3), 389–407.

Boas, I., & Rothe, D. (2016). From conflict to resilience? Explaining recent changes in climate security discourse and practice. *Environmental Politics*, 25(4), 613–632.

Bolnick, J., Kayuni, H. M., Mabala, R., McGranahan, G., Mitlin, D., Nkhoma, S. . . . van Donk, M. (2006). *A pro-poor urban agenda for Africa: Clarifying ecological and development issues for poor and vulnerable populations* (Vol. 2). London: IIED.

Brisman, A., McClanahan, B., South, N., & Walters, R. (2018). *Water, crime and security in the twenty-first century: Too dirty, too little, too much*. London: Springer.

Campbell, J. R. (2015). Development, global change and traditional food security in Pacific Island countries. *Regional Environmental Change*, *15*(7), 1313–1324.

Carrington, K., Hogg, R., & Suzzo, M. (2016). Southern criminology. *The British Journal of Criminology*, *56*(1), 1–20.

Castells, M. (2011). *The power of identity* (Vol. 14). Cambridge: John Wiley & Sons.

Castells, M. (2015). *Networks of outrage and hope: Social movements in the Internet age*. Cambridge: John Wiley & Sons.

Chambers, R. (2006/1989). Vulnerability, coping and policy (Editorial introduction). *IDS Bulletin*, *37*(4), 33–40.

Chmutina, K., Lizarralde, G., Dainty, A., & Bosher, L. (2016). Unpacking resilience policy discourse. *Cities*, *58*, 70–79.

Clarke, M. (2019, August 13). Tuvalu's PM says Australia's climate funding for Pacific "not an excuse" to avoid emissions cuts. *ABC News*. Retrieved from www.abc.net.au/news/2019-08-13/australias-climate-funding-pacific-islands-forum-tuvalu/11408930

Connell, R. (2014). Using southern theory: Decolonizing social thought in theory, research and application. *Planning Theory*, *13*(2), 210–223.

Dalby, S. (2015). Climate change and the insecurity frame. In S. O'Lear & S. Dalby (Eds.), *Reframing climate change: Constructing ecological geopolitics* (pp. 83–99). London: Routledge.

Davies, S. (1993). Are coping strategies a cop out? *IDS Bulletin*, *24*(4), 60–72.

Dawson, M. (2012). Reviewing the critique of individualization: The disembedded and embedded theses. *Acta Sociologica*, *55*(4), 305–319.

Elliott, L. (2015). Human security/environmental security. *Contemporary Politics*, *21*(1), 11–24.

Fair, H. (2015). Not drowning but fighting: Pacific Islands activists. *Forced Migration Review*, *49*, 58.

Forsyth, T., Leach, M., & Scoones, I. (1998). Poverty and environment: Priorities for research and policy. In *An overview study prepared for the United Nations Development Programme and European Commission*. Sussex, UK: Institute of Development Studies.

Glover, L. (2012). More fossil fuels and less carbon emissions: Australia's policy paradox. In L. Anceschi & J. Symons (Eds.), *Energy security in the era of climate change* (pp. 198–213). London: Springer.

Goldstein, D. M. (2005). Flexible justice: Neoliberal violence and "self-help" security in Bolivia. *Critique of Anthropology*, *25*(4), 389–411.

Goodman, J., & Salleh, A. (2013). The "green economy": Class hegemony and counter-hegemony. *Globalizations*, *10*(3), 411–424.

Gray, L. C., & Moseley, W. G. (2005). A geographical perspective on poverty–environment interactions. *The Geographical Journal*, *171*(1), 9–23.

Hanlon, D. (2009). The "Sea of little lands": Examining micronesia's place in "our sea of islands". *The Contemporary Pacific*, *21*(1), 91–110.

Hau'ofa, E. (1994). Our sea of islands. *The Contemporary Pacific*, 148–161.

Heath, L., Salinger, M. J., Falkland, T., Hansen, J., Jiang, K., Kameyama, Y. . . . White, I. (2014). Climate and security in Asia and the Pacific (food, water and energy). In M. J. Manton & L. A. Stevenson (Eds.), *Climate in Asia and the Pacific: Security, society and sustainability* (pp. 129–198). London: Springer.

Hernández Castillo, R. A. (2010). The emergence of indigenous feminism in Latin America. *Signs: Journal of Women in Culture and Society*, *35*(3), 539–545.

Huggins, M. K. (2000). Urban violence and police privatization in Brazil: Blended invisibility. *Social Justice*, *27*(2(80)), 113–134.

Joseph, J. (2013). Resilience as embedded neoliberalism: A governmentality approach. *Resilience*, *1*(1), 38–52.

Kabeer, N. (1999). Resources, agency, achievements: Reflections on the measurement of women's empowerment. *Development and Change*, *30*(3), 435–464.

Kabeer, N. (2005). Gender equality and women's empowerment: A critical analysis of the third millennium development goal. *Gender & Development*, *13*(1), 13–24.

Kaldor, M., & Rangelov, I. (2014). *The handbook of global security policy*. West Sussex: John Wiley & Sons.

Kapur, R. (2014). Gender, sovereignty and the rise of a sexual security regime in international law and postcolonial India. *Melbourne Journal of International Law*, *14*(2), pp. 1–30.

Lyons, K. (2019, August 13). Australia's coal use sharpens Pacific tension as Scott Morrison arrives for forum. *The Guardian*. Retrieved from www.theguardian.com/world/2019/aug/14/australia-coal-pacific-tension-scott-morrison-forum

Mahmood, S. (2011). *Politics of piety: The Islamic revival and the feminist subject*. Princeton, NJ: Princeton University Press.

Manton, M. J. (2014). Introduction. In M. J. Manton & L. A. Stevenson (Eds.), *Climate in Asia and the Pacific: Security, society and sustainability* (pp. 1–16). London: Springer.

Mar, T. B. (2016). *Decolonisation and the Pacific*. Cambridge: Cambridge University Press.

Masys, A. J., & Lin, L. S. (Eds.). (2017). *Asia-Pacific security challenges: Managing black swans and persistent threats*. Cham: Springer.

McGranahan, G., & Satterthwaite, D. (2002). Environmental health or ecological sustainability? Reconciling the brown and green agendas in urban development. In R. Zetter & R. White (Eds.), *Planning in cities* (pp. 43–57). Warwickshire: Practial Action Publishing.

Meo-Sewabu, L. (2016). "Na Marama iTaukei Kei Na Vanua": Culturally embedded agency of indigenous Fijian women-opportunities and constraints. *New Zealand Sociology*, *31*(2), 96.

Nadkarni, M. V. (2000). Poverty, environment, development: A many-patterned nexus. *Economic and Political Weekly*, *35*(14), 1184–1190.

Oels, A. (2015). Resisting the climate security discourse: Restoring "the political" in climate change politics. In S. O'Lear & S. Dalby (Eds.), *Reframing climate change: Constructing ecological geopolitics* (pp. 188–202). London: Routledge.

Ohlsson, L. (2000). *Livelihood conflicts: Linking poverty and environment as causes of conflict*. Department for Natural Resources and the Environment: Swedish International Development Cooperation Agency.

Ombati, M., & Ombati, V. F. O. (2016). Resilience of children and youth negotiating urban vulnerabilities and livelihoods in the Langas slums of Eldoret, Kenya. *Urbana: Urban Affairs & Public Policy*, *XVII*, 1–13.

Parker, A., & Grossman, Z. (2012). *Asserting native resilience: Pacific Rim indigenous nations face the climate change*. Corvallis: Oregon State University Press.

Parpart, J. L., Rai, S. M., & Staudt, K. A. (Eds.). (2003). *Rethinking empowerment: Gender and development in a global/local world*. London: Routledge.

Ratuva, S. (2014). 'Failed' or resilient subaltern communities?: Pacific indigenous social protection systems in a neoliberal world. *Pacific Journalism Review*, *20*(2), 40–58.

Sirven, N. (2007). De la pauvreté à la vulnérabilité: Évolutions conceptuelles et méthodologiques. *Mondes en développement*, *25*(140), 9–24.

Smith, L. T. (2013). *Decolonizing methodologies: Research and indigenous peoples*. London: Zed Books Ltd.

Stromquist, N. P. (2015). Women's empowerment and education: Linking knowledge to transformative action. *European Journal of Education*, *50*(3), 307–324.

Tazreiter, C., Weber, L., Pickering, S., Segrave, M., & McKernan, H. (2016). *Fluid security in the Asia Pacific: Transnational lives, human rights and state control*. London: Springer.

Tilly, C. (1995). Citizenship, identity and social history. *International Review of Social History*, *40*(Suppl. 3), 1–17.

Tilly, C. (2003). Political identities in changing polities. *Social Research*, *70*(2), 605–620.

Titifanue, J., Kant, R., Finau, G., & Tarai, J. (2017, July). Climate change advocacy in the pacific: The role of information and communication technologies. *Pacific Journalism Review*, *23*(1), 133–149.

Tschakert, P. (2009). Digging deep for justice: A radical re-imagination of the artisanal gold mining sector in Ghana. *Antipode, 41*(4), 706–740.

Vanuatu Climate Action Network. (2019, August 7). *Civil society is fighting for Pacific leaders to seek advice from International Court of Justice on the climate emergency.* Media Release. Retrieved from https://drive.google.com/file/d/1-f05ilGENHEjZENKs-U8Ao3fnoP1NKAu/view

White, R. (2013). *Crimes against nature: Environmental criminology and ecological justice.* London: Willan.

Index

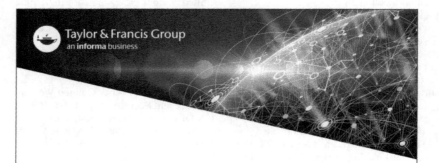